The Sword and the Centuries

ALFREDUS HUTTON. F.S.A. ÆTATIS SUÆ LXI

The
Sword and the Centuries

OR

OLD SWORD DAYS AND OLD SWORD WAYS

BEING A DESCRIPTION OF THE VARIOUS SWORDS USED IN CIVILIZED EUROPE DURING THE LAST FIVE CENTURIES, AND OF SINGLE COMBATS WHICH HAVE BEEN FOUGHT WITH THEM

BY

ALFRED HUTTON, F.S.A.

Late Captain King's Dragoon Guards

AUTHOR OF

"COLD STEEL," "OLD SWORD-PLAY," ETC.

WITH INTRODUCTORY REMARKS

BY

CAPTAIN CYRIL G. R. MATTHEY

London Rifle Brigade

ILLUSTRATED

WRENS PARK

The Sword and the Centuries
or
Old Sword Days and Old Sword Ways
By Alfred Hutton
New Introduction by Paul Hilts

First published 2003 by Wren's Park Publishing, an imprint of W. J. Williams Publishing & Son Ltd.

British Library Cataloguing in Publication Data available
A catalogue record for this book is available from the British Library

ISBN 0905-778-84-7

This edition is reproduced as the original Grant and Richards, 1901, including all illustrations, a new select bibliography and a new introduction by Paul Hilts

Printed and bound in Great Britain by Creative Print and Design Group, Ebbw Vale, Wales

To

MY BRIGHT

BRAVE-HEARTED LITTLE CHILD-FRIEND AND PUPIL,

CHARLIE SEFTON,

I INSCRIBE THIS VOLUME.

THE AUTHOR.

INTRODUCTION

Lovers of the art of fence, to whom the name of Alfred Hutton has long since become a household word, may well have been pardoned had they thought that this expert and author, after the production of his various masterpieces on the swordsmanship of all ages, had exhausted even his apparently limitless power to instruct further in this fascinating subject. They must, however, now confess that although the present work has no pretension to actual technical instruction in the handling of weapons, it is nevertheless full of interest, and therefore almost necessarily instructive, even though indirectly.

As the title indicates, the author has traced the sword and its use from the earliest forms, through all its changes and developments, up to its most perfect state of the present day.

Many will doubtless be tempted to object on the ground that there is nothing new in this, and that the histories of swordsmanship and duelling, either separately or combined, have already been exhaustively treated by such authors as Olivier de la Marche, Embry, Fougeroux de Campigneulles, Coustard de Massi, Millingen, Sabine, Steinmetz, Merignac, and others.

There is certainly much truth in this, but in the present case the subject has been handled on such totally different lines as to constitute a marked difference from the works of these authors, and perhaps for this very reason to call for remark. There is no attempt at a history of duels in chronological order, or at an essay on the development of the sword and its manipulation. Captain Hutton's idea has been from the outset simply to trace the gradual changes in the sword and its accompanying accessories, and at the same time in the form of narrative to give examples of its actual use at different periods, without technicalities of any kind. These instances constitute the chief charm of the book, as all without exception are authenticated facts, many of them being taken from the description of eye-witnesses of the occurrences described, and often given in their own words.

The difficulty experienced by the author in finding an instance of an encounter with every form of weapon—especially the earlier ones—such as the lance, the axe, the sword, the estoc, the two-hand and the bastard sword, must have been enormous; and the fact that he has succeeded vouches for his deep research into ancient works and manuscripts, which alone should attract and interest the true antiquary, be he a swordsman or not.

In addition to the bare record of the details of the different encounters described, and the circumstances to which they owed their origin, points of etiquette are constantly cropping up and explained, which tend most forcibly to illustrate the remarkable social conditions under which men have lived and died. Though the manners and customs of past times are properly speaking a subject quite distinct from that of the book, they come into such close relationship with it that they cannot well be overlooked in this connection, and the author's knowledge of them must in consequence frequently strike the reader as profound.

Commencing with the Age of Chivalry, in which the knightly weapons consisted chiefly of the lance, the axe, and the sword, with the shield for defensive purposes, in addition to the body armour worn, there are given most interesting accounts of both "combats de courtoisie" and "combats à outrance," which thoroughly exemplify the use of these various weapons.

"The Ancient Method and Usage of Duels before the King," or judicial combats, reproduces an old manu-

script verbatim, which sets forth with great minuteness the ceremonies observed on such occasions between knightly opponents. But to show that the judicial combat was by no means confined to men of rank, the author introduces the combat of cudgel and shield, used in like case by the lower orders; as also, which is still more interesting, a reproduction of Sloane MS. 1710, *f.* 152, *which sets forth that "a ffellon may wage bataille, with the order thereof."*

The chapter on the Two-hand Sword contains a verbatim reproduction of Harleian MS. 3542, *ff.* 82-85, *on "The Vse of the Two Hand Sworde," probably one of the oldest treatises on fence in existence.*

The Age of Chivalry ends with the ceremony of degradation of recreant knights and nobles.

Proceeding with the Period of the Rapier and its auxiliaries, we are brought into contact with the most picturesque and the most deadly form of fence ever attained. Numerous examples are given of the treacherous expedients resorted to at this epoch to insure success in an encounter, whether premeditated or by chance, which were only too frequent, but, as Captain Hutton shows, happily relieved from time to time by truly gallant conduct on the part of opponents, which prove that, though the true age of chivalry was past, it was not as yet entirely extinct.

Here, again, in order to find instances of encounters with all the forms of weapons, whether offensive or defensive, in vogue during the Rapier Period, such as the rapier, the case of rapiers, the dagger, the buckler, the great gauntlet, and later, during the Transition Period, the flamberge and early small sword, the author's research must have proved almost endless, though ultimately successful.

The period of the true small sword contains a sketch of the three greatest exponents of it, namely, Saint Georges, Eon de Beaumont and the great Angelo, besides much other interesting matter.

Following this is a minute account of the Prize-

players and Prize-fighters, a subject of which but little is known to the general reader. Captain Hutton in this little volume has certainly brought forward much that is new and interesting to the swordsman, but little that is more so than this, and that his research has been deep and accurate is evident from the reproduction of many old documents of that period, dealing with the manners and customs of the prize players and fighters of the sixteenth century. As the author truly remarks, these two classes should not be confounded with one another, the prize-player being a man who qualified before a jury of experts, whereas the prize-fighter was an individual (of either sex) who competed in public for prizes.

Hence the broadsword gradually leads up to the Nineteenth Century, wherein the duelling sword and sabre of the present day are treated of, the work closing with a chapter on the now obsolete British sports of cudgelling, backswording, and singlestick.

Captain Hutton is to be heartily congratulated on the production of this most interesting little volume, to which I can only wish every success.

CYRIL G. R. MATTHEY.

PREFACE

NOT so many years ago the weapons, and especially the swords, fashioned and fought with in bygone centuries were only to be seen, and then scarcely even looked at, in museums and collections; people passed them by as merely quaint old rusty things, and went on to admire some piece of faded tapestry or curious enamel. But during the last decade a few members of the London Rifle Brigade, under the guidance of an enthusiastic student of old arms and old fighting, began to study the methods of playing with those swords of long ago, which they found out from old Italian books, old French books—ay, and here and there an old English book as well. Of these the most prominent were Captain Cyril Matthey, then a young subaltern in the regiment, who has since won his spurs in the literary world by his admirable reproduction of "The Works of George Silver"; Captains Stenson Cooke and F. H. Whittow, Mr. E. D. Johnson, and Mr. W. P. Gate, most of whom now hold officers' rank; but when they began to interest themselves in this ancient work they were mere boys in their teens, but they attained to such proficiency in the handling of two-hand swords, rapiers, and the like, that they were able to visit various schools and to enthuse the boys by exhibitions of fighting with all kinds of weapons, which were made the more intelligible by short lectures given by the lads themselves. At Bradfield College, in particular, their efforts produced a most happy effect; for the following year an exhibition was given by the boys of the college in their Greek theatre, consisting mainly of Shakespearian fights, with action and dialogue, in which the weapons used were all of the Elizabethan period.

The fame of the London Rifle Brigade fencers found its way abroad, and in 1894 the same party were invited by the Cercle d'Escrime of Brussels to play the leading fighting rôles in a magnificent display at the Théâtre de la Monnaie, known as "L'Escrime à travers les Ages," which consisted of ten combats of various periods in the history of the sword; and to increase the interest of them a short playlet was written round each event, the chief of them being a "combat aux armes courtoises" between Jacques de Lalain and Thomas Qué, of whom more anon. This scene was most superbly mounted; the famous old society of fencers, the Chef-Confrérie de Saint Michel of Ghent, lent their historic banner to adorn the pavilion of their "Bon Chevalier"; and there were a good two hundred people on the stage. There was a fierce fight with two-hand swords, and another, beautifully framed by its little playlet, with the less well-known "case of rapiers"; an encounter at night in the days of Louis XIII. between two gentlemen armed with rapier and cloak, who found themselves among a party of friends who thought fit to amuse themselves with ridiculing the commands of that not very formidable monarch. But they forgot his great Minister; they drew lots about who were to fight: the winners were delighted, and they had the impudence to set to work under the light of the very lantern under which the edict of the Cardinal, the terrible Richelieu, was suspended. They fought beautifully, and neither of them was hurt, for the town guard came on to the scene, commanded by their Captain, who promptly arrested the pugnacious pair and haled them off to prison; the rest of the act took place "behind"—we know Richelieu! And then, last but not least, there was a great fight between three Mignons, those precious pets of Henri III., and three equally pretty fellows attached to the Duke of Guise, the famous "Balafré," only two of whom survived.

Our English public has seen but little of these old-world encounters, embellishments though they be to any costume piece where fighting has its place. Miss Esmé Beringer gave a rare example of it one afternoon as Romeo, the very Romeo that Shakespeare created—a boy in his teens, and not a gentleman in his fifties, and such a gallant boy! How cleverly he wielded his long rapier and his dagger, and sent Tybalt to his ancestors with his *passata sotto!* and how gracefully he played the brief tussle with Paris in the tomb, killing him in fair fight, instead of knifing him, as we have seen it done, without giving him so much as a chance of asking for his life! A year or two later Mr. Tree and his friends showed us a number of fine examples of what the Musketeers could do with rapier, cloak, and dagger, when they played in the Quadrangle scene almost every trick of fence known to Capo Ferro and Alfieri.

When we come to examine the various systems of hand-to-hand fighting, there is no need to go back to the remote ages of nations dead and gone; the Assyrians, the Egyptians, the Greeks, and the Romans all wore armour, and all fought with spears and swords and shields, differing more or less in fashion and in form, but in their use varying scarcely at all from the weapons of the armour-clad knights of the Middle Ages; so it is in the fifteenth century that we may commence our research, and then we find ourselves face to face with no less than five of these periods, each possessing arms in the main peculiar to it, and each teeming with the history of interesting single combats.

It is not our intention to weary our readers with technical details or with cut-and-dried lessons of the fencing of olden time, because it has already been done; and were we to trench on that preserve we might be regarded as literary poachers, and the poacher's lot, when he is caught, is not usually a happy one; if he only steals the title of your book, the finger of scorn may mark him down; and if he helps himself to too much of the inside of it without the judicious use of inverted commas, the rough grip of justice may close on him. No, we will not be poachers! We will show our friends the weapons used in ancient times; we will present to them the courtly encounter of the armoured knights of the fifteenth century, who played, and fiercely, too, at arms for the love of their fair ladies; we will let them see the grim fight to the death for the saving of knightly honour, and the ugly, gruesome, judicial combat between common fellows, in which it was honestly believed that the Deity Himself descended from high heaven to help the innocent and to make known the truth; and in this the immortal Shakespeare gives us some assistance. We shall merge into the day of the long Hispano-Italian rapier; we shall see how and when the chivalrously fair combat in the lists changed itself into the bloodthirsty private meeting in distant field or secluded coppice, in which there were many deeds of "supersticerie"—how very apt is that old Elizabethan word! it conveys a mean, sneaking, murderous act, done with unfair advantage. Such things were common in those days, and were not so badly looked on, either, for that dear, delightful old gossip Brantôme goes so far as to apologize for some of the perpetrators, whose very exploits he has just recorded, by saying that such and such a gentleman, so well known to himself, could hardly have been guilty of such a piece of wickedness. We shall find a fellow go to the field with secret armour under his shirt, and another, knowing that his enemy, trusting to his honour and integrity, will come to the rendezvous alone, will be there before him attended by a party of his friends, who at once set upon the solitary man and despatch him without form or ceremony. And these people were "gentlemen" in the days of Henry the Great! So for the mere sake of self-preservation it was necessary that each of the quarrellers should bring with him a second and a third and a fourth, and sometimes even a larger number; and it became the fashion—we shall see how presently—for all these people to fight with one another, the principals because they had to, the seconds because they chose to, the thirds because it was a horrid cold morning and they wanted to warm themselves, and the fourths because they both agreed that people might say disagreeable things about them if they did nothing but stand twiddling their thumbs when all their friends were fighting. Seeing this, can we wonder that during the reign of that one King alone no less than four thousand French gentlemen lost their lives in private quarrel?

And now we pass on to the fine old fighting times of the Musketeers, of whose exploits Mr. Tree has recently given us such vivid examples. When a party of some four gentlemen had made an engagement to meet another party of the same number (mind you, only two of these eight had any quarrel at all), one of the first-mentioned quartette did not make his appearance—perhaps his stomach had failed him—so they were reduced to three; and as they passed along the street they happened on a solitary gentleman, a perfect stranger to them, who was about his own private business. They took off their great broad-leaved hats and gravely saluted him, and one of them said: "Good sir, behold we are in a great strait; they are four, and we are suddenly reduced to three. The odds are against us. Could you and would you lend us your assistance?" To which the gentleman—such was the fashion of the time—with a great sweep of his magnificent plumed hat, replied: "I' faith, gentlemen, I am much beholden to you. You do me an honour of which I feel scarcely worthy. Nevertheless, my sword and myself are entirely at your service." So off he went with them, and gaily fought with a gentleman whom he had never seen, or even heard of, before, and it was lucky for him if he got home without an extra hole in his skin.

But when Louis XIV., "le Roi Soleil," the Sun King, as he delighted to be called—and, of course, was so—got free from Mazarin, and made up his mind to be his own Prime Minister, he determined to put down the duel. He objected to it greatly: not that he had any objection to people being killed, but he would have them killed on his account, and not on their own. He was a masterful monarch, and he very promptly put a stop to the fighting of seconds, thirds, and fourths, and, for the matter of that, of principals too, by the simple method of hanging a few specimens of them.

During the reign of the great Louis, the form of the sword affected by fashionable people underwent a radical and apparently rather sudden change. The large handsome rapier of the Mignons and the Musketeers disappeared, and its place was taken by a decidedly short weapon, the early form of that which is known among us men of to-day as the small or Court sword. The sword-makers were sorely puzzled to invent for it a blade entirely satisfactory, and it took a hundred years for them to reach its perfection in the shape of the light, elegant, wicked little triangular bodkin of about the year 1770. The earliest form of this small sword-blade was flat and double-edged—a sort of miniature rapier blade; but this proved to be too whippy, and they thickened it into a diamond section, which made the sword so clumsy and ill-balanced that it very soon fatigued its owner to such an extent that he was fain to hold it with both hands. And several masters of the period taught their disciples how this was to be done. Their works are still extant.

Of course, this change in the fashion of the sword necessitated a change in the manner of using it. The masters were equal to the occasion, and invented a system of fence which was the parent of the foil fencing of our own time. But those masters had to teach their pupils to fight, and not merely to play a graceful academic game, so they retained much that was useful of the old rapier principles, especially that of the use of the left hand in parrying a thrust and in overpowering the enemy by seizure of his sword or person. From this time forward the number of weapons needful to be understood was very much curtailed. The long rapier, the bastard sword, "the case of rapiers," and the two-hander, were relegated to the walls of the ancestral castle or the glass case of the museum. The dagger was retained by the soldier, for he fastened it to the end of his musket, and hence the bayonet. The swords which remained were the broadsword for the officer, as well as for the "gladiating" prize-fighter, and the small sword for the civilian.

We now approach the eighteenth century. The "Grand Monarque," who, though old and religious, was still alive, had completely crushed out the evil habit of fighting among the seconds, and, with his rigorous discipline, had made it dangerous even for the principals to void their differences as best it pleased them, so that in France, erstwhile the happy hunting-ground of the duellist, such encounters were rare, and even when they occurred they had to be conducted with the greatest secrecy, so it is to England that we must turn to see what the sword was doing. During the two previous centuries the rage for private fighting was not so pronounced here as it was across the water. It was always attended with more or less risk, for even in Elizabeth's reign killing in a duel was something of a hanging matter; but in the days of the early Georges gentlemen sometimes dined or supped more well than wisely, words flew out, tempers flew out, out flew the swords, and then there was trouble!

That pretty little silver-hilted small sword was as necessary an appendage to the dress of the eighteenth-century gentleman in all weathers as is the umbrella, when the barometer is falling, to that of the gentleman of the twentieth. The civilian arm was the small sword. Then there was the soldier, whose business it was to hack and hew his King's enemies, and he did it with a mighty cut-and-thrust weapon supplied to him by his country. And last, but not least, there was the "gladiating" prize-fighter, who fought his "battles" on the public stage for money and nothing much else. This man had to have skill at his business, and it is him that we have to thank for the preservation of the art of broadsword play in Old England.

In the nineteenth century we must again look to France for examples of sword work; for although the duel still existed in England, it had degenerated into the pistol duel, and the attitude of the seconds had also degenerated. Originally their first duty was, if possible, to accommodate matters and bring their principals to an agreement; but these fire-eaters of the later Georgian times took upon themselves instead the office of inflaming the matter as much as possible, and even of forcing young fellows to kill each other when there was no just quarrel at all, so it was high time that in England the duel should be stamped out once and for all.

CONTENTS

LIST OF ILLUSTRATIONS

NEW INTRODUCTION

The reader looking into the history of the art of self-defence with the sword will find a striking paradox awaits. Although some form of fencing in this manner has been practiced continually for more than 1000 years, there remain more misconceptions than facts in the popular imagination: that only nobles fought single combats; that single combats never included grappling, as in Ju-Jitsu; that whatever use of weapons took place in Europe was undisciplined, and never taught in organized fashion before the age of the rapier, about 1600; that thus, the Oriental martial arts are much older as organized forms than their Occidental counterparts.

Alfred Hutton's *The Sword and the Centuries* holds a unique place in history in this respect. Writing at the end of the 19th century, when History was only newly established as an academic discipline, Hutton, a captain of the King's Dragoon Guards, and a respected expert on and collector of antique weapons, wrote a book that addressed many questions at once. Hutton described the evolution of weapons, and changing attitudes about the use of arms and personal combat; attitudes about the nature of chivalry, and how different classes used weapons in Europe before 1700. In doing this, he established a new kind of history, a new idea of evolution—actual, extensive quotes from primary sources; but also a unique blend of entertainment and historicity, a light tone—"Ye gods and little fishes!" he exclaimed in denouncing the lack of renown of an Italian adventurer to "unfencerlike

England" in Elizabethan times—combined with a rigorous approach to what constitutes evidence in history: He described how D'Artagnan came to meet the Three Musketeers, but took his narrative from D'Artagnan's own memoirs, not from Dumas's novel.

The Sword and the Centuries might almost be seen as a direct response to Egerton Castle's influential 1884 text, *Schools and Masters of Fence*, which declared that all fighting before the age of the rapier (late 16th–early 17th century) was not systematic, but "rough, untutored" brawling, and that "the theory of fencing has reached all but absolute perfection in our days..."

Castle's views fit perfectly with the 19th century view of history—a teleological explanation, a steady progression from a barbaric past to the glories of Victorian civilization. (This view of History also goes far toward explaining why Darwin was, and is, so consistently misunderstood—that a true understanding of biological evolution describes not progress upward from ape to Man, but change without the values of "good" or "bad", or "higher" or "better" attached.) In this respect, *The Sword and the Centuries* is one of the first history texts of the 20th century.

Hutton points out, in the style of a 20th century scholar, that many texts exist from as early as the 13th century, mainly from Germany and later Italy (with a handful each from France, England, Spain, Holland, and Belgium), that prove there were schools of fence and famous teachers all throughout the late middle ages and into the Renaissance. Castle and his followers, therefore, were ignoring a large body of works that showed that the modern conception of the art of self-defence, including prize-fighting as well as fencing, was part of a long, rational development over centuries of both technological and social change, rather than an Athena sprung lately and fully formed from the minds of a few 19th century masters of fence.

Hutton displays his own thorough mastery of the extant texts and powers of research, finding contemporary accounts of combats with almost every form of edged and pointed weapon—broadsword, backsword, estoc, smallsword, bastard sword, two-hander, dagger, lance, sabre, rapier, two-sword, or case of rapiers, longsword, even executioner's "Sword of Justice"—without bogging the reader down in technical discussions nor in arguments concerning who was first to use them. He delights in stories of George Silver, the famous Elizabethan master and "father of English swordsmen," whose 1599 *Paradoxes of Defence* he characterizes as both the first printed English text on fence, and "mainly a fierce attack upon the unsound teaching of the then fashionable Italians," (which Hutton derides as "frog-pricking thrusts" with the rapier, rather than the "good old English custom of . . . honest downright blows with sword and buckler.") He also never loses sight of the fact that his is an entertainment, and thus he concentrates on narratives, at first- and second-hand, that illustrate the mind-set of contemporaries, rather than merely quoting the early texts ("fechtbucher," literally, in German, "fight books") that describe the techniques involved in use of various forms.

Hutton stresses forms of and attitudes toward combat in many different classes, not just among gentlemen. In this way, he exposes striking misconceptions, stating matter-of-factly that "in the days of chivalry, the art of fencing was confined to the lower orders . . ." The true expression of nobility thus lies not in mastery nor teaching of formal techniques of combat, so much as in that only gentlemen would fight solely for pleasure–combat "à la plaisance"—for the entertainment of and only until the satisfaction of, the gentles involved. Hutton describes two different types of Judicial Combat, fondly remembered in popular history as the manner in which a great knight such as William Marshall proved his innocence of unjust charges.

Pointing out that duels among the lower classes had

to be "à la outrance," to the death, because the lower classes were not allowed to bear arms at all, let alone use swords for pleasure, Hutton tells of a combat between two tailors of Valenciennes. The two are of such base state that they must fight on foot with shield and cudgel, clothed in suits of cuir bouilli, boiled leather armour. (He includes an illustration from Hans Talhoffer's 15th century text; interestingly, other editions of Talhoffer show and describe combat between a man and a woman, the male attired and armed as above, but fighting from within a waist-high pit, with the female also attired in leather suit, but armed with a stone in a sack, standing at the edge of the pit.) In this sort of duel, which Hutton says is usually associated with an accusation of murder, one combatant must kill the other, demonstrating the rightness of his claim. The loser's corpse is then delivered to a hangman, for "execution", having been proved guilty of either murder or false accusation.

By way of contrast, Hutton reproduces *The Ancient Method and Usage of Duels Before the King*, the minutely detailed formal rules for a duel between two nobles. Included are lengthy descriptions of how the combatants are to be attired, and how to make their entrance into the field of honour, and how to make their pleas for redress before several court officials, the number of attendant knights and squires each shall have, as well as such provisions as the king's ability at his pleasure to declare a judgement in the quarrel between the two, and that they "be Friends without any further controversy."

Evidence of the evolution Hutton describes (and Castle ignores) continued to be available right through the American Civil War. The McClellan Bayonet Drill, which, following the example of Hanko Doebringer's explanation of Johannes Liechtenauer's 1389 system of dividing the opponent's body into four target areas, divides the target areas for attack and defence into Prime, Segund, Tierce and Quart, was adapted from a French manual of arms, itself derived directly from a fencing manual, probably developed for the spear or polearm in the Swiss-Burgundian wars of the 17th century.

That Hutton's ideas continue to be influential is undeniable. The last decade of the 20th century saw an explosion of interest in edged weapons and their use in Western martial arts. Hutton continues to inspire the work of a generation of modern historians including Brian Price, Stephen Hick, Michael Lacy and Sydney Anglo. The Royal Armouries' Senior Interpreter Andrew Deane is developing a coherent school of martial arts based on illustrated works of the Renaissance, and offering courses in the manner of the old Masters in conjunction with Dr. Jeffrey Forgeng of the Higgins Armory Museum in Worcester, Mass.

Recent translations or new editions have appeared of Talhoffer (Mark Rector's 2000 edition *Medieval Combat* is the first-ever in English), the anonymous 15th century *Jeu de la Hache*, Sigmund Ringeck's, Peter von Danzig's, Fiore di Liberi's 15th century texts, and Jacob Sutorium (Sutor) von Baden's 1612 work; Christian Tobler has published an illustrated work based on the fechtbucher of Johannes Leichtenauer and Ringeck; and there are moves to bring out a translation of the first known medieval martial arts manual, the Royal Armouries' anonymous 13th century Ms I .33.

To be sure, there are still large areas for research. Among the most glaring omissions, neither Hutton nor the fechtbucher discuss in detail the proper use of the shield, especially the larger (Crusader-style) "heater" forms. Indeed, all the fechtbuch illustrations show combatants with smallish bucklers, or else a large, pavise-style with thrusting points top and bottom. And much discussion remains concerning the intended use of the fechtbucher—their elliptical, secretive texts raise the question of whether they were merely extended advertisements for their masters' schools, or notebooks for refreshing students on techniques before attending classes.

Whether read as pure entertainment, or as a seminal academically-based work establishing the new science of History, *The Sword and the Centuries* is bound to bring modern audiences a treasure of delight as well as challenging ideas. Both the casual reader and the devoted historian will find entertainment and sources for further research.

Paul Hilts, New York 2003

THE

SWORD AND THE CENTURIES

BOOK I

THE AGE OF CHIVALRY

THERE are those who pretend that previous to the sixteenth century, the age of the rapier, fencing did not exist except among the lower orders, and that the great ones of the earth, the nobles and knights, despised it altogether, and trusted only to the brute force of their strong right arms and to the splendid temper of their plate armour, and this they did to a very considerable extent, especially in the mounted combats, where the lance was used; but we find these very knights arming themselves for defence with shields, and wherever we see the attack warded by any kind of defensive weapon we have to recognise the art of fence, albeit in an archaic form; while the *hâche d'armes*, or the poleaxe, as people call it, which was about five feet in length, and was used with both hands, had evidently something like a system of fence of its own. This axe was as much favoured as the sword in the tournaments and *pas d'armes*. The smaller people, whose means did not admit of their providing themselves with armour, were compelled to cultivate personal skill, their weapons being for the most part the hand-buckler for defence, and the sword, or at times a stout wooden "wafter," or cudgel, for attack, which also served, as does our latter-day single-stick, as a means for instruction in the use of the steel sword. The dagger or sheath-knife of some description was carried by all, both high and low, and the practice of it was taught by the masters of the time.

The swords of this period were, broadly speaking, the heavy two-hander, the "hand and a half," or bastard sword, a weapon heavy, certainly, but which could be wielded with one hand, and it had a grip so long that the left hand could be used as an auxiliary in dealing a "swashing blow"; and the ordinary one-hand sword, which from its comparative shortness and lightness was the most convenient for personal wear. The blades of all these were double-edged and pointed, and were furnished with a heavy pommel, which served as a balance, and at close quarters proved itself a most crushing and deadly means of attack. To these we must add the estoc, with its long stiff blade, usually pointed only, whose object was the penetration of the strong plate armour. Most of these swords, even the clumsy two-hander, originally belonging to the fifteenth century, outlived also that which followed, as we find Alfieri, an Italian master of the seventeenth century, devoting an entire treatise to it.

The historian Olivier de la Marche, an official at the Court of Philippe le Bon, Duke of Burgundy, has left us in his "Memoirs" an infinity of anecdotes, many of them told with remarkable exactness of detail, of single combats which he himself had witnessed, deadly fights and courteous encounters in the knightly lists, and certainly one instance of the judicial combat, in which it was believed that the Deity Himself intervened to protect the innocent.

CHAPTER I

How the Lord of Ternant and the Spanish Esquire Galiot de Balthasin fought on Foot and on Horseback for Knightly Honour.

We are in the year of grace 1445, and we are at the Court of the good Duke Philip of Burgundy. It was the custom in those days for knightly personages to travel in foreign countries in search of adventure, and accordingly Galiot de Balthasin, a noble esquire of Castille, who was Chamberlain to Philip Maria, Duke of Milan, craved permission, which was readily granted, to quit the dukedom for awhile in order that he might see the world, and if occasion offered it might gain glory for himself with his lance and with his sword. He set out accordingly with a goodly retinue, and in course of his wanderings we see him arrive at the town of Mons, in Hainault, where the Burgundian Court happens to be, and here should be an opportunity for gratifying his ambition. But it chanced that at that time the relations between the two Dukes were of a most cordial nature, and Galiot had received orders from his master that he was on no account to take up arms against any of Duke Philip's subjects unless the initiative came from them, and then only with the consent of the good Duke himself. It must be noted that a single combat, whether to settle once for all some deadly quarrel or only to enhance knightly renown, was absolutely forbidden unless permission was granted by the monarch or some other personage duly authorized by him; which done, the lists were prepared with as much pomp and circumstance as the position of the combatants might require. These lists formed the arena, which for mounted combats was about sixty paces in length and forty in width, and was usually enclosed with a double set of rails, with an entrance at each end.

Galiot, having in his mind the orders he had received, much fears that at the Hainault Court he may not find anyone ready to do him pleasure, and decides that, if it be so, he will cross the seas to England, where the difficulty will no longer exist. He is presented to the good Duke, who sees before him a valiant fellow in the early prime of his years, with a handsome, frank face and a tall, graceful figure, with the strength of the bull and the suppleness of the panther. He is of noble blood, too, and of high renown, and such a man goes straight to the heart of the good Duke, who receives him right cordially, and appoints him lodging suited to his rank. He is still, however, hampered with his Milanese commands; but this soon reaches the ears of the famous Lord of Ternant, a Knight of the Order of the Golden Fleece, and one of the Duke's most cherished warriors. Ternant delights in a passage of arms, and he is very willing to assist Galiot towards the realization of his desires. He accordingly, by permission of the good Duke, mounts on his left arm the badge of his lady-love, which is of itself a challenge to all and sundry to dispute the beauty of the fair damsel, and he sends the King-at-Arms of the Golden Fleece with a courtly message to Galiot to the effect that he wears the badge with special reference to him, and that should he desire to touch it and to

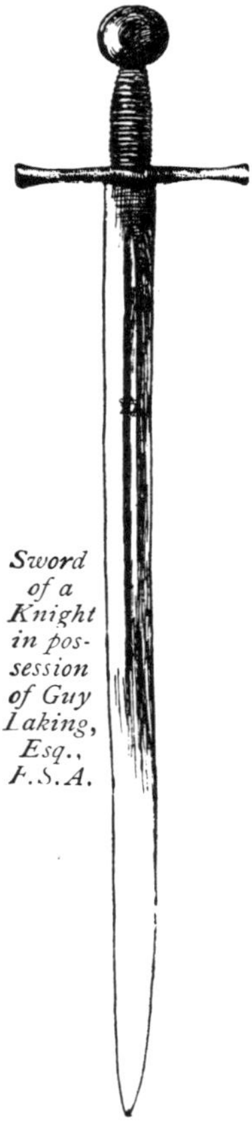

Sword of a Knight in possession of Guy Laking, Esq., F.S.A.

take up the challenge, he will find him one hour after mid-day in the great hall of the castle, in the presence of his highness his lord and master. Now, it was the privilege of the person taking up such a knightly challenge to determine how far the combat should be of a serious nature, and this was shown by the manner in which he touched the badge. Galiot inquires of the Kings-at-Arms and Heralds what is the custom of their country in this respect, when Toison d'Or informs him that indeed it is the idea of the Lord of Ternant to contend for chivalry alone, but that the decision must rest with himself: that if he tears off the badge or handles it roughly, they must fight to the death; but that if he touches it with gentleness and courtesy, then the encounter will be for love of ladies and for knightly honour.

Galiot, having received permission from the good Duke, approaches Ternant with much ceremony, and gently lays his hand upon the badge, saying: "Noble chevalier, je touche à vostre emprise, et au plaisir de Dieu vous fourniray et accompliray tout ce que je sçauray que desirez de faire, soit à pied, soit à cheval." The Lord of Ternant bids him right welcome, and thanks him graciously, promising that in due course he will advise him of the weapons which it is his intention to use, and they are on foot the pike, the estoc, or *espée d'armes*, and the great axe, and on horseback the lance and the sword, while the good Duke arranges that the passage of arms shall take place in the town of Arras in the month of April, 1446, in order to give Galiot time to return to Milan to arm himself and to make his preparations.

The long-looked for day has arrived, the spacious lists are prepared in the great market-place, and on one side of them a large covered stand is erected for the accommodation of the good Duke and his Court; at one end is the pavilion (we humble moderns would call it a dressing tent) of the Lord of Ternant, and a very grand affair it is too, being of blue and black damask with his arms on the crown of it, and surrounded by numerous banners and pennons, and the silken tent of Galiot is equally rich. About an hour after mid-day the good Duke, attended by his son, the Count of Charolois, the Count of Estampes, and many other nobles, enters the stand, bearing in his hand the white staff of the judge, and takes his seat on the throne. The trumpets sound and a party of eight men-at-arms enter the arena. They are armed cap-à-pie, but have no other weapons than white staves, and their duty is to part the champions should the need arise. Of the combatants, the Lord of Ternant, being the challenger, is the first to arrive. He is on horseback. The trappings of his horse are embroidered with his arms, and he himself is wearing his surcoat. He is armed at all points, with his helmet on and his visor raised. He is a dark man with a strong black beard, and in good truth his appearance is such as to inspire respect. He is accompanied by the Lord of Beaujeu and the Count of Sainct-Pol, who act as his seconds or advisers. He dismounts, makes his obeisance to the good Duke, and proceeds to his pavilion. Galiot de Balthasin next rides in. He, too, is in complete armour. He is an agile fellow and intends it to be known, and he vaults clean off his horse as lightly as if he had on nothing more heavy than a silken doublet. He makes his reverence to the Duke, and retires to his tent to prepare for the fray.

The passage of arms is commenced with the combats on foot. The initial ceremonies having been completed, the Marshal of the Lists proceeds to the pavilion of Ternant and demands the pikes which he proposes to use. They are similar in every detail, and he takes them to Galiot, who selects one. At three o'clock the trumpet sounds and the champions appear in complete armour with their visors closed. Ternant advances steadily, holding his pike in both hands. Galiot assumes a much more lively manner. He has his weapon in his right hand only, and plays with it as if it were no heavier than an archer's arrow, and makes one or two leaps in the air so light and so quick that it is clear his armour is no hindrance to him. They charge with such vigour that Galiot breaks the point of his pike on Ternant's breastplate, while the latter strikes so fiercely on his opponent's helmet as to force it open. The white wanded guards appear on the scene and cause the combatants to retire a few paces, when, the damage having been repaired, they charge again, and again a third time, when Ternant's point is broken off and Galiot's pike shivered. Both now retire to their pavilions, the number of thrusts agreed upon having been delivered, for it must be understood that in this affair it had been arranged that each combat should cease after a given number of blows had been exchanged.

They again issue forth armed with the long stiff estoc. In a subsequent story we shall see what a terrible weapon this was, when used in deadly earnest, but our champions of the moment are contending only for knightly honour, just as we ourselves play a friendly bout with the foils in the fencing-room.

Galiot, as before, chooses his weapon, and the encounter commences. The Lord of Ternant, who is fond of fine clothes, and has changed his surcoat for one of white satin embroidered with gold, advances, covered with his round shield, and delivers so furious a thrust that he again forces open his adversary's helmet; but when they charge again, Galiot pierces the arm-guard of Ternant and carries it away on the point of his sword; the armourers adjust it there and then, and when again they meet they both break the points of their swords and have to be supplied with others. After this Ternant plays a more careful game, and deals Galiot such a blow on his helmet that it fairly staggers him; but he recovers himself and pays it back with a thrust on the gauntlet which twists it quite round, to such a degree that the spectators think the wrist is dislocated, but fortunately no serious harm has been done, and they retire to their pavilions, where Ternant takes advantage of the short delay to again change his costume. The Marshal of the Lists now supplies each with a great axe; these axes are exactly similar, about five feet in length, but they have no spikes, as it has been agreed that this combat is to be one of downright blows only. Galiot springs forward and charges Ternant furiously, who steps aside, and, as his assailant is carried forward by the impetus of his advance, deals him such a blow on the back part of his helmet that he makes him reel again; but he quickly recovers himself, and attacks Ternant with such a rain of blows that he is obliged to give back four or five large paces. This is closely watched, and the requisite number of blows having been exchanged, the good Duke throws down his white staff and so terminates the encounter. The guards separate the combatants and conduct them, each with his visor raised and his axe in his hand, to the presence of the Duke, who expresses his pleasure at their prowess and bids them retire.

But their passage of arms is not ended, and the combat on horseback with lance and sword must shortly take place. Monday, May 2, 1446, is the day chosen by the good Duke for Galiot and Ternant to accomplish the remainder of their feats of arms, and something after mid-day he and his Court take their seats, the eight guards make their appearance mounted on the finest coursers that the ducal stables can produce, each one bearing in his hand a short strong staff with which it is again their duty to part the combatants should necessity arise. The Lord of Ternant is the first to come on the scene; he is in complete armour, and both he and his horse are, as usual, magnificently arrayed, the crest, mane, and tail of the latter being interplaited with threads of gold. He makes his obeisance to the Duke and takes his place at his end of the lists. Galiot de Balthasin now appears on a powerful charger which is covered with a species of clothing of buff leather, and he carries on the "chanfrain" and on the "poictral" great sharp spikes of steel. No sooner does the Marshal of the Lists perceive these spikes than he draws to them the attention of the Duke, who, in his capacity of judge, directs the King at Arms to inform Galiot that in his country such things are not permissible; Galiot apologizes most courteously and the offending spikes are removed. He makes his salute to the Duke and proceeds to his place opposite to Ternant. The Marshal now takes the lances and the swords which have been provided by the challenger and presents them to Galiot, who makes his selection. The trumpets sound and the combat commences; they advance at a rapid pace, lance in hand. Ternant has girt himself with his sword in the usual fashion, but Galiot holds his weapon ready drawn in his left hand along with his bridle, and one can see from their manner of approaching each other that Ternant intends to bring his lance into play, while Galiot, who is very powerfully mounted, evidently aims at the contact of the horses themselves, in which the aforesaid spikes would have been very useful. The two champions collide with a tremendous crash, which forces Ternant's charger backwards on to his croup, but both horse and man are equal to the occasion. Unfortunately, however, a hanger of his sword-belt breaks, the hilt of the sword swings free and rests on the horse's croup; but it cannot be said that he is actually disarmed, as the weapon is still in its scabbard, and the scabbard is still more or less attached to his person. He attempts to draw the sword, but he cannot reach it; Galiot takes advantage of this, and rushes upon him with furious blows of edge, point, and pommel. Ternant parries as well as he can with his steel gauntlet, gives his horse the spur, causing it to bound in the air, which frees the sword-hilt, and the weapon slips out of the scabbard on to the ground. He is now completely disarmed, through no fault of his own, and the guards interfere, separate the combatants, and restore the sword to its owner. It is now Ternant's turn to assume the offensive, and after delivering two fierce blows on the helmet he aims with his point at the open joints of Galiot's armour, but the shirt of mail below is serviceable, and no injury is inflicted. By this time the number of blows agreed upon have been accomplished, the good Duke throws down his white staff, and the combat ceases. The champions are conducted to his presence, when he compliments them on their skill and courage, and commands them to embrace and be friends, and thus ends a *pas d'armes* as fiercely fought and as highly thought of as any recorded by the chroniclers of old.

CHAPTER II

How the Good Knight Jacques de Lalain and the English Esquire Thomas Qué fought with the Great Axe.

OF all the warriors who formed the Court of Duke Philip of Burgundy, the most renowned for his chivalry was the good knight Jacques de Lalain, whose "gestes" are amply recorded by George Chastellan, King at Arms of the Golden Fleece. He, like Galiot de Balthasin, conceived a desire for foreign travel and foreign fame, and having received permission from his liege lord, he betook himself to Scotland, accompanied by his uncle, Messire Simon de Lalain, Lord of Montigny, and an esquire of Brittany named Hervé de Meriadet, where they were honourably entertained by the King, James II., who granted them the lists, in which they were opposed, Lalain to James Douglas, Simon to the Lord of Haguet (Halkett ?), and Meriadet to another, and the affair, in which the great axe was the chief weapon, terminated in favour of Lalain and his party.

They next proceeded to London, and presented themselves at the Court. That not very brilliant monarch Henry VI. was still on the throne, and he not only accorded them a very poor reception indeed, but, further, absolutely refused to permit any of his subjects to take up their challenge. Annoyed by such treatment, and disappointed at the failure of their enterprise, they decided to quit England as soon as possible, repaired to "Sand-wyc," and had scarcely embarked on board ship, when they were overtaken by a young English esquire, named Thomas Qué,

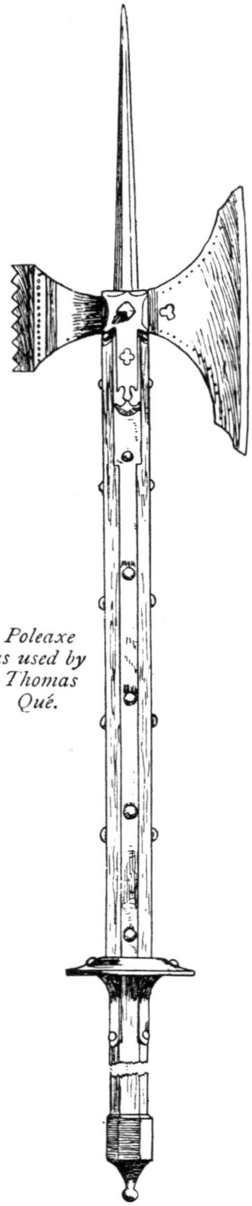

Poleaxe as used by Thomas Qué.

who had been absent from the Court during their short visit. He expressed his regret that so noble and famous a knight as the Chevalier de Lalain should have been so unceremoniously treated, and should have been balked of the object of his ambition, and informed him that he would make arrangements in six weeks' time to cross the sea and take up the challenge, hoping that the combat would take place in the presence and under the personal control of the good Duke Philip himself.

There was joy at the Court of the good Duke, and more than all in the heart of the brave Lalain, when letters were received from the English esquire announcing his speedy arrival, in order to accomplish the feat of arms exactly as it had been proposed by Messire Jacques, namely, that each should wear the harness he was accustomed to use in the lists, and that they should contend on foot with the great axe and with the sword until one or other should measure his length on the ground.

Messire de Lalain immediately approached his master, requesting the ducal license and permission to accomplish his undertaking, which license was generously and gracefully accorded, and commands issued that the lists should be prepared in the market-place of Bruges with such pomp and circumstance as should do honour to the combatants.

The important day arrived; the old market-place was gaily decked with pennons and banners, and the windows of all the houses thronged with richly dressed strangers. In the centre were placed the lists, the enclosed space in which the contest was to take place, at each end of which was a pavilion or retiring tent. And around this space were canopied platforms for the more privileged spectators, while in the centre was placed the ducal throne. The Duke himself then appeared, attended by a brilliant court of great nobles, knights, and esquires, with many great ladies.

Messire Jacques, having been informed of the arrival of the Court, immediately presented himself in the lists accompanied by his two uncles, the Lord of Crequi and the Lord of Montigny, that same Simon de Lalain who had been his companion in Scotland, and numerous other friends, made his obeisance to the Duke, and then retired to his pavilion. The English esquire then entered, attended by two knights whom the Duke had, according to the usual custom, appointed to act as his seconds, or rather advisers, and after having saluted His Highness betook himself to his tent to assume his armour.

It was the custom that the weapons of each combatant should be duly examined, and there was some discussion on the axe brought by the Englishman, which was something more dangerous in form than those usually employed in the tournament. It was furnished with a large cutting blade, a heavy warhammer on the reverse side, and a very long spike, while the "tail" was also armed with sharp steel. The head of Lalain's weapon was composed of a hammer, a "bec de faucon" (a sort of pick resembling a falcon's beak), and a short spike for thrusting. Even Messire Jacques himself drew attention to the disparity of the weapons, but Thomas Qué begged so persistently to be allowed to retain the one which, as he said, he had brought from England on purpose, that Lalain, out of his courtesy and good nature, withdrew all objection, unfortunately for himself, as we shall show.

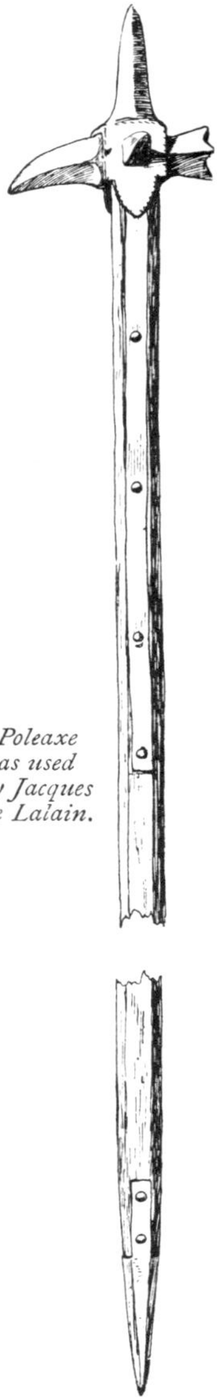

Poleaxe as used by Jacques de Lalain.

The ceremonies usual in tournaments having been completed, the champions issued from their pavilions, that of Lalain being most sumptuously appointed, and adorned with thirty-two banners, containing the arms of all the noble houses with which he was connected by descent. He was armed at all points, but bore on his head only a small "sallade" with neither gorget nor visor, so that his face and neck were completely exposed. His only offensive weapon was his axe, which he held at the balance close to his person, so that he might be able to attack or to defend with either end of it. Qué, on the other hand, wore on his head a strong helmet with the visor closed and firmly fixed, and he carried his axe in such a way that it was clear that he intended to rely mainly upon the head of the weapon in his assault. He was also "girt with his sword."

The combat commences. Messire Jacques delivers a fierce thrust with the tail-spike of his axe at the visor of his opponent's helmet, but it does not penetrate; Qué replies with a rush and a charge, aiming blow after blow with edge, hammer, and point at the fair mark of Lalain's unarmoured face. Messire Jacques, however, is an active man, well skilled in his passes and traverses. He deftly evades the furious onslaught until it somewhat slackens, and his light, open headgear allows him to breathe freely, while his adversary, half smothered in his heavy, close-visored helmet, is at something of a disadvantage. The Flemish knight seizes his chance, lands a furious swinging stroke well on the helmet of Qué, and follows with a veritable rain of such ponderous blows that a weaker man must have succumbed to them. But Thomas Qué is valiant, strong of limb, with much good old British beef and ale in his composition, and the fierce onslaught of the Fleming but makes him moderate his ardour somewhat, and he guards and parries with the greater coolness, until Messire Jacques again attempts to penetrate his visor with the tail of his weapon. Qué parries it upwards with the head of his axe, but by mishap the point of his long sharp "dague" enters the left wrist of Lalain, where his gauntlet is unarmoured, and pierces it through and through. The fight is not over, though, for neither champion is down. The good Chevalier draws back his injured hand, which bleeds copiously, retires a pace or two, and tries in vain to grasp his axe with it. He raises it on high and shakes the gauntlet as if he hopes in some way to check the bleeding. He places the head of his weapon underneath his left arm, and with the tail-end beats off the "doubly redoubled blows" of the English esquire, when fortune at last favours him, for at the moment when Qué is aiming a terrific blow, with both arms held aloft, he charges him at the unarmoured joint of the armpit, with his right hand grasps the back part of his helmet, and with a vigorous wrench drags him forward, when, his armour being very heavy, his balance is lost, and he falls with a crash at full length, with the sharp conical visor of his "pig-faced" helmet buried so deep in the ground that he is unable to regain his feet without the assistance of the attendant guards. The victory is awarded to Lalain by the good Duke Philip, and so ends one of the most picturesque encounters with the historic *hâche d'armes*.

CHAPTER III

How Two Tailors fought to the Death with Shield and Cudgel.

OUR former gallant scene is played and the curtain down. Ring up again, Mr. Prompter! And what now meets our eye? No longer the brightly-decked market-place of old Bruges, with its canopied platforms thronged with lovely dames and their attendant knights. No, we are in the highly-privileged city of Valenciennes. True, the place is a public one, but the drama we are to witness is grim and ghastly, such as no woman or child is allowed to see. And who are to be the chief actors in it? Not the Bon Chevalier, the courtly Lalain, and his brave English opponent Thomas Qué, who fought a friendly fight for the love of their fair ladies and for their own knightly honour. Our champions to-day are a pair of common journeymen tailors, of such base sort that they may not wield a sword, but must fight out their quarrel with weapons suited to their low condition. And they must fight to the death, for in the times in which we find ourselves it was firmly and earnestly believed that the Deity Himself would descend from heaven to protect the innocent. And once more rare old Olivier tells us the story.

Among the "liberties" which had been granted by the Emperors and the Counts of Hainault to the worthy burghers of Valenciennes was a very peculiar one. Any person, gentle or simple, who might have the misfortune to take the life of another in self-defence could claim sanctuary on declaring that the fight had been a fair one, and that he was ready to maintain the same with his body in the lists; and this done, all process of law against him had to cease, nor was any person allowed to molest him except by taking up his challenge. The weapons, too, were curious. They consisted of a stout wooden club and a shield of wood something in the form of that used by the Crusaders—that is to say, nearly triangular. These were imposed upon all, both high and low, and the only favour conceded to the high-born combatant was that he

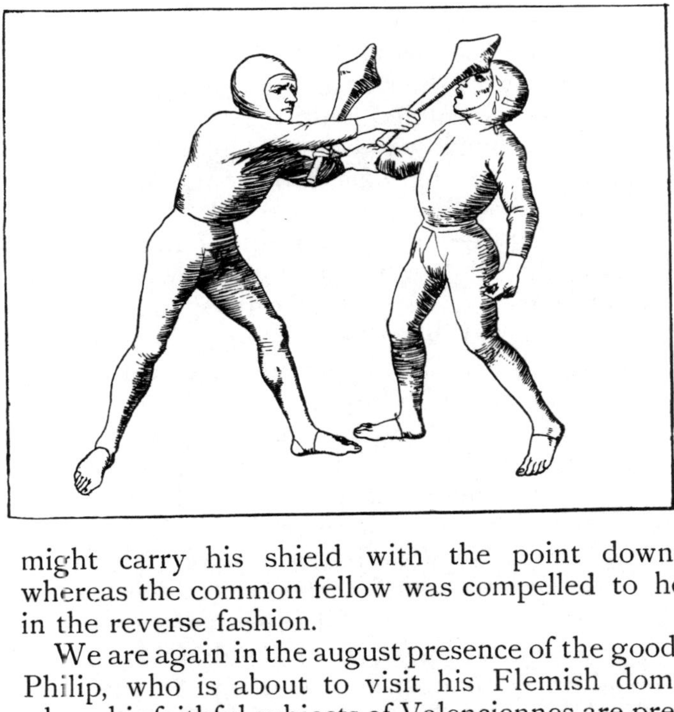

Costume worn by common men in the judicial combat. From "Talhofer's Fechtbuch."

might carry his shield with the point downwards, whereas the common fellow was compelled to hold his in the reverse fashion.

We are again in the august presence of the good Duke Philip, who is about to visit his Flemish dominions, where his faithful subjects of Valenciennes are preparing a special treat for him, one of such rare occurrence that even to so potent a Prince it ought to be a novelty.

It so happened that a tailor named Mahuot had come to words with another fellow, whose name does not appear, and from words they proceeded to blows, which ended in the death of Mahuot's enemy. There were no witnesses. The survivor told the story in his own way, and things were going well with him, when a relative of the deceased man, a spiteful fellow named Jacotin Plouvier, took the matter in hand, and set current a rumour that the fight had not been a fair one, and that his unfortunate cousin had been treacherously murdered. He finally set the law in motion against Mahuot, formally accused him of the crime, and declared his readiness to prove his case in the lists, club and shield in hand. The two litigants were promptly arrested, and kept safe but separate; they were well cared for, too, and bountifully fed, that they might be strong on the day of their battle, and in state to show good sport to the assembled multitude.

The day has arrived. The good Duke Philip, with his son the Count de Charolais, is present, but although he is the Sovereign, he is not the judge on this occasion. This duty devolves by right of their ancient charter upon the high officials of the town, Messire Gilles de Harchies, Lord of Beilligniers, the Provost, and Merciot du Gardin, the Mayor, who are also charged with all the arrangements and ceremonies incident to this strange spectacle.

The lists are dressed in the market square, and so great is the crowd of eager witnesses that Nicolas du Gardin, who commands the guards at the Hôtel de Ville, has much ado to preserve order. On occasion of a serious combat such as this, it was forbidden to all to make any sign or sound which might serve as a warning to either champion, and no man was permitted so much as to speak, or even to cough or to sneeze, under penalties of a most severe nature. And when the worthy Nicolas sees that the people are inclined to transgress, he lays about him vigorously with a huge staff which he carries, crying, "Gare le ban!" an exclamation which quiets the noisy ones right speedily, and, indeed, it is needful, for all the people side with Mahuot, their fellow-townsman.

The arena is a peculiar one. It is circular, and not, as usual, square, and it has but one entrance. Inside it are placed, facing each other, two chairs draped with black, on one of which Mahuot, who is the first to appear, takes his seat, followed immediately by Jacotin Plouvier.

The toilet of the two champions is also a strange one. Their heads have been shaved, they are bare-footed, and the nails of both their fingers and their toes have been carefully pared, while their bodies and limbs are clothed in garments of dressed leather (*cuir bouilli*), so tightly fitting that they had to be actually sewn upon their persons. The myrmidons of the law now make their appearance, accompanied by a priest, who bears a large missal, on which he causes them to make oath that their cause is a just one; that is to say, Mahuot swears that he killed his man in fair fight, while Jacotin swears precisely the contrary. To each man is now presented his shield, with the point of it upwards: it is painted red, and bears on its surface the cross of St. George; and next his club of tough wood, the two clubs being of exactly the same size and weight. The men now request that three things may be supplied to them, namely, grease, wood ashes, and sugar, and anon are brought two large basins full of grease, with which their tight-fitting leathern garments are besmeared. They are followed by two basins of wood ashes, with which they remove the grease from their hands, the better to hold their shields and clubs. And lastly there is placed in the mouth of each a lump of sugar to prevent thirst.

The chairs are now removed, the men of the law retire, and the champions are left facing each other, on which the Mayor rises from his seat, exclaiming, "Let each man do his duty!" The fight begins, and they charge each other vigorously. Mahuot, seeing that he is something overmatched by the size and weight of his enemy, attempts a ruse. He picks up a handful of sand, with which the lists are plentifully strewn, and dashes it into Plouvier's face, following the action with a blow of his club on the forehead, which causes the blood to flow freely. This, however, only serves to enrage Jacotin, who is a sturdy, powerful fellow, and he attacks Mahuot so furiously as to make him fall headlong, whereon he springs upon him, tears his eyes out of their sockets, finishes him with a tremendous blow on the head, and finally, taking him in his arms, flings him over the railing into those of the executioner, who promptly hangs him on the gibbet which has been erected for the accommodation of the vanquished man.

Vulson de la Colombière records that in England and France, when judicial combats of this kind took place, common men were armed with the club only, as the shield, being that part of the armour on which its owner's heraldic devices were painted, was considered doubly noble, and it must in no way be contaminated with the touch of plebeian hands. In Edward III.'s time there was such a battle between Hamon le Stare and Walter Blowberne, very uninteresting persons, certainly, being nothing better than a pair of thieves who had fallen out about their booty. There exists a picture of them, a copy of which forms the frontispiece to the Selden Society's "Crown Pleas." They are armed with a peculiar kind of club, and are without shields. Hamon was vanquished, and was, as usual, promptly hanged.

Shakespeare also, in the second part of "King Henry VI." (Act II., Scene iii.), places such a scene on the stage, and Halliwell records that it was founded on fact; that the real names of the men were William Catour the armourer and John Davy his apprentice; and that the lists were duly prepared, the cost of erecting them being £10 8s. 9d., which would represent in these days a much larger sum. Shakespeare names his armourer "Horner," and his apprentice "Peter Thump," and he places the scene in a hall of justice, arming the men with sandbags attached to staves. These two arrangements seem to have been made to suit the convenience of the stage in Shakespeare's time, for the great hall of a castle is the very last place in which we can imagine such a contest taking place; the lists were always erected in the open air, and the sandbag must have been employed as being less dangerous for theatrical work than a heavy club. The fight in the play has something of a comic effect at the commencement, for the armourer's admirers ply him to such an extent with sack, charneco, and strong beer that he is quite incapacitated; and after a little preliminary skirmishing, in which the tipsy fellow reels about all over the arena, the apprentice manages to get in a sound blow which brings him to the ground, on which he confesses himself to be in the wrong. The end of Horner was, of course, the customary one, for an item in the accounts runs, "Also paid for 1 pole and nayllis, and for settyng up of ye said mannys hed on London Brigge, v*d*."

The thorough belief in Divine intervention is shown by the King's speech at the end of the scene:

"Go, take hence that traitor from our sight,
For by his death we do perceive his guilt;
And God in justice hath reveal'd to us
The truth and innocence of this poor fellow
Which he had thought to have murder'd wrongfully."

CHAPTER IV

How the Good Knight *Sans Peur et sans Reproche* fought in the Lists with the Estoc against the Spaniard Sotomaior, and slew him.

BAYARD! What noble thoughts does this name call up! this hero for all time, famed alike for his courage in fight, his courtesy in camp and in castle, his piety, his generosity, and his patriotism. Put the life of the good Chevalier into the hands of a young boy and bid him strive to be a Bayard, and you need bid him nothing more!

We are in the dawn of the sixteenth century, the most romantic period of the history of the sword, from the chivalrous weapon of the armour-clad knight to the murderous rapier of the silken-coated Mignon.

In the year 1503 we find King Louis XII. of France at war with the then Spanish ruler of Naples, and the Good Knight without Fear or Reproach one of his most trusted officers; he is at this time in command of the fortress of Monervino, from which place one fine day he thinks fit to make a reconnaissance, in which he encounters a troop of Spaniards whom he defeats without the loss of a single man of his own party. True, some five or six of his people have been wounded, and a couple of horses killed, but as a set-off for this he has taken several prisoners, among whom is the Spanish commander himself, Don Alonzo de Sotomaior. During the journey home he discovers that his prisoner is of a noble family, and therefore on arrival at his castle assigns to him one of its handsomest chambers, and, to add to his comfort, provides him with suitable apparel from his own wardrobe, saying to him: "My Lord Alonzo, I am informed by some of the prisoners whom I have taken that you come of an illustrious house, and that, which renders you in my eyes still more to be honoured, you are of high renown for your prowess in arms. I would not, therefore, treat you as a prisoner, and if you will give me your faith not to quit the castle without my permission, I make you free of the whole. It is spacious, you can amuse yourself as you will, and I and my officers will be right glad of your company until such time as you shall have arranged and paid your ransom, about which matter you will not find me difficult." Sotomaior replied: "Captain, I thank you for your courtesy, and assure you on my faith that I will not depart hence without leave from you." But he failed to keep his promise, and he afterwards paid dearly for his treachery.

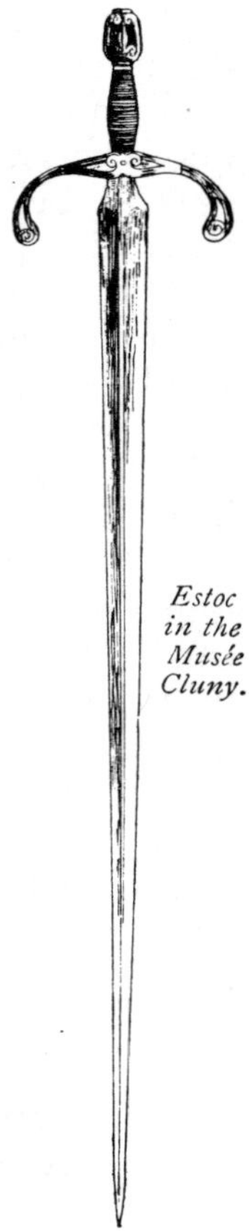

Estoc in the Musée Cluny.

Some fifteen or twenty days does the Spanish noble remain at Monervino, during which time he arranges his ransom at a thousand crowns; he and his companions are treated most hospitably, and he roams about the castle as suits his pleasure without so much as a challenge from a sentry. One day he finds himself in conversation with a certain Albanian, an avaricious fellow and easily tempted, and he says: "Look you, Theode: you can do me a good turn, and if you will do it I give you my word that you shall want for nothing so long as I live. My sojourn in this place irritates me, and the more so that I have no news of any of my people; if you will procure me a horse to-morrow morning, I can slip away easily, and in four hours gain a garrison of my friends. I will take you with me, I will provide you with the best of employment, and will give you in addition fifty golden ducats." Theode, greedy as he is, has some misgivings, and remarks: "But I hear you are on parole, and if you do this thing our Captain will have a quarrel with you; and, in good truth, he is not a man to trifle with." Don Alonzo replies: "I am not about to break my faith; I have arranged my ransom at a thousand ducats, which I shall immediately despatch to your Captain." "Good!" quoth the rascal; "at daybreak to-morrow without fail I shall be outside the castle gate with two horses; when the gate opens, make you pretence to come out to take the air, and then to horse and away." This arrangement the worthy pair duly carry out, but the good Chevalier, who was never a sluggard of a morning, comes down early into the lower courtyard and asks for Don Alonzo, but no one knows anything about him, except the porter, who had seen him at daybreak near the gate. The alarm-bell is sounded and search is made, but neither Sotomaior nor Theode the Albanian can be discovered anywhere. Bayard, greatly annoyed, turns to one of his men named Le Basque. "Mount at once," says he: "take with you nine others, spur towards Andria, and if you find our prisoner, bring him back dead or alive; and if you catch that rascally Albanian bring him also, that he may hang from the battlements as a warning to others." A misfortune now happens to Don Alonzo; his girths give way, and he is obliged to dismount in order to rearrange them. Le Basque and his merry men appear upon the scene; the treacherous Theode, knowing well what his life will be worth if he is taken, puts spurs to his horse and rides as hard as he can to Andria, which is only distant about two miles. The Spaniard also tries to mount, but his saddle turns with him, and he is captured, put on his horse, and taken back to Monervino, where he is brought before the good Chevalier, who says: "How now, my Lord Alonzo? You pledged me your faith that you would not quit the castle without my leave, and this is how you keep your promise; such is not the act of an honest gentleman, and I can no longer trust you." Don Alonzo tries to explain that he meant no harm, that he would have sent the ransom within the space of two days, and that he only ran away because he was weary at not receiving any news of his friends. At such paltry excuses the good Chevalier is more angry than ever, and shuts him up in a tower, where he keeps him a fortnight, without, however, loading him with chains or subjecting him to any other annoyance, and the food and drink supplied to him are such as he can in no way complain of. At the end of this time the ransom arrives, and Sotomaior, to his astonishment, sees the good Chevalier divide the whole of it among his men, after which he is permitted to depart.

On arriving at Andria, Don Alonzo meets with a most marvellous reception from his companions in arms, for, to tell the truth, there was not a man in the Spanish army more esteemed as a warrior. He was greatly disgusted at his captivity, and his friends console him as well as they are able, pointing out that, after all, it is the fortune of war sometimes to win and sometimes to lose, and that they ought really to thank Providence for having sent him back to them safe and sound. They ask him many questions about the good Chevalier. "What sort of man is he? What is his mode of life? How did he treat you when you were his captive?" Don Alonzo answers: "By my faith, my friends, I know not in the world a more hardy gentleman nor one with less of the sloth about him; for when he is not about some fighting business or other, he is for ever taking his share in the games of his men, such as wrestling, leaping, throwing the bar, and such-like manly exercises; and as for his generosity, in that matter he has no equal, for when my ransom arrived, with mine own eyes I saw him divide the whole of it among his soldiers without keeping so much as a crown piece for himself. But as for the treatment I received, whether it was by his orders or not, his people did not treat me like a gentleman ; indeed, they were so much more rough with me than they need have been that I never can forgive it." Some of his friends, knowing the good name borne by Bayard, are amazed at this ; others say : "Oh, well, nobody quite likes being a prisoner"; and some even go so far as to think that he had himself to thank for it, so there is a good deal of talk in the garrison of Andria, in which the name of the good Chevalier is rather severely handled, and this is brought to his ears by a returned prisoner of war.

The good Chevalier is greatly astonished, and he calls his people together and addresses them : "See, gentlemen, here is this Don Alonzo complaining among his Spanish friends that I have treated him more vilely than words can express ; you all know what has happened, and for my part I do not think that any prisoner of war could have been used more generously, until he thought fit to break his faith with me and attempt to escape ; and, in good truth, if I thought I had done him any wrong I would willingly make him all the amends in my power. But, by my faith, I will write to him and tell him that, although I am suffering from quartan fever, if he still ventures to say that I have treated him ill, I will prove the contrary in single fight, my body against his, on foot or on horseback, whichever of the two may please him." The letter is written, and conveyed to Andria by the Lord of La Palisse, known among his friends as La Lune. Don Alonzo reads it, and without consulting anyone sends back a somewhat rough answer, to the effect that he is not the man to retract anything he may have said, and that he accepts the combat, which must take place in a fortnight, within two miles of the Castle of Andria, or elsewhere, should the other party wish it. The good Chevalier chooses for his seconds or advisers La Lune and his old comrade Bellabre.

The day appointed has arrived, and the Lord of La Palisse, accompanied, as has been agreed, by two hundred men at arms, conducts his principal to the field mounted on a fine powerful courser, and dressed in white in token of humility; but Don Alonzo is not yet present, so La Lune proceeds to hasten him, when he inquires in what array the good Chevalier may be, to which the answer is, "On horseback as a man at arms." "How so?" says Alonzo; "is it for me to choose the arms and for him the field?"—ignoring the fact that the field had been chosen by himself, and that in not too polite a fashion either—"go and tell him that I intend to fight on foot." In fact, Don Alonzo, who has by this time heard a good deal more about his man than he knew before, would have little objection to get out of the affair altogether; he fancies that the good Chevalier will refuse the proposed combat on account of the fever from which he is suffering, and that even if he consents, he will be in so weak a state that all the advantage will be on the side of Sotomaior. When this news is brought to the good Chevalier, he remains in thought for a moment, for he had that very morning suffered from an attack, but, having the courage of a lion, replies: "La Lune, my friend, bid him make haste, for with God's help I will this day defend mine honour."

They now busy themselves with preparing the lists, which are not railed in as usual, but are simply formed of rows of large stones. The good Chevalier now enters accompanied by the Lords of La Palisse, Humbercourt, Fontrailles, and many other valiant Captains, who all pray to our Lord that He will vouchsafe to aid their champion. Don Alonzo now finds that fight he must, so he appears, followed by a numerous retinue, takes his place in the field, and sends to Bayard the special weapons with which he intends to fight, namely, an estoc and a dagger, with a gorget and a steel cap. The good Chevalier scarcely troubles to make any choice, but when all is prepared he kneels down and offers up a prayer; then, prostrating himself, kisses the ground, and as he rises makes the sign of the cross, and marches straight towards his enemy as gaily as if he were in a palace among a bevy of fair ladies. Don Alonzo now advances, saying: "Lord of Bayard, what would you with me?" To which our hero replies: "I would defend mine honour." And without more ado they attack each other briskly with various fierce thrusts, one of which slightly wounds the Spaniard in the face, and causes him to be more careful in his fight and to cover his face as much as possible. The good Chevalier, finding him thus difficult, resorts to a ruse: when Don Alonzo raises his weapon to deliver a thrust, he also raises his as if he were about to give a counter, but he keeps it steady, and when the attack of his enemy is finished, and no harm done, he finds him entirely open, and plants such a tremendous thrust on the centre of his gorget that, notwithstanding the excellence of the steel, his estoc pierces it through and through and penetrates four good fingers' breadths into his throat, and the point is fixed so hard and fast that he cannot withdraw it. Sotomaior, feeling himself mortally wounded, attempts to wrestle with his enemy, and both fall together, when Bayard, alert and active, draws his dagger and, placing the point against the nostrils of the fallen man, calls upon him to yield. But he is dead already. His second, Don Diego de Quiñones, exclaims: "Lord of Bayard, he is no more; you are the victor." The good Chevalier is much grieved, for he would have given a hundred thousand crowns, if he had possessed them, to have conquered his enemy alive; nevertheless, recognising the hand of Providence in his victory, he kneels down and gives humble thanks to God, after which, according to the usual custom, he seizes the corpse by the foot and drags it out of the lists, saying to Don Diego: "You know that it is my right to deal with this according to my good pleasure, and it is my pleasure to render it to you; and indeed I would, my honour being saved, that matters were otherwise."

The Spaniards bear away the body of their champion

with lamentable cries, while the French conduct their hero to the sound of trumpets and clarions in triumph to the castle of the good Lord of La Palisse; and so ends a fight which has rendered the name of the great Bayard more glorious than ever for his courage and the nobility of his soul.

CHAPTER V

How the Baron d'Aguerre fought with the Lord of Fendilles with the Bastard Sword, and what came of it.

THERE has been a controversy among "kernoozers," collectors, and other wise men as to what manner of sword the "bastard" really was, but it was recently set at rest at the Society of Antiquaries by the production of a very rare book, "The Schoole of the Noble and Worthy Science of Defence," by Joseph Swetnam, an Elizabethan fencing master, who describes it thus: "The Bastard sword, the which sword is something shorter than a long sword, and yet longer than a short sword." Vulson de la Colombière also alludes to the two weapons used in the combat presently treated of as "Deux espées bastardes, pouvans servir à une main et à deux, les gardes d'icelles faites à une croisette seulement, et pas d'asne ouvert." This is the sword recognised by the above-mentioned wise men as the "hand and a half sword," but the name seems to be a modern invention. The story of D'Aguerre and Fendilles is taken partly from Colombière, who has evidently based his work on the *procès verbal* itself, and partly from the "Discours sur les Duels" of that delightful old gossip Brantôme.

At the Court of Henri II., in the early days of his reign, there was a terrible scandal which greatly affected the honour of Claude d'Aguerre, Baron of Vienne le Chastel, and it arose from certain statements made against him by Jacques de Fontaine, Lord of Fendilles, a young man who was regarded among his acquaintance as something of a mad-brain and something of a bully; but the accusations were of so serious a nature that nothing but blood could wipe them out, and the matter became still more complicated from the fact that acts of violence had been committed, Fendilles having given the lie to D'Aguerre and boxed his ears into the bargain. After having consulted with their friends, they applied to the King for permission to void their quarrel by mortal combat; but Henri II., who had been greatly chagrined at the recent death of his friend Chastaigneraïe, killed in single fight by the Sieur de Jarnac, at which event he himself had acted as judge, and had registered a solemn vow that he would never again permit such an encounter to take place, flatly refused his consent; but they found the Duc de Bouillon more accommodating, and he granted them the lists in his own country, where he held sovereign rights.

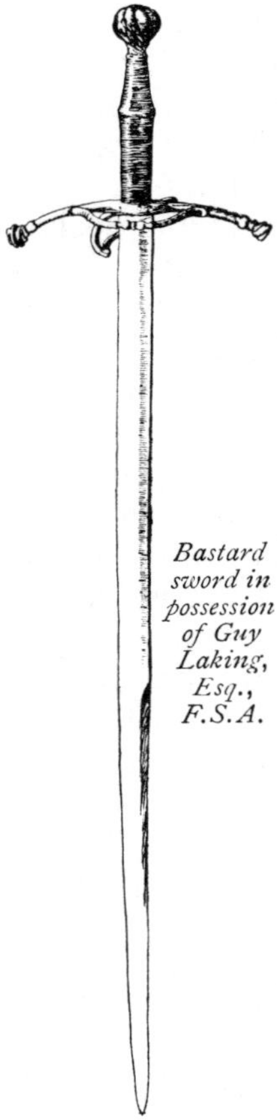

Bastard sword in possession of Guy Laking, Esq., F.S.A.

The day fixed for the event is August 28, 1549, and the "camp" is arranged in the lists of Sedan, and four officials, M. de Louppy, M. de Miremont, M. de Mebrich, and M. de Sisieulx, are charged with the preparations about which they are busy before sunrise, at which time D'Aguerre the challenger is introduced by his second, the Vidame of Chartres, accompanied by some two hundred of his company clad in his colours of scarlet and white, and he is conducted to his pavilion, which has been erected close to his entry, and where he is expected to remain until his appearance is required within the lists. Fendilles has been commanded to make his appearance within one hour after the arrival of the challenger, and he gives evidence of his truculent nature by causing to be prepared a gibbet and a great fire for the accommodation of D'Aguerre when he shall have vanquished him; for, according to the laws and customs which regulated these combats, the person of the conquered man, whether alive or dead, was the absolute property of the victor, to treat as best it might please him. But Fendilles seems to have but little stomach for the fight after all, and his delay in arriving causes the friends of D'Aguerre to make complaint and to demand that judgment may be given against Fendilles, and that he may be declared vanquished by default, with all the attendant unpleasant circumstances, among which would be conspicuous the gibbet and the fire provided by himself. At length, however, he is produced by his second, the Duke of Nevers, attended by some thirty or forty retainers dressed in his colours, white and green, and he is conducted to his pavilion. Each combatant is now arrayed in his armour, is brought into the lists, and is conducted to a seat at his own end of the arena. He is now required to make oath that his quarrel is a just one, and that of his enemy unjust, and that he has about himself and his arms no kind of charm or magical contrivance wherewith to hurt his enemy, and that he trusts only in the justice of the Deity, his good right hand, and the excellence of his arms. The choice of the weapons falls to Fendilles, whose second, the Duke of Nevers, selects one of them; they are "bastard" swords, which may be used with either one hand or both hands. Their hilts are furnished with plain cross-guards, or *quillons*, and *pas d'âne* unprotected by rings or counter-guards, and their blades are broad and heavy, with double edges and sharp points; each of the seconds provides himself with a sword of similar make, to be held in readiness in case the weapon of either combatant should be broken. The champions are still seated in their chairs.

The Herald now enters the lists and makes the following proclamation: "In the name of my Sovereign

Lord I make express command to all that, so soon as these present combatants are engaged, all persons shall maintain silence, shall abstain from speaking, coughing, or spitting, and shall make no sign with foot, hand, or eye which may aid, injure, or prejudice either of the aforesaid combatants. And I further command, in the name of my said Sovereign Lord, to all and sundry, be their quality what it may, that they shall not on pain of death set foot in the lists, or in any way interfere with either of the said combatants, be his necessity what it may, without the permission of my said Sovereign Lord and of the Masters of the Lists."

The trumpet sounds, and the Herald cries : " Laissez les aller, laissez les aller, laissez les aller, les bons combatants !" when they rise from their chairs, D'Aguerre the first, who for a moment fixes his gaze upon his enemy; then, raising his eyes to heaven, kisses the cross of his sword, as also does Fendilles, when they move towards each other with rapid strides. For an instant they halt, but advance again, each with his point levelled at the other; D'Aguerre attacks and so presses his man that he nearly drives him against the barriers, which are of cords, hoping to force him altogether out of the lists, and so to claim the victory ; but Fendilles eludes him and deals him a severe stroke across the thigh, causing, from the great weight and breadth of the sword-blade, a huge gaping wound, from which the blood flows in such great abundance that D'Aguerre fears his strength may fail him. He lets fall his sword, and being an expert wrestler (for be it understood that no one in those days was considered a complete man-at-arms unless he was proficient in the wrestling art), he throws his enemy, holds him down, and, having disarmed him of his morion, deals him many severe blows on the head and face with it, so that he is covered with blood and bruises; but the morion slips from his grasp, and he finds himself unarmed. He feels his strength still ebbing, when the

3

attention of Judge, Masters of the Lists, seconds and everyone is diverted by an unforeseen accident. A large scaffold which has been erected for the accommodation of certain of the spectators of a sudden gives way; it is crowded with dames and demoiselles, nobles and knights, who have come to enjoy the cruel sport. It falls with a terrible crash, all the wretched people are precipitated into the ruins, and the noise caused by the groans of the injured and the screams of the terrified is such that scarce anything else can be heard; while the remaining spectators hesitate between seeing the end of the fight and going to the assistance of the unfortunate victims. Taking advantage of the uproar, some of his friends cry out to D'Aguerre, "Jettez lui du sable dans les yeux et la bouche," a thing which under other circumstances they would not have dared to do for their lives. Now, the ground is, as usual in such cases, plentifully strewn with sand, and the Baron, who is growing weaker and weaker, takes the hint, and throws such quantities of sand into the face of Fendilles that he nearly suffocates him, crying out to him: "Rends moy mon honneur, rends moy mon honneur, ne me tiens tu pour homme de bien?" To which Fendilles, in despair, at last replies: "Oüy, oüy, je te le rends de bon cœur, et te tiens pour homme de bien, tel que tu es.'

This confession of Fendilles is reported by the Masters of the Lists, the seconds and others to the Judge, who declares him to have been vanquished by force of arms, and attainted and convicted as a false accuser; whereon he is stripped of his armour by the Heralds and flung over the barriers to the outside of the lists, as being a person unworthy to make his exit as does the victor, while D'Aguerre, after his wound has been dressed, is conducted to the sound of trumpets and drums to his lodging with triumph and great pomp.

CHAPTER VI

The Two-hand Sword.

UNLIKE the "bastard" sword, which may be wielded with one hand or with both, as occasion may serve, the two-hander was of such a ponderous nature that it was no easy matter for even a stout fellow to manœuvre it well, and that was of necessity always with both hands. It approached six feet in length from pommel to point; it was double-edged, like most of the swords of its period; its hilt was furnished with a guard, consisting of long quillons, with very often a ring at each side, and about a foot or so above this guard the heavy broad blade was furnished with two "lugs," which in a measure protected the hand when the grip had to be shifted from the handle to the forte of the blade, and the part between the quillons and the lugs was very often covered with leather. It does not appear to have possessed any scabbard, but the soldier carried it naked at the "slope," with the flat of the blade resting on his shoulder. From its immense weight, it could only be entrusted to the biggest and strongest men-at-arms, some of whom used often to be detailed to act as escort to the Auncient, or Standard-bearer.

It possessed a system of fence of its own based very largely, as George Silver says, on the fight of the "short staf of cõvenient length," which was a simple traveller's staff, something in the form of an alpenstock, and of a length suited to the height and powers of its owner. Its practice is largely entered into by Joseph

3—2

Swetnam (1617), and by George Silver (1599), whose works have been recently edited by Captain Cyril Matthey. Foil swords of steel were also used for the instruction and practice of the two-hander. There exists also in the British Museum a very curious and interesting fifteenth-century manuscript* giving detailed lessons in the use of the two-hander, the transcript of which here follows :

The Vse of the Two Hand Sworde.

The ferste pleyng & begӯnyng of the substansce of ye too honde swerde / ye ferst gronde be gynyth[1] wt an hauke[2] beryng inwt ye foote wt a double rownde wt . iij . fete howtewarde & as meny homward makyng ende of ye play wt a quarter cros smetyn wt an hauke snach settyng down by ye foote.

The . ij . lesson ys . ij . haukys wt . ij . halfe haukys cleuӯg ye elbowys wyth ye same . ij . doubylrowndys forsayde wt . iij . foote owtward . & as meny hamward.

The . iij . lesson ys a sprynge vpward . wt an hauke quarter . downe by ye cheke . wt . ij . doubylrowndys stondӯg borne on ye hed . wt a dowbylrownde born in wt ye foote . wt . iij . outwards.

The . iiij . lesson . ys wt a dowbil hauke wyth . ij . doubil rowndis[3] berӯg inwt a step vp on bothe feete.

The . 5 . lesson ys wt an hauke menyd[4] our ye hede . but bere ht vp wt a step . breke of ye erthe wt rēnyng rowndis on ye hede wt . ij . halfe havkis born wt . ij . koc stappis[5] of ye foete.

The . 6 . lesson bere ovte ye erthe wt . iij . koc stapps & so come home ovte of danger a gayne.

The . 7 . lesson ys . Smyte an hauke cros . cros our ye elbovys wt a bak stop & so smyte ht on ye fet.

[T]he . 8 . lesson ys wt . an hauke cros smytӯ

[1] *Beginneth.*
[2] *A blow.*
[3] *Circular cut.*
[4] *Managed* (?).
[5] *Nimble steps.*

* British Museum, Harleian MS. 3542, ff. 82-85.

wt a bakstep born wt bothe fete & a contrary hauke hamward born wt . ij . steppis.

These ben stroke & revle of ye . ij . hondswerd to make hys hond & ys foete a corde.

[T]he pley of ye . ij . hondswerd

by twene . ij . bokelers ys . fyrst take a sygne of ye gonde ther ye pley by twene . ij . bokelers . make ferst a sygne to hē wt a large hauke down to ye grownde . wt . iij . rollyng strokis[6] . wt an hauke to ye oder side.

[T]he . ij . lesson ys a chase . or an hauke wyt a quartr born in wt a kocstep & an hauke born in wt a chase foyn[7] . y made vp wt a lygte sprȳg.

[T]he . 3 . lesson ys . a chase[8] . wt . ij . havkys cleuyng ye elbovis.

[T]he . 4 . lesson . ys a chase smetȳ wt . ij . half rowndis . wt . ij . kocstoppis . a qrter wt a steppe an hauke wt a chase foyn . wt ye stroke a venture[9] smetȳ on . iij . fete . & made vp wt a rake[10] down . & bore vp wt a dovbil hauke . & so serue ye stroke aūetur vp on bothe fete.

[T]he . 5 . lesson . ys a chase wt an hauke & wt a bakstep stondȳg on ye foote . & playng on yt othr syde a qrter & ye same chase . & an hauk wt a step . & an hauke wt a chase foyn contry smyten . & so smyte in wt bothe feete i made vp wt . ij . halfe hauke . wt . ij . bakstoppis . & wt ye rēnyng.

[T]he . 6 . lesson ys . ij . hauke qrters rovnys wt a brokyn halfe hauke a leyng dovn to ye foete wt a contrary honde ys is ye fyrst leyng a dovne.

[T]he . 7 . lesson & ye fyrst takyng vp ys . iij . rakys vpward & . iij . dovneward . & gan inwt a grete steppe . wt doubyl qrter wel smytȳ . berȳg ovte wt ye foete a brokyn halfe hauke settȳg downe ye swerde by ye foete.

[T]he . 8 . lesson & ye secnde leȳg a dovne of thy swerde . ij . haukys wt a qrter & iii wt ye foete wt a brokyn hauke . a leȳg dovne to ye foete wt a cōtrary honde.

[T]he . 9 . lesson & ye secnde takȳg vp of thy swerde ys . iij . haukys on euych[11] syde stondyng on ye erthe stil wt a stop bor menyd on ye erthe

6 *Moulinets.*

7 *Thrust.*

8 *A charge. An attack made to drive back the enemy.*

9 *A stroke made at a chance opening shown by the enemy.*

10 *Rake is a blow given at the fullest reach.*

11 *Each.*

. w^{t} an hauke quart^{r} born w^{t} a step . and w^{t} a doubyl qrter honde & foete born ou^{r} ye hede . an hauke menyd settyng thy swerd by thy foete.

[T]he . 10 . lesson & y^{e} . iij . leyng dovne of thy swerd ys a qrter & in w^{t} ye foete & an hauke brokȳg at ye cheke & then a doubil hauke a bovte ye hed brokyn . & then in w^{t} a sprȳge of ye foete . w^{t} a stroke auēture . w^{t} a qrter & w^{t} a snache . leyng to ye erthe w^{t} a cōtrary hond.

[T]he . 11 . lesson & ye iij . takȳg vp ys w^{t} a sprynge w^{t} y^{t} on hond rigte vp on to ye visage w^{t} an halfe rounde brokȳ in to a step w^{t} a reuence to ye cros of thy hilte w^{t} a long cartar stroke smetȳ flat dovne by ye bak . w^{t} a doubil brokȳ spryng bak ye foete a drawyng . & in w^{t} a long rake dobil . in wyth ye foete walkyng & on eche foete . ij . rakys . & at ye alurys ende smyte in . iiij . rakys doubille born into a step . & so ye other rakys in to ye alure ende . & dovbil y^{t} on in to a step . a gayn turnȳg in w^{t} a long dovbil rake w^{t} a step . & w^{t} y^{t} oth^{r} hond spryng vp thy swerd to thy rygt shulder & smyte thy stroke auētur w^{t} an hauke settȳg dovne thy swerd by thy foete.

To Incounter wth the Two Hand Sworde.

And as for ye first contenance of y^{e} . ij . hōd swerd . thou shalt walk in w^{t} . iij . foete to thy adu^{r}sary w^{t} a bold spyrte & a mery herte w^{t} a sengyl qrter . & a sengil quart^{r} wastyd[12] w^{t} a cart^{r} stroke, and thus smyte thy conter bothe of & on & lete thy hond & thy foet a corde to geder in goede afense.

12 *Well laid on.*

[T]he . ij . conter ys w^{t} a doubil quart^{r} w^{t} thy foete goyng . & a dobyl quart^{r} wastid in to a step & in w^{t} thy foete & smyte a large hauke vp in to ye skye . w^{t} a doubil snache.

[T]he . 3 . lesson of ye covnter ys . a rake on eche foete goyng till thou come to thy adusary . w^{t} a doubil quart w^{t} hole defense born w^{t} an oth^{r} dobil qrter w^{t} hole defense breke in & a sygne a toche w^{t} a large sprynge & smyte w^{t} fers stroke menyd w^{t} hole defence & so smyte ys cowntr bothe of & on . & bovre[13] thy strokis of eche of thy cowntris.

[T]he . 4 . cownt ys . ij . halfe rovndys. Wyth a tnye[14] foyne . beryng in ye foyne wt a qrter . & an hauke at ye skye wt a snache wt thy hole defence born a for the . & ths cowntr most be smete wt tnsposyng of thy erthe of bothe fete for surenesse of defence.

[T]he . 5 . cownt is an halfe rownde of ye secnde foete . & than smyte . ij . dobil haukys & bothe sides hole . & brokē enter hȳ wt ye ferst foete . wt a dobil qrter . & so smyte a cartr stroke but tne[15] hym wt a stroke auēture wt hole defence . & thvs smyte ths cownter bothe of & on . & lete thy eye . thy foete . & thy honde a corde in thy defence . ye cause of stroke auēture is callyd . for a mā tnyth hys bak to hys enmy.

[T]he . 6 . cowntr ys beryng in wt . iij . foynys on bothe fete . & loke thou tñe hond & foete & smyte a large qrter . & ber in a stop wt thy bak nakyd born . & smyte a large hauke wt fers hert & draw hym sor vp to ye skye.

[T]he . 7 . cowntr ys menyd wt . iij . menyd foyns & trāspose hā bothe goyng & comyng . & smyte thy foynys wt in thy sengyl quart . & at ye last quartr smyte a large sprynge wt a lusty stop a fore & then a chace foyne.

The Play with the 2 Hand Sword in Verse.

Man yt wol to ye to hond swerd lern[16] bothe close & clere /
He most haue a goode eye both fer & nere
& an in stop . & an owte stop . & an hauke qrter. A cantel . a doblet . an half for hys fere
Too rowndys . & an halfe wt a goede cher . This ys ye ferst cownter of ye too hond swerd sere[17]
Bynde hē to gedere & sey god spede . Two qrters & a rownde a stop thou hȳ bede
A rake wt a spryng yer thou hȳ a byde . ffalle in wt an hauke & stride nogte to wyde

13 *Bear.*
14 *Turning.*
15 *Turn.*
16 *Learn.*
17 *Sore, terrible* (?).

Smyte a rēnȳg qrter owte for hys syde
ffal a pō hys harneys yf he wole a byde
Come in w^{t} a rake in euy a syde
An hole rownde & an halfe . Wath so h^{t} be tyde
. iiij . qrters & a rownd . & aueture stroke wyth
Bere vp hys harnes & gete thou ye gryth
Dobyl vp lygtly & do as y seye
ffal in w^{t} an hauke & ber a goede eye
A spryng & a rownde & stap in wyth
Spar nogth ā hauke yf he lye in thy kyth
Smyte a rēnȳg qrter for owte of thy honde
A byde a pon a pēdent & lese not thy londe
Smyte in ye lyfte foete & cleue rygt dovne
Geder ovte of thy rygte hond & smyte a hauke rovnde
ffresly smyte thy strokis by dene[18]
And hold wel thy lond thath hyt may be sene
Thy rakys . thy rowndis . thy qrters a bowte
Thy stoppis . thy foynys . lete hē fast rowte
Thy spryngys . thy quarters . thy rabetis[19] also
Bere a goede eye & lete thy hond go
ffy on a false hert y^{t} dar not a byde
Wen he seyth rovndys & rakys rēnyng by h^{s} side
ffle not hastly for a lytil pryde
ffor lytil wote thy adusary wath hȳ shal be tide
lete strokys fast folowe aft^{r} hys honde
And hauk rovnde w^{t} a stop & stil y^{t} thou stond
Greue not gretly thov y^{u} be tochyd a lyte
ffor ā aft^{r} stroke ys bet^{r} yf thou dar hȳ smyte
A gode rovnde w^{t} an hauke & smyte rygt dovne
Gedyr vp a doblet & spar not hys crovne
W^{t} a rownde & a rake a byde at a bay
W^{t} a rēnȳg[20] qrter sette hȳ oute of hys way
Thys beeth ye lettr y^{t} stondȳ in hys sygte
To teche . or to play . or ellys for to fygte
These beeth ye strokys of thy hole grovnde
ffor hurte . or for dynte[21] or ellys for dethys wonde.

[18] *Skill.*
[19] *Recoveries.*
[20] *Furious.*
[21] *Heavy stroke.*

How Sir Patrick Hamiltoun fought with the Dutch Knight and vanquished him. And how the Italian "Rocko" was constrained to fight with Austen Bagger, and was sore hurt.

Lindsay of Pitscottie tells a story of a Dutch knight, whom he names "Sir John Cockbewis," in the fifteenth century, at the time when Jacques de Lalain flourished, who, like many others, set out on his travels in search of adventure and renown, and he relates a notable combat in the lists between this knight and Sir Patrick Hamilton, in which the two-hand sword had its part. This encounter was none of the mortal kind, as some of those already described, but, like that between the Lord of Ternant and Galiot de Balthasin, for love of ladies and for knightly honour.

The narrative of Pitscottie is not so replete with interesting details as those of La Marche, Brantôme, D'Audiguier, and Colombière, but he gives us a fair general idea of the fight, which we will allow him to describe in his own quaint style: "Thair cam ane Duch knyght in Scotland, called Sir John Cockbewis, and desired fighting and justing with the lordes and barrones thairoff. But none was so apt and readie to fight with him as Sir Patrick Hamiltoun, being then strong of bodie and able to all thingis, and yitt for lak of exercisoun he was not so weill practised as mister had beine, though he laked no hardiment, strength, nor courage. Bot when the Duchman and he was assembled togidder on great horsis, under the castle wall of Edinburgh, in the barrace; so efter the sound of trumpet, the rusched verrie rudlie togidder and break thair spears on uther, and immediatlie gatt new speares and encountered againe. Bot Sir Patrickis horse utterit witht him and wald on nowayis encounter his adversar againe, that it was force to the said Sir Patrick Hammelltoun to lyght on footte and gif the Duchman battell; and thairfor quhene he was lichtit doune cryit for ane two handit sword, and bad this Duchman lyght frome

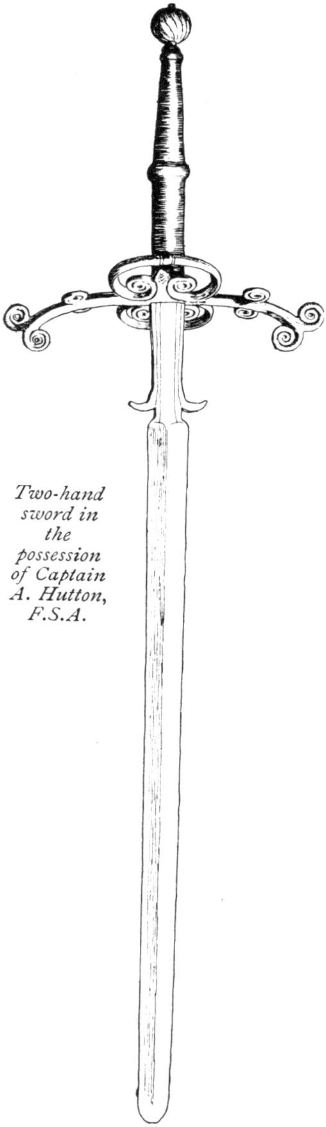
Two-hand sword in the possession of Captain A. Hutton, F.S.A.

his horse and end out the matter, schawand to him ane horse is bot ane waik weapon quhene men hes maist ado. Then both the knightis alighted on thair foott, and joyned pertlie togidder with rightawful countenance; each on strak uther and foight the space of an hour with uncertaine victorie, quhill at the last the said Sir Patrick rusched rudlie upon the Duchman, and strak him on his knies, and the Duchman being on his knies, the king kest his hatt over the castle wall, and caused the judges to stay and red thame; but the heraldis and trumpeteris cryed and soundit, saying the victorie was Sir Patrikis."

George Silver gives a curious account of an encounter between one Signor Rocco, an Italian professor who came to England about the year 1569 to teach his art, and an English swordsman named Austin Bagger, who had the reputation of being a good fighting man, and to have seen "manie tall fraies," but does not appear to have been in any sense a professional. Silver's story is as follows:

"This Signior Rocko came into England about

some thirtie yeares past: he taught the Noblemen and Gentlemen of the Court; he caused some of them to weare leaden soales in their shoes, the better to bring them to nimblenesse of feet in their fight. He disbursed a great summe of money for the lease of a faire house in Warwicke lane, which he called his Colledge, for he thought it great disgrace for him to keepe a Fence-schoole, he being then to be the onely famous maister of the Art of armes in the whole world. He caused to be fairely drawne and set round about his Schoole all the Noblemens and Gentlemens arms that were his Schollers, and hanging right under their armes their Rapiers, daggers, gloves of male and gantlets. Also he had benches and stooles, the roome being verie large, for Gentlemē to sit round about his Schoole to behold his teaching. He taught none commonly under twentie, fortie, fifty or an hundred pounds. And to know how the time passed he had in one corner of his schoole a Clocke, with a verie faire large Diall, he had within that schoole, a roome the which was called his privie schoole, with manie weapons therein, where he did teach his schollers his secret fight after he had perfectly taught them their rules. He was verie much beloved in the Court.

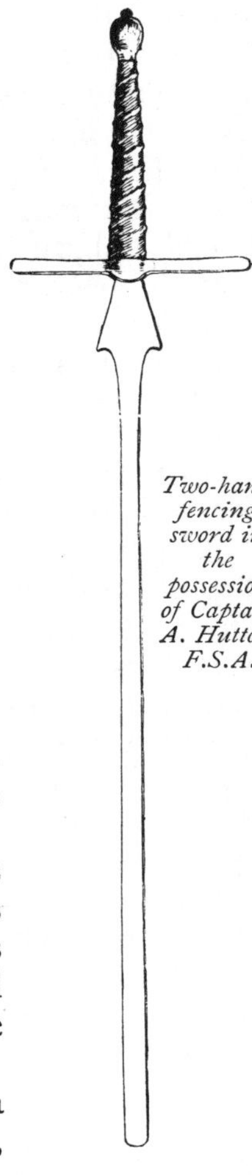

Two-hand fencing sword in the possession of Captain A. Hutton, F.S.A.

"There was one Austen Bagger, a verie tall gentleman of his handes, not standing much upon his skill, but carying the valiant hart of an Englishman, upon a time being merrie amongst his friendes, said he would go fight with Signior Rocco, presently (*i.e.*, that very instant) went to Signior Rocco his house in the Blackefriers, and called to him in this maner: Signior Rocco, thou that art thought to be the onely cunning man in the world with thy weapon, thou that takest upon thee to hit anie Englishman with a thrust upon anie button, thou that takest upon thee to come over the seas, to teach the valiant Noblemen and Gentlemen of England to fight, thou cowardly fellow come out of thy house if thou dare for thy life, I am come to fight with thee. Signior Rocco looking out at a window, perceiving him in the street to stand readie with his Sword and Buckler, with his two-hand sword drawne, with all speed ran into the street, and manfully let flie at Austen Bagger, who most bravely defended himselfe, and presently (instantly) closed with him, and stroke up his heeles and cut him over the breech, and trode upon, and most grievously hurt him under his feet: yet in the end Austen of his good nature gave him his life, and there left him. This was the first and last fight that ever Signior Rocco made, saving once at Queene Hith he drew his Rapier upon a waterman, where he was throughly beaten with Oares and Stretchers, but the oddes of their weapons were as great against his Rapier, as was his two-hand Sword against Austen Bagger's Sword and Buckler."

The two-hander was recognised as worthy of something more than mere respect when employed against any weapon of lighter make, although assisted by a buckler or other defensive arm. Its ponderous, sweeping strokes must have needed a very strong man indeed and a very active one to stop them even by parrying "double," and Austen Bagger was certainly a gentleman of this type.

CHAPTER VII

Of the Sword and Buckler, and how the Sieur de Jarnac fought in the Lists with the Lord of Chastaigneraïe and how he slew him.

THE sword used in such a fight was the double-edged sword commonly worn on the person, whether on foot or on horseback, and on ordinary occasions the hand-buckler, a small round shield about eleven inches in diameter, having but one handle at the centre, which was held in the fist, was the usual defensive auxiliary. These weapons were the constant companions of the average English gentleman in his daily walks, and very useful he found them in the sudden quarrels in street and tavern, which were common in the somewhat boisterous times in which he lived. But in the more serious prearranged combats in the lists a larger shield, quite two feet in diameter, was employed, which, when it was furnished with the single handle, never mind what its size might be, was recognised as a "buckler"; but when it was attached to the forearm by two bands of steel or straps of leather, through one of which the arm was passed, while the second was grasped in the hand, it was known as the "target" or "rondache." It covered the forearm and hand, but although from its great breadth it protected a considerable part of the person, it was not so handy in fight when wielded by an active, skilled fencer as was the smaller shield.

In the year 1547, the last year of the life of King Francis I. of France, two young nobles were prominent at his Court, whom Colombière states to have been of much the same age, and neighbours in the part of the country from which they came. They had both been brought up as royal pages in the King's household, and had since borne arms in His Majesty's service, exactly as had their fathers before them. They were constantly together, and were understood to be on almost brotherly terms. The one was François de Vivonne, Lord of Chastaigneraïe, a younger son of André de Vivonne, Grand Seneschal of Poictou. He was greatly admired, honoured — ay, and redoubted too, not only for the high favour he was in with King Francis, and afterwards with King Henri II., but also for his great natural beauty, his varied accomplishments, and his magnificent stature, and still more for his generous heart, his invincible spirit, his experience in arms, and his confidence in his own splendid dexterity. The other was Guy de Chabot, eldest son of Charles, Lord of Jarnac, Monlieu, and Saint Aulaye. He was such a favourite with King Francis that he always addressed him as "Guichot," from the particular affection he felt for him. He was known at the Court as the Sieur de Jarnac. The title Sieur appears to have been applied to the eldest son of a noble house in old France very much as that of Master is in Scotland.

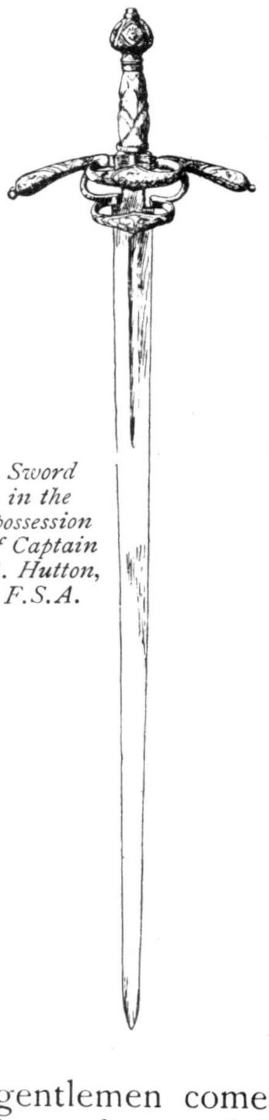

Sword in the possession of Captain A. Hutton, F.S.A.

The friendship between these two gentlemen comes to an untimely end, owing to the imprudence of Vivonne, who relates to the King a scandalous tale, which seriously affects the fair name of Jarnac, and still more seriously the honour of a certain lady nearly connected with him by marriage, the details of which I refrain from recording. Francis, not alto-

The "Coup de Jarnac," after Wulson de la Colombière.

gether believing the story, unfortunately treats it as a joke, and in a manner twits Jarnac about it. He, however, sees nothing at all to laugh at, and is in such high dudgeon that he accuses Chastaigneraïe to the King of falsehood. Moreover, he makes a public statement that whosoever has made the statements against the lady and himself lies in his throat like the wretched scoundrel that he is, and he takes care that Chastaigneraïe shall be made well aware as to whom this statement applies. The latter now takes umbrage at having been given the lie, and seeing a fine opportunity for fighting the young Jarnac, whom, confident in his dexterity and his experience in arms, he assures himself that he will speedily crush, he appeals to King Francis to grant him the lists in order that he may fight his enemy to the death, and Jarnac, on his side, is equally anxious for the encounter, in order that by force of arms he may clear his own honour and the fair fame of the lady. But Francis, feeling himself perhaps something to blame in the matter, peremptorily refuses this; but the obstacle is removed shortly afterwards by his death, when he is succeeded by Henri II. Chastaigneraïe stills pursues the affair, and, assuming the rôle of challenger on account of the lie given him, applies to the new King for permission to finish the quarrel in the lists, and he, seeing that the difference, owing to the entire absence of anything in the shape of evidence, can in no other way be adjusted, grants the request, ordaining that the combat shall take place in his presence within the space of thirty days, and that the vanquished man, both in himself and in the heirs of his body, for ever shall be degraded, regarded as ignoble persons, and deprived of all the rights, privileges, and prerogatives usually enjoyed by the nobles of his realm.

The two enemies have now a month in which to prepare themselves. Chastaigneraïe, with his overweening confidence in his own powers—for, in addition to his renown as a man at arms, he is so skilled in the art of wrestling that there is not a professional wrestler in all Brittany that can stand against him—takes but little trouble either to practise with his weapons or to attend to his religious duties, for when he finds himself near a church he passes by it lightly, and the idea of hearing Mass scarcely enters his head; while Jarnac, on the contrary, not only frequents the churches and monasteries, begging the good people there to pray for him, but further enlists the services of an Italian fencing-master of much skill and resource, by name Captain Caizo, who, judging from the nature of the instruction which he imparts to his pupil, must be an adept in the precepts of the renowned Achille Marozzo, whose work has been published only a few years. We shall shortly see the result of the Captain's teaching.

King Henri has decided that the combat shall take place on July 10, 1547, and that the lists shall be duly prepared at Saint Germain-en-Laye, where His Majesty is staying. The old Lord of Jarnac having been advised of the behaviour of his son in this matter, is greatly pleased with him, and says openly that if his boy had not taken up the quarrel he would, notwithstanding his age, have fought Chastaigneraïe himself, the which greatly encourages the younger Jarnac, who in due time presents himself at Saint Germain, accompanied by his second, M. de Boizy, the Grand Escuyer, as does also his enemy, attended by the Count of Aumalle. The lists are arranged near to the park of Saint Germain, according to the directions of the Connestable, the Marshals, and the Admiral of France, who are with the King, and the Herald makes the usual proclamation to the spectators, to the effect that no person shall make any sign to either champion which may either assist him or hinder his enemy.

The Lord of Chastaigneraïe has, in his over-confidence of victory, made certain preparations, even as did Fendilles, one of the heroes of the "bastard sword" fight, although not of quite so gruesome a character. He has erected outside the lists a splendid marquee, in which is prepared a magnificent banquet, to which he has already invited the King and the whole of his Court, in order to duly celebrate the event, and, to do the more honour to his royal master, to say nothing of himself, he has had recourse to all his friends for the loan of such vessels of gold and silver, rich armour, carpets and tapestries, as they may be able to supply.

The challenger is now brought from his lodging by his second, attended by a company of 300 of his men dressed in his colours of scarlet and white, who conduct him with drums and trumpets to the entrance of the arena, when the Count of Aumalle leads him to his pavilion, which is pitched on the right-hand side of the King's stand, and which he must not quit until his entrance into the *champ clos*. The defender Jarnac now appears, accompanied by his second and a band of retainers clad in black and white, to the number of about sixscore. Each champion is attended, in addition to his second, by certain friends or "confidants," whose duty it is to see to his wants and to render him such service as the laws of the combat may allow; namely, on the side of the challenger the Sieurs of Sansac, Monluc, Aureille, Fregoze, and the Count of Berlinchière, and on that of the defender the Sieurs of Clervaut, Castelnau, Carrouge, and Ambleville.

Jarnac, as the defender, has the right to decide what armour and weapons shall be employed, and he selects for armour a corselet, a pair of gauntlets, a shirt of mail, a large steel buckler, and a morion, all of which are accepted by the other side as arms in general use among gentlemen; but he further imposes, by the advice of the cunning Caizo, a peculiar "brassard," or armpiece, for the left arm, which is made without any joint, and so fashioned that it keeps the arm quite straight and rigid, so that the combatants can use their bucklers for defence, but anything in the shape of seizing the opponent and throwing him is quite impossible. Chastaigneraïe's friends object to this "brassard" as being an unusual piece, but he himself haughtily accepts it. It is now the turn of Jarnac and his party to be hopeful, and it happens that when his esquire is fixing the aforesaid armpiece on to Chastaigneraïe's arm he hurts him slightly, and he exclaims angrily, "I'll make you pay for this when the affair is over!" to which the esquire replies, "Oh, there will not be much left of you to frighten me when my master has done with you." And so, indeed, it happened. Moreover, it was rumoured in Paris three hours before the combat actually took place that Chastaigneraïe had been killed, and the wily Caizo moved about among the intending spectators, engaged in what we vulgar twentieth-century people would call "making his book" on the possibility of there being a ham sliced before sunset.

The Herald again makes his proclamation respecting non-interference on the part of the spectators, after which the challenger is introduced into the *champ clos* by his second, and following him the defender, who now sends to him the offensive weapons which he has determined to use, and of which there is one provided for each combatant; they are, a one-hand sword, double-edged and very sharp, a large dagger to be carried in its sheath at the right side, and a smaller one to be worn in the boot somewhat after the fashion of the Highlander's skene dhu, and he selects which of each pair suits him. Each of them is now required, according to the usual custom, to swear on the four Gospels that his quarrel is a just one and that of his enemy unjust, and that he carries neither on his person nor on his arms any charm or magical device with which he may unfairly hurt his enemy.

This ceremony completed, the champions are conducted to their seats at opposite ends of the lists, and the Herald enters, on which they rise, their seconds take leave of them, and the Herald cries: "Laissez les aller, laissez les aller, laissez les aller, les bons combattans." They advance to meet each other, Chastaigneraïe with furious mien and disordered steps, Jarnac cool and confident in the sound instruction he has received from Caizo. Several fierce thrusts and blows are given and parried on both sides, when Jarnac shifts his ground, feints a swashing blow at his enemy's head, and so draws up his shield to defend it, and as it rises dexterously passes his point behind the unfortunate man's left knee, holding his hand in pronation, and with a quick movement snatches it back, bringing the sharp false edge into contact with the lower part of the ham. This slight cut startles Chastaigneraïe, but before he has time to move Jarnac repeats it in a much more serious fashion, severing sinews, veins, muscles, and everything down to the very bone. Chastaigneraïe falls to the ground, and Jarnac approaches him, calling to him: "Render me mine honour, and cry mercy of God and the King for the fault you have committed;" and perceiving that it is utterly impossible for the wounded man to regain his feet, he advances towards the King and asks if his honour is secured, in which case he will gladly give Chastaigneraïe to His Majesty. But the King is angry at the discomfiture of his favourite, and makes no reply. Meanwhile the fallen man is trying to struggle to his feet in order to attack Jarnac, when the latter presents his point, crying: "Move not, or I kill you." Chastaigneraïe falls back, exclaiming: "Kill me, then." After some further discussion the King accepts the wounded man, whose credit is saved, since he has not yielded, but he has the victor to thank for his act of mercy. His friends now draw near to give him help, and his wounds are dressed by the surgeon; but he is so chagrined at his defeat after so much boasting that he tears off the bandages, and thus dies.

But what of the splendid marquee, and the magnificent banquet, and the plate, and the tapestry, and all the beautiful things that his friends have lent him? Well, the very unexpected collapse of the great Chastaigneraïe falls like a bombshell on the King, the

Court, the seconds, and all the vast concourse that had assembled to enjoy the edifying spectacle of two gentlemen engaged in cutting each other's throats. All is confusion; the common people spread like a flood over the ground, trampling down the barriers and tearing down the stands; nor do they spare the marquee: they invade its precincts, they devour the dainties which have been prepared for their betters, they pull down the tapestries and pull up the carpets, and the lucky ones of them make off with the gold and silver cups and vessels, and when the myrmidons of the law at last make their tardy appearance on the scene, the place is a mass of wreckage, and there is nothing left for them to save. It is an evil day for Chastaigneraïe, and for his friends likewise.

In later times an idea got abroad that there was something unfair about this hamstringing cut, and the term *coup de Jarnac* came to be applied practically to any sort of cut made at the leg with the sword, and metaphorically to any underhand attack of what kind soever. This is a libel on the fair name of Guy de Chabot, who certainly did not invent the trick, as it was regularly taught by the fencing-masters of the day, most of whom, like Caizo, were Italians, and the chief of them all, Captain General Achille Marozzo, in his famous work, the first of its kind of any practical value, is most emphatic in his advocacy of the use of it, and with good reason, seeing that, when a man was clad in complete armour, almost the only uncovered part of him was the hinder part of the upper leg, the best way to attack which was to adopt the exact course pursued by Jarnac; and, indeed, we have records of other duels in which this cut was used with success. In the very same year, 1547, two Englishmen named Newton and Hamilton fought, one of them receiving a wound in the ham; the details of their fight are so like those of the Jarnac-Chastaigneraïe affair that to relate them would be but irksome repetition.

Again, when the great Duke of Guise was in Italy a

certain Gascon Captain named Provillan, who had the unlucky habit of letting his tongue run wild, made certain remarks highly derogatory to the honour and morality, not merely of an individual, but of the Italian people as a whole, when an Italian Captain, a fine tall fellow and a right good man-at-arms, determined to take the matter up and with his own sword purge his nation of the affront. So he sent him a challenge ; M. de Pienne was second to Provillan, and Paolo Giordano to his enemy. They entered the lists, and as soon as the usual ceremonies were completed they commenced operations, when the Italian gave the Frenchman such a huge ugly stroke across the ham that he dropped at once and hastily recanted the unpleasant remarks he had made about the victor's fellow-countrymen ; and although the Italian generously gave him his life, he was well punished, for he remained a cripple to the end of his days. In good truth, Jarnac was not in any way to be blamed, but rather to be complimented on the masterly manner in which he profited by the teaching he had received.

CHAPTER VIII

The Ancient Method and Usage of Duels before the King.*

"When upon the exhibiting the Bill of the Appellant in Court before the Constable, the Appellant fails in the proof of his Appeal, and cannot by Witness nor any other manner make the right of his Demands appear, He may offer to make proof of his intent upon the Defendant by his Body, by Force; and if the Defendant will say he will so defend his Honour, the Constable, as Vicar General in Arms under the King, hath power to join this Issue by Battel, and to assign the time and place, so that it be not within forty Days, unless by the agreement of the Parties they give themselves a shorter day.

"And upon the joining of the Issue by combat, the Constable shall signify to them their Arms, which are a Gauntlet, a long Sword and a short Sword and a Dagger: and then the Appellant and Defendant shall both find able pledges for their Appearance at a certain time of a day set, before the Sun be come to some one degree certainly named, to acquit their pledges, and the Plaintiff to make the best defence he can for his honour. And that in the mean time neither of them by themselves, nor by any Wel-willers of theirs shall lye in Ambush to assault or work any grievance to the other.

"The King shall find the Field for the performance

* From an old MS. of Elias Ashmole, Esq., quoted in "Miscellanea Aulica" (1702).

of the Duel, which must be sixty Foot in Length, in Breadth forty. It must be a hard and a firm ground, nothing stony, and listed about by the devise of the Marshal with good and serviceable Railing.

"There must be two doors, the one in the East, the other in the West; each of them of the height of seven feet or more, so that a Horse cannot leap over them, and these Doors are kept by the Sergeants at Arms.

"The day of the Battel the King shall sit in a Chair mounted on a Scaffold, and a low Seat shall be made for the Constable and Marshal at the foot of the descent from the Scaffold; and sitting there they demand the Pledges of the Appellant and Defendant to come into the Lists, and render themselves the King's prisoners, until the Appellant and Defendant are come in and have made Oath.

"When the Appellant comes to the Field, he shall come to the door in the East, armed and so appointed as the Court did order, and shall there attend the coming of the Constable to bring him in.

"And the Constable shall demand of him who he is, that comes thus armed to these Lists, what name he bears, and the cause of his coming.

"The Appellant shall answer, *I am such a Man A. of B. the Appellant, who am come armed and mounted to the Door of these Lists to demand an Entry, to make an endeavour to prove mine intent against C. of D. and to acquit my Pledges.*

"Then the Constable taking up his Beaver, so as suring himself that he is the same Person who is the Appellant, shall throw open the Door and bid him enter in his Arms with his Victuals, and other necessary Attendance, and his Councel with him, and shall then bring him before the King, and thence to his seat, where he shall attend until the Defendant come.

"Then the Appellant shall make a request to the Constable and Marshal to discharge his Pledges, and the Constable and Marshal shall inform His Majesty that since the Body of the Appellant is entered the

Lists to make proof of his Appeal, his Pledges by Law ought to have a discharge, and, after leave granted by the King, the Constable shall discharge them.

"If at the time appointed, the Defendant come not in his defence, the King doth command the Constable to call him by the Marshal, and the Marshal shall command the Lieutenant, and the Lieutenant shall command the Marshal of the Heralds of the South, if it be in the March of *Clarencieux;* and if the Marshal of the Heralds of the South be not there, then a Herald of the March of King *Clarencieux* shall call him, and if the performance of the Battel be on the North side of the River *Trent* in the March of King *Norroy*, the Marshal of the King of the North shall demand him, and in his default one of the Heralds of the March of King *Norroy* shall call for the Defendant thus.

"*O yes, O yes, O yes.*

"*C. of D. Defendant come to your Action, which you have undertaken this day, to acquit your Pledges in the presence of the King, Constable and Marshal, and to defend yourself against A. of B. Appellant in that he shall question and charge thee.*

"And if he appear not, he shall be in like manner thrice demanded at the four Corners of the Lists, only at the second time he is Proclaimed, at the end the Herald shall say, *The day is far passed.*

"So at the third time the Herald, at the half hour after Three of the Clock in the Afternoon, by the Commandment of the Constable, shall thus summon him.

"*C. of D. Defendant save your Honour, and come in to your Action, which you have undertaken at this day; the time is far gone, the half hour is spent, come in to the Lists upon the peril that shall follow thereon, or else you come too late.*

"Then when they have both appeared, the Register of the Constable's Court shall in writing observe their entrance, the order, and time, and the manner, whether on foot or mounted, their Arms, the Colour of their Horses, and how their Horses are harnessed, least the Horses or their Harness should be changed, or otherwise imbezelled.

"Then the Constable shall know whether it will please the King's Majesty to appoint any of his Nobles to Councel and advise them.

"The Constable shall imploy two Knights, or Esquires, to the Appellant to keep him standing, and to take care that he use no Charm, Spell, nor other ill Arts, until he hath made Oath. And with the like Charge two shall be dispatched to the Defendant.

"And when the Constable hath asked his Majesty's Pleasure, whether his Highness will receive their Oaths in Person, or that the Constable and Marshal take them in their Lists, calling for the Appellant with his Councel, shall demand of the Councel if they will make any further protestations, that they should now put them in, for this time is peremptory, and hereafter no protestation shall be received.

"Then the Constable shall have a Clerk ready by him, with a Book, and shall cause his Register to read the whole Bill to the Appellant, and shall say to him.

"*You A. of B. do you know this to be your Bill, and the Complaint which you exhibited in Court before me, laying your right hand upon this book, you must swear the truth of your Bill in all points, from the first to the last Charge in it, and that it is your Intent to prove upon C. of D. the Contents thereof to be true, so aid you God.*

"The form of it is thus.

"*Thou A. of B. y'is y'i Bill is soye in ayell Pointe and Articles fro the beginninge Contenwitt yer enn unto the ende, and y'is yinne Intent to Prove y'is day on the aforesaid C. of D. so God yee helpe, and his halloweth.*

"This done, the Appellant remanded to his stand, the Defendant shall be in the like manner sworn upon the truth of his defence.

"And this their first Oath they ought to do kneeling, but by the favour of the Constable and Marshal they sometimes do it standing.

"Then the Constable shall by the Marshal call the Appellant before him, and tender this second Oath to him, which, if the Constable give him leave, he may do sitting.

"*A. B. laying your hand on the Book this second time, you must swear that you come no otherwise appointed, than by me the Constable, and Marshal assigned, with a short Sword and a Gauntlet, and a long Sword and a Dagger, that you have not any knife, nor any other pointed instrument, or Engine, small or great, no Stone, or herb of vertue, no Charm, Experiment, nor other Enchantment, by whose power you believe you may the easier overcome your Adversary, who within this List shall oppose you in his defence, and that you trust not in anything more than in God, your Body, and the Merits of your Quarrel: so God you help.*

"Then being conducted to his place, the Keeper of the List shall be put out, and the Defendant in the same manner shall be demeaned.

"Then the Constable and Marshal shall send for them both before them, and the Constable shall name the Appellant and Defendant, and shall say to them both:

"*Take ye each other by the right Hand, and I defend that neither of you be so hardy violently to handle one another upon your peril,* and laying their left Hands on the Book, the Constable shall say, *I Charge you A. of B. Appellant, by your faith and your right hand which is enclosed in the hand of your adversary C. of D. that you use your power, and make use of all advantages, to make good your Appeal upon C. of D. your Adversary the Defendant, to force him to a Rendring of himself unto your hands, by demanding a Parley; or with your own hand to kill him before you part off these Lists, by that heighth of the Sun and Age of the day you have assigned to you by us the Constable and Marshal by your faith: and so God you help.*

"The same form shall be observed on the part of the Defendant, and then they shall be brought each of them to their places, the List cleared of the Councel on both sides.

"The Oaths thus past, a Herald by the Command of the Constable and Marshal, shall make *O yes* thrice and shall say:

"'We the Constable and Marshal, in the King's name, Charge and Command every Man, of what quality and condition soever he be, that he approach not within four foot to these Lists, nor that he speak any word, make any noise, give any sign, nor by his Countenance, or otherwise direct either of these parties A. of B. or C. of D. the Appellant and Defendant, to take any Advantages the one upon the other, by any sign so given. upon pain of life and member, and the forfeiture of his Chattels.'

"Next the Constable and the Marshal assign the place where the Kings at Arms, and the Heralds standing may have a full sight of all the Action within the Lists: for now they are to attend the Appellant and Defendant, and minister to them in what they shall command them. And if either of them faint, or have any desire to eat or drink of their Victuals they bring with them into the Lists, it is the office of the Herald to be attending on them.

"If the Appellant will either eat or drink he must first desire the good leave of the Defendant, which shall be by a King at Arms signified to the Constable and Marshal, and they to attend the King with the desire of the Appellant, and consent of the Defendant, and pray his Majesty's allowance of it. And if either the Appellant or Defendant have a necessity to do any other thing, the Heralds and Poursivants shall attend them.

"After that the Constable and Marshal shall free the Lists from people of all conditions, except a Knight, and two Squires of the Constable's Train, and the Lieutenant, a Knight and two Squires of the Marshal's

Retinue; which shall be in Armour, bearing Launces in their hands, which are not to be barbed with any Iron, to part and divide them when his Majesty shall give the Word.

"The Knights and Squires are to bring neither Swords, Knives, Bowes, nor Daggers with them into the Lists.

"They of the Constable's side are to keep one Corner of the Lists, and there lay themselves flat upon the ground: and in like manner shall they of the Marshal's side bestow themselves at another Corner of the Lists, for none may appear upright in the Lists, save the Constable and Marshal.

"And if the King be not present, then the Constable and Marshal shall sit in the place of the King, and the Lieutenant within the Lists.

"But if the King be present, then the Constable, sitting upon a Seat before the King within the Lists, as the King's Vicar General, shall command his Lieutenant to accompany the Appellant; and the Marshal, or his Lieutenant, with the like respect shall accompany the Defendant, and the Constable sitting at the foot of the Seat Royal, shall speak with a loud voice, *Let them go, let them go, to do their endeavour.*

"This said, the Appellant going to the Defendant, standing in the presence of the King, shall with all his strength assault him, and the Defendant shall be as wary as he can in his defence.

"The Constable and Marshal, or their Lieutenants, ought to be within hearing, as also within sight, that if any of them speak or make any sign he will renounce his Quarrel, or if the King's Majesty say but *Ho*, or give any other signal, then they who are within the Lists with the Constable and Marshal, throwing their Launces between the Appellant and Defendant, so parting them, they shall not give way to either of them to assault the other, until the King command they be free, or that the Constable declare his Majesties pleasure to be so, saying, *Let them go, the King wills it.*

"Notwithstanding that the Constable hath given the Defendant a set time to come in to his performance, yet, in case he cometh not according to the appointment of the Constable, right Judgement shall not pass against him upon his default, until the first half hour after three of the Clock be clearly passed, Let the cause be treasonable or otherwise.

"But the Appellant, whose suit it is, ought to be there at his precise time, when the Constable shall first demand him; else his pledges have forfeited their security.

"The Appellant and Defendant shall be searched by the Constable and Marshal, their Weapons and Arms questioned at all points, that they be avowable, and no Engine or Device not honourably Justifiable in them, and if they find any such practice the party shall be outed of that weapon; For Reason, Civility, and the Law of Arms, will upon no Condition in Acts of this high performance admit of Treachery or base Conspiracy.

"The Appellant and Defendant shall, as they themselves agree, Cloath their Bodies; for that is left to themselves; only the Constable shall examine that they both have the same Armour, or other defence upon their Bodies.

"If the one of them desire his Sword should be shortened, so that it is shorter than the measure of the Standard; the other is not bound to abate the length of his Weapon; but if they once agreed to fight with Swords longer than the Standard, allowed at the day of the Accounts within the Lists, either of them may demand to have his Weapon made to answer the Measure of this Standard, and the other is in honour bound to make his conformable, being a demand lawful, not upon fancy, and tasting of no private way or advantage.

"Now the Constable and Marshall are to be attentive to the King, if his Majesty shall please to Command the Combatants should be parted, to take breath, or for any other purpose, and in any case they must take much care how they part and divide them, and that at the Time they Interpose they be both of them in the same degree or possibility, and neither of them at the Mercy, nor in the hand of the other.

"The Constable and Marshal shall not suffer them to whisper, nor have any private discourse, for they are the Witnesses, and in their Breasts lies the record of their Words, and in no other place.

"And if the Battel be grounded on a cause of Treason, he that is convicted and discomfited, shall be disarmed by the Command of the Constable and Marshal: one Corner of the List broken down in disgrace of the party becoming Recreant, and being fastened to a Horse, shall be dragged from the place where he so lost his Arms to the block, and have his Head severed from him, or be hanged by the Neck or otherwise according to the several usages of the Country.

"It is the office of the Marshal to accompany the party to the place, and there in his view to see Execution done, and all the sentence performed, and that as well on the part of the Appellant as the Defendant: for good Conscience, Equity, and the Law of the Field, do exact that the Appellant, in case he be convicted, and becometh a man vanquished in his own proof, that he incur the same pain and hazard the Defendant shall do.

"But if the Cause be another Crime than Treason, he that is so by the Body of his Adversary convicted, shall lose his Arms within the Lists, and thence led out to the place of his suffering, which is directed by the usage of the Country, and this as well of the Appellant as the Defendant, as afore is said, only he shall not be dragged, nor the Rails broken, unless it be in Treason, and not otherwise.

"But if it be meerly an Act of Arms, a Tryal by Challenger allowed by the Grace of the King, Constable, and Marshal, he that in that confesseth himself vanquished, shall be disarmed, degraded, and being led to the skirt of the Lists, shall be tossed or thrown over, without any other punishment.

"If it please the King to take the difference and the Judgment of it into his hands, and command them to be Friends without any further controversy, then the Constable taking the Appellant, and the Marshal the Defendant, shall bear them both before the King, and the King shall by the Constable signify his pleasure to them.

"Then they shall be both of them led together unto one of the Gates of the Lists in all points, as they entered the Lists, and be so conveyed out of the Lists in the same Article of Time, that of them no man may say a First out or a Last within the List, since the King hath into his own Hand taken the Consideration of the Quarrel.

"It were dishonourable that either of the sides in a Battel, drawn by the Word of the King, should suffer any dishonour, the one more than the other: And the Ancient Tenet and Opinion hath been, that he that is first out of the Lists suffers a diminution of Honour. The Field being his in Honour, that is last Possessor of it, for he makes it good.

"There ought to be double Lists for the Servants of the Constable and Marshal, and for the Serjeants at Arms of the King, where they are to attend, and to defend that no Offence, Affray, Outrage, or other Misdemeanor, against the Crys made openly in Court be committed, or suffered, or any affront that way be meant against the King's Majesty, the Law and honour of Arms. These men ought to be in Compleat Arms.

"The Constable and Marshal may bring what power they please with them into the Field, and those either Armed or otherwise, at their Election.

"The King's Serjeants at Arms shall be the Keepers of the Doors and Portals of the Lists, and to make all arrests by Command of the Constable and Marshal, and them so arrested to assure.

"The Fee of the Constable is their Steeds and Arms, all that they bring with them into the Lists, save only those wherewith they fight. And of the party overcome, all his Arms and other things of the Combate are the right of the Constable.

"The Fee of the Marshal is only the Lists, Bars, Seats, and other works for that Spectacle."

That a ffellon may wage battaile, with the order thereof.*

One James Lees, beinge Indited of ffellony And callid to ans[wer] to the same Inditement, hath confessed the ffellony in the Kings Benche, And therevppon hath appeached one Richard Herberde to have bene present wth him at the comyttinge of the same fellony as a principall, And therevppon the said Herberd hath bene put to answere And pleadith that he is not giltie of the same ffellonye, And for his Triall hath waged Battaile as he may do by the lawe. And herevppon daie is given the iij^{de} daie of may next to performe the Battaile at Tothill, aboute the wch theis things followinge are to be done.

ffirst by the order of the lawe both the parties must at theire owne charge be armed w^{th}oute any yron or long armoure, their heades bare and bare handed and bare footed, every one of them having a Baston horned at ech ende of one length, And euie of them must haue a Targett or Sheeld wth iiij corns w^{th}oute any other armoure wherewth thone may grete thoth[er.]

Itm the Justice of the Kings Bench must sit alone vppon some highe and meete place in theire Robes and coyfes, as they do in the Bench yf the Triall were by xij men, to see the battaile and to give theire iudgement accordinge as the same shall fall owt vppon the vanquisshinge of the one or the other.

Itm there must be prepuracion of Lysts w^{th}in th

* British Museum, Sloane MS. 1710, f. 162.

wch the parties must fight, And the fild kept by therle marshal or vnder mshall.

Itm there must be proclamacion made before the fight begonne, that no person be so hardie, other then those two that shall do the fight, to move them selves nor make any noice or shoute whereby the battaile may be disturbed.

Proclamacion in duells.—The Justice Commandeth in the Quenes ma^{ties} name that in person of what estate degree or condicion that he be beinge present how he be so hardie to give any token or signe by counte^{n}ance speach or language either to the pursuer or to the defender, whereby thone of them may take any advantage of thother. And that no person remove but kepe still his place. And that eurie person and persons kepe theire Staves or theire Weapons to them selves, And suffer neither the said pursuer nor the defender to take any of theire weapons or any other thinge that may stand to the said pursuer or defender any availe, vppon paine of fforfeiture of Landes Tents goods Cattells, ympr.sonment of theire boddies, making fyne and ransom at the Quenes will & pleasure.

Oath enforced in duells.—This here yow Justice that I haue this daie neither eaten n^{r} dronk, nor have vppon me niether bone Stone ne gresse nor any . . . enchauntment Socercy nor witchcrafte wher throughe the po[wer?] & the woord of god might be enlessid or diminysshed, and the dev[il's?] power encreassid And that myne appeale is true so helpe me go[d] & his Saincts And by this booke——

[This makes it clear that the use of the shield, in such an encounter as this, was not always denied to common men, as Colombière states.—The Author.]

Of the Degradation of recreant Knights and Nobles.

We have watched in several instances the events of the *champ clos*, we have accompanied the victor in his triumphal return to his home, and we have perhaps bestowed a passing thought on the vanquished; but these combats have been either courteous encounters for love of ladies and for knightly honour, or they have been fights to the death for the voidance of some private quarrel. Before we bid adieu to the days of chivalry, it should be worth our while to see how justice was meted out to those recreant knights who had com-

Ceremony of Degradation. From Columbière.

mitted grave offences against their Sovereign or against the laws of justice or morality. They were tried and condemned by competent authority, and sentenced usually to death; but before they were handed over to the executioner they were compelled to undergo public degradation from their estate of knighthood and from all honours whatsoever that they might be possessed of. The ceremony of this degradation was a grievous and a terrible one, and such a scene we are now about to witness.

A court consisting of twenty or thirty knights or esquires without reproach is convened. The traitor knight is brought before it and accused by the King-at-Arms or the Herald, who recites at length all the details of the crime and produces his witnesses, and the court, after hearing both sides of the question, and after due deliberation, condemns the man, and ordains that previous to his execution he shall be publicly degraded from the honours of knighthood and nobility, and shall be deprived of the decorations and insignia of whatsoever order he may have before received, and he is taken back to prison.

For the due execution of the sentence two scaffolds are erected, which face one another, one of which, furnished with canopy, carpets, and rich seats, is prepared for the knights and esquires, who form the tribunal, attended by the Kings-at-Arms, Heralds, and Pursuivants, clad in their tabards and heraldic colours; the other scaffold, of plain rough wood, with a post at the end, which faces the judges, is destined for the punishment of the culprit, and on this post is placed his escutcheon, which is smudged with black and hung upside down. The judges take their seats, and the wretched man is brought from his prison and compelled to ascend the scaffold prepared for him, where he is placed on his knees in front of the tribunal. He is dressed in complete armour, and wears all his orders and decorations. On each side of the scaffold there are seated twelve priests clad in their surplices. The Herald reads aloud the sentence of the court, and the priests commence the recitation of the entire Vigils of the Dead from the *Dilexi* to the *Miserere*, and at the end of each Psalm they make a pause, during which the Heralds strip the guilty man of some portion of his armour, beginning with his helmet, which they hold on high, crying with a loud voice, "Behold the helmet of the traitor and disloyal knight!" The helmet is now broken to pieces, and the priests commence the next Psalm, and the ceremony is continued until he has been deprived of his collar, or gold chain, his gauntlets, his cuirass, his sword, his gilt spurs, and all the various parts of his armour ; and finally his escutcheon is taken down from the post on which it has been exposed, and broken into three pieces with a hammer and whatever instruments may be needed for the work, and on the completion of this the priests rise and chant over the head of the miserable wretch the 109th Psalm, "Deus laudem meam ne tacueris," which contains certain maledictions and curses upon traitors.

As it was the ancient custom for those who were about to receive the order of chivalry to enter a bath to purify their bodies and to pass the entire night in a church to purge their souls, so water—that is to say, foul water—forms part of the ceremony of degradation. Accordingly, the Pursuivant approaches with a basin filled with the disagreeable liquid The King-at-Arms demands three times the name of the despoiled knight, whom the Pursuivant describes by his name and titles of nobility. The Herald informs him that he has been deceived, and that the person named by him is a disloyal traitor, and, to make the truth of this apparent to the assembled multitude, he demands in a loud voice the opinion of the judges, the eldest of whom replies that, by the sentence of the knights and esquires here present, it has been ordained that the traitor named by the Pursuivant shall be for his crimes degraded from his noble rank and condemned to death. On this the Pursuivant empties the contents of the basin upon his head. The judges now descend from their scaffold, and, having assumed robes of mourning, proceed to the church. The degraded man is also compelled to descend, but not by the stairway by which he had entered on the scene. A cord is passed under his arms, he is flung to the ground, placed upon a hurdle, and covered with a pall, as if he were already a corpse, and so dragged to the church, the priests chanting over him the prayers for the dead, after which he is delivered to the Provost, and by him consigned to the public executioner, who promptly carries out the remainder of the sentence. The Kings-at-Arms and the Heralds declare his children and descendants born after the commission of the crime to be degraded, ignoble, and base, unworthy to bear arms or to present themselves at any jousts, tournaments, armies, courts, or other royal assemblies, on pain of being stripped naked and severely whipped as rogues and persons of infamous character.

BOOK II

THE PERIOD OF THE RAPIER.

CHAPTER IX

The Rapier and its Auxiliaries.

THE person who most felt the death of the Seigneur de la Chastaigneraïe was King Henri II. himself. He had granted the lists already refused by his predecessor, and his promised presence had encouraged both the combatants to pursue their quarrel to the bitter end. The slain nobleman had been a great personal friend of his, and he was so grieved at the issue that he made a solemn vow that during his life he would never again permit such an encounter to take place, nor did he ever do so, and it was on account of this sentimental vow that Fendilles and D'Aguerre, of "bastard sword" fame, were obliged to betake themselves to the country ruled over by the Duke of Bouillon.

In the knightly days single combats were confined to the *champ clos*, which was never granted where the quarrel was of a frivolous nature, and only the monarch himself, or some great noble the governor of a province, and so holding viceregal powers, had the authority to grant it. The arrangements were, as has been shown, carried out with much pomp and solemnity, and so serious were they sometimes considered that on certain occasions women and children were not permitted to be present, while for two men to take the law into their own hands and to fight a duel without permission was a matter of high treason. Thus, such encounters were held in check, and took place rarely. But this ill-considered vow of Henri II. changed the aspect of affairs; various gentlemen applied for permission to settle their quarrels in the good old-fashioned manner, but invariably met with a prompt refusal, so they ignored the King's vow and his edicts, and the laws of the land as well, and introduced, in place of the solemn combat in the *champ clos*, the *duello alla mazza*, as the Italians called it. They went out into the woods and fields, sometimes with seconds and sometimes without them, which latter imprudence opened the way to

A duel "à la Mazza," after Alfieri.

abuses: a combatant would wear chain mail underneath his clothes, for they no longer fought in armour, but in their shirts; and it did so happen that, when one of the quarrellers had even less stomach for a fight, men were placed in ambush to intercept the enemy on his way to the field, and the possibility of such an arrangement caused both parties often to come to the ground attended by a number of friends and partisans. This, again, led to other abuses, and to much sad slaughter of valiant gentlemen. But here and there we find in history a few bright examples of chivalrous courtesy and almost Christian charity, and such cases are worthy of record.

This period, which lasted from the middle of the sixteenth to the middle of the seventeenth century, was the most prolific in the variety of weapons favoured by the higher classes of fighting men. The great armour-smashing poleaxe has practically disappeared, although some of the seventeenth-century professors of the art reckoned it along with the two-hander as an arm with which anyone wishing to be considered a complete man-at-arms ought to be acquainted. So we have still the two-hand sword, the "bastard," and the more portable and convenient one-hand or short sword, of which we have since the time of Henry VIII. the varieties of the close-hilted and the back sword, both of which possessed basket hilts; again, there existed a peculiar combination of swords known in England as the "case of rapiers," but on the Continent as "the two swords." These were not rapiers by any means, but were more like the short sword; they were kept together side by side in the same scabbard, and were too inconvenient for personal wear, so that their practice was somewhat neglected, and their use is but little recorded in history. The dagger was employed mainly as an auxiliary weapon for defence, and when used alone was usually drawn in hot haste in some sudden quarrel, although a prearranged duel with a brace of daggers is related by Brantôme. The defensive weapons we meet with (it must be noted that we are now in the days of "parry and riposte") are the buckler, the dagger, the cloak, the great gauntlet, and the ordinary gauntlet of everyday wear. But the typical sword of this period was the long Hispano-Italian rapier, with its usual adjuncts, the poniard or the cloak.

This rapier calls for especial notice. It was not an invention; it was a development. It commenced its existence as the plain cross-hilted sword of the knightly times, in wielding which a man was accustomed to place his forefinger over the quillon in order to attain a stronger grip; but the finger, being entirely unprotected, occasionally got hurt, and to prevent this a small curved piece was added to the upper side of the cross-guard, which for the sake of symmetry was afterwards added to the other quillon. Again a "ring" of steel came to be placed on the outside, followed by a second one, and other defences for the hand appearing to be needful, they gradually developed themselves into the complete graceful arrangement of quillons, *pas d'âne*, and counter-guards to be seen in the "swept"-hilted rapier of the latter half of the sixteenth century.

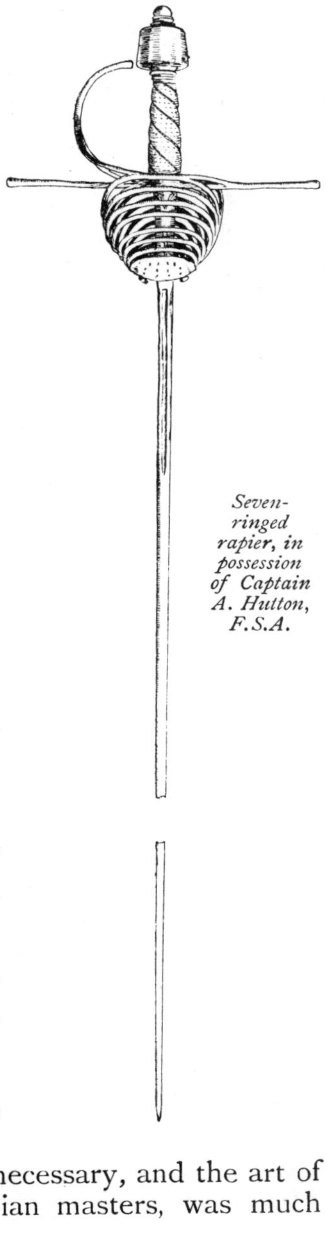

Seven-ringed rapier, in possession of Captain A. Hutton, F.S.A.

During the seventeenth century the "swept" hilt, passing through various modifications, arrived at its most perfect form, that of the cup, which, seeing how the weapon was handled, was an admirable defence for the sword hand; while the dagger came to be furnished with a solid triangular shell, which equally well guaranteed the safety of the hand which wielded it.

In the private quarrels with which this period is rife, armour was no longer worn. The combatants engaged each other stripped to their shirts, and, seeing the deadly nature of the thrusts of the rapier, the acquirement of personal skill became necessary, and the art of fencing, as taught by the Italian masters, was much cultivated. The rapier itself was long and unwieldy, seldom less than four feet in length from pommel to point, and sometimes even exceeding five feet; its attacks were therefore somewhat slow and by no means of a complex nature, while when it was used alone its strokes were avoided as much by movements of the feet and evasions of the body as by direct parries of the sword itself. These movements of the feet were steps or paces forward, backward, or to either side (when they were known as "traverses"), executed with more or less rapidity as occasion required. The dagger was the most favoured weapon of defence; the parries with it were not more than three or four in number, and were extremely simple, and it was not used for attack except when the men found themselves in close contact with each other. This rapier and dagger fight was the most romantically picturesque of all the varied combats recorded in the history of the art. When the cloak took, as it occasionally did, the place of the dagger, it was rolled twice round the left arm, and the thrusts were dashed aside by its pendent folds, and it was sometimes thrown in various ways in such a manner as to completely envelop the person, or so to entangle the sword of the enemy that he was for the moment entirely at the mercy of the thrower. This fight was very easy to acquire, and Swetnam says that in a very few lessons a boy of fifteen can learn to defend himself against any man

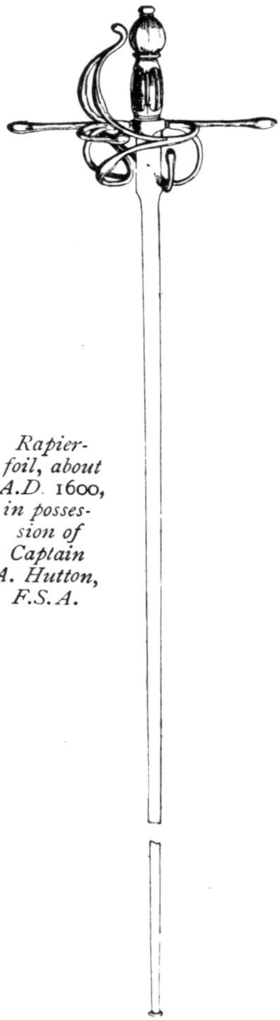

Rapier-foil, about A.D. 1600, *in possession of Captain A. Hutton, F.S.A.*

Duel with Rapier and Cloak, after Cappo Ferro.

whatsoever ; and, indeed, we ourselves know a little boy of that age, Master Charles Sefton, who more than holds his own with the gentleman who has taught him.

The period of the rapier was, in good truth, the most quarrelsome period in history ; the "point of honour" was carried to such an extreme point that men would fight to the death for almost any trivial reason, and sometimes even without any at all, but from pure light-heartedness, for the mere fun of the thing and for nothing else. Shakespeare, who lived in those lively times, gives us an idea of it in the speech of Mercutio to Benvolio, who, by the way, is about the only tolerably peaceable person in the whole play of "Romeo and Juliet": "Come, come! thou art as hot a Jack in thy mood as any in Italy. Nay, an there were two such, we should have none shortly, for one would kill the other. Thou! why thou wilt quarrel with a man that hath a hair more or a hair less in his beard than thou hast. Thou wilt quarrel with a man for cracking nuts, having no other reason but because thou hast hazel eyes. What eye, but such an eye, would spy out such a quarrel? Thy head is as full of quarrel as an egg is full of meat. Thou hast quarrelled with a man for coughing in the street, because he hath wakened thy dog that hath lain asleep in the sun. Didst thou not fall out with a tailor for wearing his new doublet before Easter? And with another for tying his new shoes with old riband?" And this is the pacific person of the period.

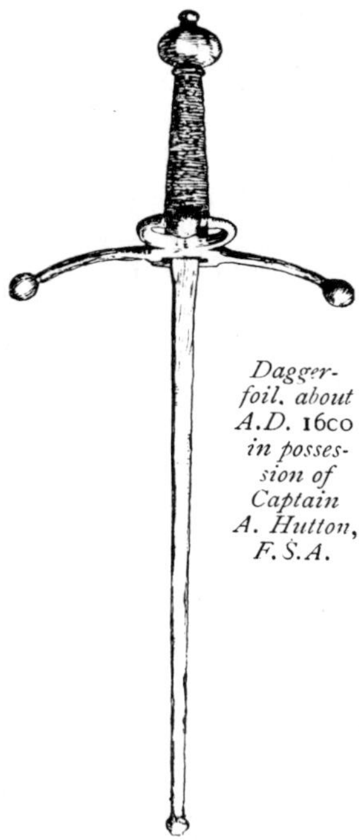

Dagger-foil, about A.D. 1600 *in possession of Captain A. Hutton, F.S.A.*

Why, these sixteenth-century people would pick a quarrel with a man for merely looking at them, as

Vincentio Saviolo informs us in "His Practise"; and he shall tell us the story in his own words:

"What is become of the gentilitie and inbredde courtesie of auncient noble Gentlemen? There be certaine undiscreet men whose grosse fault I cannot overslip without blaming: these men use as they either stand or go in streets, so to stare and looke men passing by them in the face, as if they woulde for some reason marke them: which breedeth such an offence unto some men so marked, that they cannot take it in good part, and therefore it is verie dangerous. For it maie happen that a man may looke so upon one that either is by nature suspitious, or by reason of some secret thing knowen to himselfe, maie suspect that hee is therefore looked upon. Whereupon great quarrels may arise, for the man so looked on maie fall a questioning with him that looketh on him, who perhaps answering him overthwartly, may both move him to choler, and be moved himself also, and so bring the matter to some dangerous point. Whereof I have myself seen a notable example, passing through the Citie of Trieste, in the uttermost part of the territories of Friule in Italy, where I saw two brethren, one a most honorable Captaine, and the other a brave and worthie souldier, who walking together in the streetes, were verie stedfastly eied of certaine young Gentlemen of the Citie, who stared the Captaine and his brother in the face something unseemely, and (as they took it) discurteouslie: whereupon they asked the Gentlemen in verie curteous manner, whether they had seene them in anie place before, or whether they knew them. They answered no. Then replied the Captaine and his brother, Why then doo you looke so much upon us? They answered, because they had eies. That (sayd the other) is the crowes fault, in that they have not picked them out. To bee short, in the end one word added on the other, and one speech following the other, the matter came from saying to doing: and what the tung had uttered the hand would maintaine: and a hot fight being commenced, it could not be ended before the Captaine's brother was slaine, and two of the gentlemen hurt, whereof one escaped with the rest, but the cheefest cutter of them all was hurt in the legge, and so could not get away, but was taken and imprisoned, and shortly after beheadded : he was very well beloved in the Cittie, but yet could not escape this end being brought thereto by following his madbrained conceits, and by beeing misled by evill company."

There was one thing, more than all others, that, in those boisterous days, a man was well advised not to do, and that was to contradict anybody else ; "contradiction did so fly to their heads," for the very slightest word of that kind given to a hot-headed, mad-brained fellow might be construed by him into the lie direct ; then out would fly the rapiers—those rapiers fitted so very loosely in their scabbards. The more pacific and thoughtful men devised, and printed too, certain gradations of the art of contradiction, as to what particular form of "giving the lie" was worthy to be fought about, and what forms of it were not so. There was the "Lie Certaine," a sure cause of quarrel, for even in our own lawyer-ridden time it might very well lead to fisticuffs ; but in good Queen Bess's golden day such a vulgar thing as fisticuffs was unknown except to the "Generall," the vulgar herd, and such-like matters were then arranged through the medium of the lordly rapier. For example, John says to James: "Thou hast said that at the Battaile of Moncontour I abandoned mine Ensigne, and cowardly ranne away. Whereof I answer, Thou hast lied"; and perhaps to make his intention the more clear, he would add the words, "in thy throat, like the theefe that thou arte." Here is a distinct and forcible contradiction, and James must assume the rôle of challenger, for he must prove with his body the truth of his accusation. Then we had the "Lie Generall"; it was "generall in respect of the Person, when no man to whom it is given is named, as thus : Whoever hath said that I have been a Rebell to my Prince, doth lie. To this manner of Lie no man is bound to make answere, because many may haplie have so said, and that so being, he that giveth the Lie should be forced to fight with them all, which were inconvenient." Next there came the "Lie Conditional." "Conditionall lies, wee call those which are uttered upon condition, as if a man should say thus: If thou hast called me a theefe, thou doest lie: or if thou shalt hereafter so say, thou liest: and how often thou hast or shalt so say, so oft I say thou hast and shalt lie. These Conditionall lies in this sort given, are the occasion oftentimes of much disputation, because they are not in force untill the Condition is verified, I meane, until it be avowed that such words have indeede been spoken. Wherefore to avoide all doubts, it behoveth Gentlemen and other persons of honor or credite, to shunne all Conditionall lies." And there were lastly the "Vaine or foolish Lies." "The common opinion is, that he who giveth the lye, looseth the election of weapons, so that hee saie unto another that he lyeth, without having regarde to the manner how he doth it, wherby he thinketh to have done great matter. And heereupon it commeth that everye daye there riseth from the common sorte new and strange foolishnesses, as he who wil give the lye ere the other speake, saying: If thou saye that I am not an honest man, thou lyest in thy throate; the folly of which speach doth plainlie appeare. Another sort of ignorant quarrellers are, that will say thus: If anie man hath said evill of me, hee hath lied; and if he will deme to have so said, he also lieth. This sillie sort of quarrelling may likewise be called a Lie foolish and vaine, whose fashion will give cause for laughter. Another sort of these Vaine lies are thus offered: Simon meeting with Lewes saith, Draw thy weapon and I will presentlie prove thee a Liar and a Varlet: Or if thou wilt not draw, then art thou a Varlet also. Or he will say to him: If thou wilt say that I am not thy equall, thou lyest. This manner of Lie is without foundation, cause or reason and therefore meete to be laughed at."

CHAPTER X

Of Certain of the Evils which arose from the Vow of Henri II.

How M. de Soëilles went alone to fight with M. Devese, and what befell him.

M. de Soëilles was married one day to Mdlle. Dupon, a pretty young lady of Languedoc, but a few days after the wedding he found himself obliged to go to Court in order to obtain some favour from the King. It was certainly rather early for a bridegroom to quit the side of his young wife, but the affair pressed, and he confided to his brother-in-law Dupon the care of his house and the guardianship of the lady. But this gentleman proved himself more clever at discovering disagreeables than at preventing them. Soëilles had a neighbour, Devese by name, who was his most intimate friend, and was constantly with him, and during his absence continued to visit at his house. Devese was young, handsome, rich, and of agreeable manners; the lady was young, pretty, and charming in every way. The result must be left to the imagination.

Soëilles now returns home. Dupon informs him of his discoveries, and there is a pretty family fracas. Soëilles sets forth to look for Devese, arrives at his house at the hour of dinner, and finds him with his father and a dozen or so of friends about to place themselves at table. He is embraced and caressed by everyone, especially by the younger Devese, whose friendly advances he affects to return. He joins the party, and they dine together in the pleasantest manner possible. The meal ended, he takes Devese unto the garden, and, as they are sauntering down one of the avenues, he says to him, "I have come here to cut throats with you, and have left a pair of swords and a pair of daggers in a certain place, whereto I request you to accompany me." "With me?" says Devese. "You must be joking. I shall be well pleased to fight your enemies, but not yourself, for whom I have always professed the closest friendship." "No, no!" replies Soëilles; "don't you deceive yourself: either I strangle you or you strangle me." "What!" says Devese, "without any quarrel? I don't understand what it is about." "Because it is my pleasure," rejoins the other. Now a black thought flashes through the brain of Devese, and he says, "Ha! since it is your pleasure, I am your man. But we should not fight to-day. This place is full of my friends, and, should fortune favour me, it might be thought that I had received assistance from them; but send me word what time and place will suit you, and you shall find me at your service." Soëilles is satisfied, returns home and the next day sends his cartel by the hand of a servant, and, trusting to the honour and loyalty of Devese, arrives at the rendezvous alone. Devese is there to meet him, but accompanied by a party of his friends, who set upon the unfortunate man, and give him so severe a thrust from behind that the rapier breaks, and the piece remains in his body, whereupon they leave him to shift for himself as best he may. His wound heals, but his health remains greatly impaired. The conscience-stricken Devese is in deadly terror of him, and makes another attempt to take his life unfairly, and the King, having heard the two stories, is so angered that

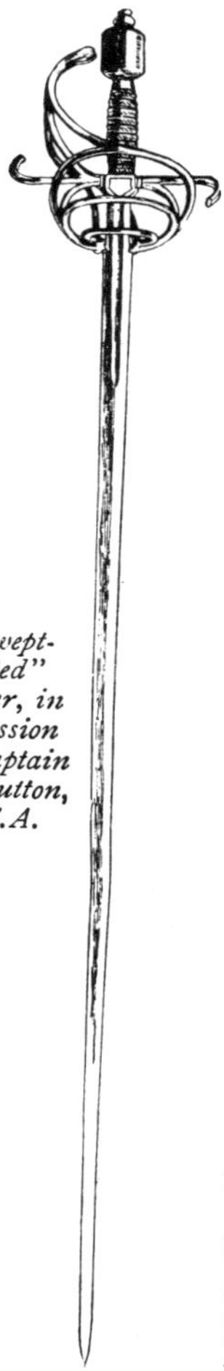

"Swept-hilted" rapier, in possession of Captain A. Hutton, F.S.A.

he cashiers Devese from the army, in which he holds a commission as Cornet in a troop of cavalry, a disgrace which completely ruins him, and places him in the position of a dishonoured person, against whom no gentleman can draw a sword. Soëilles was afterwards completely cured by an Italian surgeon whom he met by chance at Montpellier.

How the Capitaine Matas spared the Life of Achon, and how Achon repaid the Courtesy.

King Francis II. went hunting one day in the Forest of Vincennes, and among his entourage were two gentlemen, one a young spark of a courtier named Achon, and the other a Captain Matas, a somewhat eccentric man in his manners and in his dress, but for all that a gallant soldier, who had served his King well in the wars, and, in spite of his peculiarities, greatly esteemed. These two come to words on some matter or other, and agree to quarrel, so they separate themselves from their companions and betake themselves to a little hill which is hard by, and commence arranging the affair by means of their rapiers. Matas, who is an old hand at sword-play, presses his man so strongly that he very soon sends his weapon flying out of his hand, and, being of a merciful disposition, and not wishing to be spoken of as a "mangeur de jeunes gens," says to him, "Go, young man, and learn to hold your sword better another time, and to beware of attacking a man of my calibre. I pardon your presumption. Take up your sword, and, as you are quite a young fellow, we will say no more about this affair." He turns to mount his horse, but before he can even think of it the treacherous Achon, whose life he had just spared, picks up his sword, runs after Matas, and drives it right through his body, so that he falls dead on the spot. Poor Matas was much regretted, as he was well known to be a brave and gallant soldier. But the Duke of Guise blamed him greatly for having thought so little of his skill at arms and his good fortune, which had placed his enemy at his mercy, that he must give him his life to no better end than to be assassinated by him. The Italian experts in the etiquette of the duel in those times were much of Guise's mind, and counselled these kindly people who would spare an enemy to at least leave him stretched on the ground, and, instead of killing him outright, so to cripple him in his arms and legs as to prevent his doing any further mischief, and, moreover, to give him a slash across the face sufficiently ugly to keep his memory alive for the rest of his days. It would have been well for Matas had he followed their advice.

How M. de Millaud fought with the Baron de Vitaux and killed him by Unfair Advantage.

The Baron de Vitaux, although the manner of his death reflected but little credit on his enemy, was a man deserving of scant sympathy, as he had a somewhat bad record so far as brutality was concerned. When at Toulouse he met with the Baron de Soupez, a young gentleman of a somewhat overweening disposition, who had the misfortune to underestimate his qualities. Vitaux was a very little man, and Soupez, being a big one, looked down upon him in more ways than one, and having some words with him one evening at supper, although the subject of the dispute was very trivial, went so far as to throw a candlestick at his head, whereupon the fierce little man clapped his hand on his sword-hilt, and was for settling matters there and then, had he not been prevented by the friends of Soupez, who were much more numerous in the assembly than were his own, so he wisely left the house. But he concealed himself hard by, with his sword ready drawn, and as the unsuspecting Soupez came out he attacked him suddenly, ran him through the body, and left him stretched on the pavement, a rather dangerous thing to do, for at Toulouse just then the laws were rigorously administered, and, added to that, the dead man had many powerful friends and relatives in the city, who, had Vitaux been taken, would have promptly set the law in motion against him. But here his small size was of service to him. He dressed himself up as a girl, got clear of the city gates without being recognised, and thus, as Brantôme, a devoted admirer of his, puts it, "bravely saved himself."

He shortly afterwards found himself in another escapade about as creditable as the above. A certain Gounellieu, a great favourite of the King, had incurred his hatred, and that justly, because this Gounellieu had killed, as it was said, with supersticery and foul advantage, a young brother of his, only fifteen years of age, a nice little lad and of great promise. So the angry Baron, having ascertained that the murderer was on a journey to his place in Picardy, attended by three companions on horseback, rode after him, accompanied by only one friend, a young Boucicault, caught him up in the level country near St. Denis, and killed him at once without any ceremony whatever, at which the King was in despair, so fond was he of Gounellieu; and he would have had the Baron's head if he had caught him, but the worthy gentleman made his escape to Italy, and did not reappear until his evil destiny brought him in touch of Millaud, who, having good reason to hate him, promptly sent him a challenge.

Now the two enemies meet in a country place near Paris, and are attended by their seconds, whose duty it is to see that neither principal has about him secret armour or any magical contrivance by which to give himself an advantage. They strip to their shirts, when the second of Millaud visits the Baron, and that of the Baron pays the like attention to Millaud, who undoes the front of his shirt, and with both hands opens it quite wide in the frankest manner possible, and the good gentleman is perfectly satisfied. The two heroes face each other and exchange a few rapid thrusts, during which the point of the Baron's rapier is a little bent. But this might easily have happened by its striking some part of the enemy's hilt, so he treats him to two such mighty thrusts on the chest in quick succession that he is fairly forced backwards three or four good paces, and the Baron, finding that he is none the worse for them, becomes suspicious, changes his tactics, and attacks him with "estramassons."

The "estramasson" (so it is spelled by Brantôme) is a peculiar downright blow aimed at the head, not with the object of cleaving the same, but of slitting the face clean down from forehead to chin. Millaud parries these downright blows, a thing which is securely done with both sword and dagger raised on high and crossed close to the hilts—it is known as parrying "double"—and, seizing his opportunity, gives him a tremendous thrust in the body, and then another, and another, and another, until he completely finishes him, without so much as giving him a chance of begging his life. The Baron had killed quite a number of people, including the father of Millaud, and his enemies said that he did not kill his people nicely, but by supersticery and foul play. Millaud knew this, and took into his confidence a certain Signor Ferrone, an Italian from Asti, who taught him not only the fence tricks of his countrymen, but also some other tricks of theirs, which were not of quite so chivalrous a nature. The Italians were then reckoned the most astute avengers of injury known to the civilized world, and they considered that an act of treachery might fairly, and without any dishonour, be paid back in similar coin. Millaud took all these lessons to heart, and got everything ready for the entertainment of the Baron before sending him his challenge. He caused to be made for himself a nice light little cuirass, which he could wear next to his skin. It was so exquisitely modelled and so beautifully painted that to a casual observer, and the second of Vitaux seems to have been an especially casual one, it appeared to be the very flesh itself, and with the assistance of this M. de Millaud avenged the murder of his father.

How M. de Sourdiac fought with M. de la Chasnaye-Lalier and killed him with Unfair Advantage.

In the reign of Henri II., that ominous reign, on March 31, 1579, a duel took place at Paris on the island of Louviers on the Seine, between M. de Sourdiac, the young Lord of Chasteauneuf, and M. de la Chasnaye-Lalier, who had recently been the young gentleman's guardian. Some tale-bearer had reported to Sourdiac that his ex-guardian had said unpleasant things about him, so he promptly sent him a challenge. Sourdiac is a young vigorous fellow, who attempts to force a fight upon a man at least middle-aged, if not elderly, and this of itself looks somewhat ill; however, on the appointed day they meet, unaccompanied by seconds. But, as it happens, the affair has got wind, and quite a number of people of all sorts and conditions are waiting on both sides of the river to see the fun. Sourdiac asks his enemy if it is true that he has made these disagreeable remarks about him, to which La Chasnaye replies, "On my faith as an honest man and a gentlemen, I never said anything of the sort." "Then," says Sourdiac, "I am perfectly satisfied." "Not so I," rejoins the elder man; "since you have given me the trouble of coming here, I mean to fight, and what indeed will all these people, who are assembled on both banks of the river, say when they find out that we have come here with our rapiers and our daggers to do nothing but chatter? Really, it would touch our reputations. Come, let us to work!"

Accordingly they strip to their shirts, and, each trusting to the honour of the other that there shall be nothing in the shape of supersticery, advance rapier and dagger in hand, and, being both of them practised swordsmen, they exchange a number of thrusts, parries, and ripostes, without any effect, when La Chasnaye plants a vigorous *imbroccata* right on the centre of Sourdiac's body, which, to his surprise, has no effect whatever, and he cries out: "You scoundrel! you have armour on; but never mind, I shall get you nicely another way." So he commences aiming at the face and the throat, and delivers such a furious side-stroke at him (for these early rapiers had sharp edges) that, but for an evasion of the body, Sourdiac would have had his throat cut; but finding himself safe he redoubles his efforts, and finally passes his rapier through the body of La Chasnaye. But his victory was scarcely a triumph, as it was beyond all doubt that he came to the field unfairly protected by secret armour.

How M. de Romefort fought with M. de Fredaignes, and how he attempted an Act of Supersticery and failed in it.

It happened in Limosin, and it is Brantôme who tells us the story. There was a lady of an uncertain sort, known as La Vauguion, whose house was much frequented by two gentlemen, M. de Romefort and M. de Fredaignes, and, as is often the case where such a lady is concerned, the two young sparks became insanely jealous of each other. Romefort takes the initiative, and confides his griefs to a gentleman not named, who has somehow or other managed to acquire the reputation of being a "tall fellow of his hands," and something of a "sad dog," but whose records in army service—and there had been plenty of opportunities open to him—were practically nil.

This friend of Romefort's takes a challenge to Fredaignes to ride out to a certain secluded spot, and there to conclude their difference without seconds or any witnesses, except the servants who were to hold their horses. And there they meet accordingly, but Romefort has arranged a pretty little trick: he has dressed up this precious "gentleman" of his in the livery of his groom, who, they have agreed, in case of his being at all hard pressed is to leave the horses to take care of themselves (there will be plenty of time to catch them again), to come to his assistance, and between them to settle the affairs of poor Fredaignes beyond the means of recovery. They choose a convenient place for their fight at a considerable distance from the spot where they have left their horses, and their servants follow them, as it were, leisurely. Fredaignes glances round, and immediately recognises the attendant of his enemy. "Ho, ho!" he says to himself, "here is treachery. I must be sudden, and despatch;" and, being a much better man at arms than Romefort had bargained for, after a pass or two lays him stark upon the ground, before his companion has time even to think of coming to his assistance. His faithful servant has brought his horse much nearer to the scene than has the sham one of Romefort, who is naturally a trifle cautious; he mounts at once and goes direct for the gentleman in disguise, who turns tail, leaves Romefort to shift for himself, and bolts off as fast as his horse's legs can carry him. Fredaignes shouts after him to go to all the devils, and troubles no more about him. He returns home in triumph, his servant carrying the weapons of the now harmless Romefort, and he has a pretty little story to tell about how he settled matters with him and hunted off the field his groom, whose name, we imagine, he does not forget to disclose.

CHAPTER XI

How the Admirable Crichton fought with an Italian Bravo at Single Rapier and slew him, and how afterwards he was slain with Unfair Advantage.

SIR THOMAS URQUHART in "The Jewel" gives the following history: "To speak now of Crichtoun, I hope will not offend the ingenuous reader, and to make report of that magnanimous act achieved by him at the Duke of Mantua's court, to the honour not only of his own, but to the eternal renown of the whole Isle of Britain. The manner whereof was thus:

"A certaine Italian gentleman of a mighty, able, strong, nimble, and vigorous body, by nature fierce, cruel, warlike, and audacious, and in the gladiatory art so superlatively expert and dexterous, that all the most skilful teachers of escrime, and fencing masters of Italy were by him beaten to their good behaviour, and, by blows and thrusts given in which they could not avoid, enforced to acknowledge him their overcomer: bethinking himself how, after so great a conquest of reputation, he might by such means be very suddenly enriched, he projected a course of exchanging the blunt to sharp, and the foiles into tucks; and in this resolution providing a purse full of gold, worth neer upon four hundred pounds English money, traveled alongst the most especial and considerable parts of Spaine, France, Italy, and other places, wherever there was greatest probability of encountering with the eagerest and most atrocious duellists; and immediately after his arrival to any city or town that gave apparent likelihood of some one or other champion that would enter the lists and cope with him, he boldly challenged them with sound of trumpet, in the chief market place, to adventure an equal sum of money against that of his, to be disputed at the sword's point, who should have both. There failed not several brave men, almost of all nations, who, accepting of his cartels, were not afraid to hazard both their person and coine against him; but (till he midled with this Crichtoun) so maine was the ascendant he had above all his antagonists, and so unlucky the fate of such as offered to scuffle with him, that all his opposing combatants who had not lost both their life and gold, were glad for the preservation of their person (though sometimes with a great expense of blood), to leave both their reputation and their money behind them. At last returning homewards to his own country, loaded with honour and wealth, or rather the spoile of the reputation of those forraigners, whom the Italians call Tramontani, he by the way, after his accustomed manner of boarding other places, repaired to the city of Mantua, where the Duke vouchsafed him a protection, and savegard for his person: he (as formerly he was wont to do by beat of drum, sound of trumpet, and several printed papers, disclosing his designe, battered on all the chief gates, posts, and pillars of the town) gave all men to understand, that his purpose was to challenge at the single rapier, any whosoever of that city or country, that durst be so bold as to fight with him, provided he would deposit a bag of five hundred Spanish pistols, over against another of the same value, which himself should lay down, upon this condition, that the enjoyment of both should be the conqueror's due.

"His challenge was not long unanswered; for it happened at the same time, that three of the most notable cutters in the world (and so highly cried up for valour, that all the bravos in the land were content to give way to their domineering, how insolent soever they should prove, because of their former victories in the field) were all three together at the court of

Mantua; who hearing of such a harvest of five hundred pistols, to be reaped (as they expected) very soon, and with ease, had almost contested amongst themselves for the priority of the first encounterer, but that one of my Lord Duke's courtiers moved them to cast lots who should be first, second, and third, in case of none the former two should prove victorious.

"Without more adoe, he whose chance it was to answer the cartel with the first defiance, presented himself within the barriers, or place appointed for the fight, where, his adversary attending him, as soon as the trumpet sounded a charge, they jointly fell to work: and although the dispute was very hot for a while, yet, whose fortune it was to be the first of the three in the field, had the disaster to be the first of the three that was foyled: for at last with a thrust in the throat he was killed dead upon the ground.

"This nevertheless not a whit dismayed the other two; for the next day he that was appointed second in the roll, gave his appearance after the same as the first had done, but with no better success; for he likewise was laid flat dead upon the place, by means of a thrust he received in the heart.

"The last of the three finding that he was as sure of being engaged in the fight, as if he had been the first in order, pluckt up his heart, knit his spirits together and, on the day after the death of the second, most courageously entering the lists, demeaned himself for a while with great activity and skill; but at last, his luck being the same with those that preceded him, by a thrust in the belly, he within four and twenty hours after gave up the ghost. These (you may imagine) were lamentable spectacles to the Duke and citie of Mantua, who casting down their faces for shame, knew not what course to take for reparation. The conquering duellist, proud of a victory so highly tending to both his honour and profit, for the space of a whole fortnight marched daily along the streets of Mantua (without opposition or controulment) in triumph: which the never-too-much-to-be-admired Crichtoun perceiving, to wipe off the imputation of cowardise lying upon the court of Mantua, to which he had but even then arrived (although formerly he had been a domestic thereof), he could neither eat nor drink till he had first sent a challenge to the conqueror, appelling him to repair with his best sword in his hand, by 9 of the clock in the morning of the next day, in presence of the whole court and in the same place where he had killed the other three, to fight with him upon this quarrel; that in the court of Mantua there were as valiant men as he; and, for his better encouragement to the desired undertaking, he assured him, that to the aforesaid five hundred pistols he would add a thousand more; wishing him to do the like, that the victor upon the point of his sword might carry away the richer booty. The challenge, with all its conditions, is no sooner accepted of, the time and place mutually condescended upon kept accordingly, and the fifteen hundred pistols deposited, but of the two rapiers of equal weight, length, and goodness, each taking one, in presence of the Duke, Dutchess, with all the noblemen, ladies, magnificos, and all the choicest of both men, women, and maids of that city, as soon as the signal for the duel was given, by the shot of a great piece of ordnance, of three score and four pound ball, the two combatants, with a lion-like animosity, made their approach to one another; and being within distance, the valiant Crichtoun, to make his adversary spend his fury the sooner, betook himself to the defensive part; wherein, for a long time, he shewed such excellent dexterity, in warding the other's blows, slighting his falsifyings, in breaking measure, and often, by the agility of his body, avoiding his thrusts, that he seemed but to play, whilst the other was in earnest. The sweetness of Crichtoun's countenance, in the hottest of the assault, like a glance of lightning on the hearts of the spectators, brought all the Italian ladies on a sudden to be enamoured of him; while the sternness of the other's aspect, he looking like an enraged bear, would have struck terror into wolves, and affrighted an English mastiff.

"Though they were both in their linens (to wit shirts and drawers, without any other apparel), and in all outward conveniences equally adjusted, the Italian, with redoubling his stroaks, foamed at the mouth with a cholerick heart, and fetched a pantling breath : the Scot, in sustaining his charge, kept himself in a pleasant temper, and made void his designes : he alters his wards from tierce to quart ; he primes and seconds it, now high, now lowe, and casts his body into all the shapes he can, to spie out an open on his adversary, and lay hold of an advantage ; but all in vain : for the invincible Crichtoun, whom no cunning was able to surprise, contrepostures his respective wards, and with an incredible nimbleness both of hand and foot, evades his intent and frustrates the invasion. Now is it that the never-before-conquered Italian, finding himself a little faint, enters into a consideration that he may be overmatched. Matchless Crichtoun, seeing it now high time to put a gallant catastrophe to that so-long-dubious combat, animated with a divinely inspired fervencie, to fulfill the expectation of the ladies, and crown the Duke's illustrious hopes, changeth his garb, falls to act another part, and from defender, turns assailant. Then it was that to vindicate the reputation of the Duke's family, and expiate the blood of the three vanquished gentlemen, he alonged a stoccade *de pied ferme;* then recoyling, he advanced another thrust, and lodged it home ; after which, retiring again, his right foot did beat the cadence of the blow that pierced the belly of this Italian ; whose heart and throat being hit with the two former stroaks, these three franch bouts given in upon the back of other ; they give us to understand, that by them he was to be made a sacrifice of atonement for the slaughter of the three aforesaid gentlemen, who were wounded in the very same parts of their bodies, by other three such venees as these, each whereof being mortal, and his vital spirits exhaling as his blood gushed out, all he spoke was this, That seeing he could not live, his comfort in dying was, that he could not die by the hand of a braver man."

James Crichton was, in addition to his skill as a swordsman, a young man of singular talents and learning, so it was no wonder that the Duke of Mantua should conceive a liking for him, especially after his glorious victory over the terrible gladiator, and seeing that Vincenzo di Gonzaga, his son, had evinced a strong taste for literature and the fine arts, he engaged him as companion and preceptor to that Prince; but Vincenzo was, unhappily, of vindictive disposition, violent temper, and dissolute habits.

As Sir Thomas Urquhart has shown us, after the public defeat of the bravo all the fair ladies in Mantua are at the feet of the victor. There should have been safety in such a crowd of them; but unfortunately there is a special one who attracts his attention far more than the rest, and, as ill-luck will have it, the Prince himself begins to have a predilection for the lady, to see a rival in his Scotch friend, and to regard him with deadly hatred. The latter has, on an occasion, been paying an evening visit to the object of his choice, and is returning home, amusing himself, as is the fashion of Italian gallants of the time, by playing on his mandoline as he goes along, when he finds himself of a sudden attacked by a party of half a dozen men, well armed and closely masked. Crichton draws his rapier and dagger, and defends himself with such skill that very quickly two of them are down. Three have taken to their heels, and he presses the remaining one so hotly that he soon disarms and seizes him, tears off his mask, and recognises the face of Prince Vincenzo, his young master. He had only disarmed his adversary, and that, too, in self-defence, instead of killing him outright; but he is so concerned at the discovery that, in an evil moment for him, he kneels and offers his sword to him. Vincenzo takes it; he is full of wine, furious at his defeat, and, being of a treacherous and revengeful nature, brutally drives it through his body, and thus perishes the Admirable Crichton at the early age of twenty-two.

CHAPTER XII

Of Chivalrous Amenities among the Rapier Men.

SURELY we have had enough of "supersticerie," of ferocity, and of foul advantage, and it will be refreshing to see that all the gentlemen of that bloody period were not of such cruel sort. It is true that the atrocious and unpunished murders of Captain Matas and of the Admirable Crichton, by the very hands of the men they had only just generously spared, were small encouragement to men of chivalrous nature to act towards a conquered enemy as their hearts dictated. But history has preserved for us a number of instances of graceful courtesy shown by the victor to the vanquished, and received by him with grateful affection, and we will tell

How the Two Captains, Peter the Corsican and John of Turin, fought with Rapier and Cloak, and how generously they behaved to each other.

The Prince Giannino dei Medici introduced to the world two brave and valiant Captains named Peter the Corsican and John of Turin, who served him loyally in his wars, and for some years lived together in perfect good friendship. But there arose a question between them: they grew mutually distrustful, and the question developed into an open quarrel. They were constantly squabbling, and as neither would own himself in the wrong—though both were so more or less—it was quite impossible, although it was true that they had not as yet come to blows, to get them reconciled. Giannino, their lord and master, perceiving this, and knowing well their brave natures, sees that when matters do reach an extremity they will fight till both are killed, for neither will give in, and then he will lose the services of two of his most cherished officers. He tries, and in vain, all kinds of artifice to bring them to accord, for so obstinate are they that they will not listen even to their Prince himself.

In despair he determines that the quarrel shall have an end. He summons them to his presence, and once more attempts to make them friends, but, of course, without success. So he calls for two rapiers of equal length and weight; he hands one to each of the Captains. He takes his own cloak from his shoulders, and with his sharp dagger divides it into halves, giving a piece to each. He now commands that they shall be shut up in a large empty hall, and that the doors shall not be unlocked until they have completely arranged their difference one way or another.

They are left together, and the keys are turned upon them. But they are not exactly alone; they are being eagerly watched by quite a considerable audience, some of whom are peeping through the keyholes, some are squinting through the cracks and crannies of the doors, while some have even gone outside and have scrambled up to the windows. The quarrel has to be ended, so they set to work, and after a few passes John of Turin effects a thrust on the forehead of his opponent. The wound is of itself little more than a scratch; but at such a juncture as this it is one of extreme importance, for the blood begins to stream into his eyes and all down his face in such a manner that he is every moment obliged to carry his hand to his head, in order to wipe it away. John says to him: "Peter of Corsica, you cannot fight with me in this state. Let us stop a moment that you may stanch your wound." The other, taking him at his word, with his handkerchief bandages his head as well as he is able, whereon they recommence their game, and play it so fiercely that the sword of John is sent flying out of his hand. The Corsican, eager to emulate the generosity with which he has been treated, lowers his point, exclaiming: "John of Turin, take up your sword; I will not harm you with such advantage;" and he gives him time to recover it.

They engage again the third time, and fight so desperately, giving and receiving so many severe wounds, that certain of the onlookers go to the Prince and implore him to separate them, lest they kill each other outright. He comes immediately, and on entering the hall finds them both stretched on the floor and unable to fight further, by reason of their terrible hurts and the vast quantity of blood which they have lost. He calls for assistance, and causes them to be carried away, and so carefully tended that in course of time they are completely cured. During their recovery they had time to think, and each so admired the chivalrous nature of the other, that from enemies they became fast friends, and lived to perform many worthy acts of service to the Prince, their master.

The vain Captain of Piedmont.

Brantôme recounts a story of a still greater courtesy, almost quixotic, indeed, in its nature, which was shown by a certain Piedmontese captain to a fellow-countryman. These two had lived together for years on the most intimate terms, but at last an unpleasantness arose between them about some trifle or other, and, as the fashion of the time was, they must needs settle their little squabble in as serious a manner as if their knightly honour had been really impugned. They met, sword in hand, and one of them had the good fortune, without receiving so much as a scratch, to so badly hurt his man as to entirely disable him. (The fine blades of the sixteenth century appear to have a remarkable objection to find themselves the only one hurt; Shakespeare makes Mercutio say, after he has received his death-wound from Tybalt, "I am sped; is he gone and hath nothing?"). But having in mind their ancient friendship, he said to him: "Look you! we have been for so long a time almost brothers together that I have it not in my heart to kill you, although, seeing what our quarrel is, no one could possibly blame me; I pray you therefore rise up and go to a surgeon to have your wound looked to, and I will assist you." The wounded man was something of a vain fellow; he thanked the victor in the most courteous terms, but added at the same time: "I implore you to extend your generosity to its fullest. I dread its being said of me that I was injured, and did nothing in return. Will you only let it be thought that you have been touched, even ever so slightly?" The successful combatant replied: "Why, that I will, with all my heart;" and he kept his word. He bedaubed his left arm with some of the blood of his fallen opponent, and there was plenty of that same to do it with, put the arm in a sling, took the gentleman to the house of his doctor, and then went about the city for some days recounting to all their mutual friends the things which had not happened. Now, was not this a good-natured fellow, and was he not to be forgiven for the fibs which he told?

Graceful Behaviour of M. de Bussy.

Louis de Clermont, the Lord of Bussy, was one of the most valiant men of his time. On an occasion he finds himself at the Court of Monsieur (the brother of the King) and in his service. Among his comrades there happens to be a certain M. de la Ferté, a very redoubtable man-at-arms, and these two, being of similar disposition, are naturally drawn together. They become great friends, and are under mutual obligations for various good offices exchanged between them; but there arrives an argument on some matter connected with the war in which they are engaged (arguments in the days of the Valois were not confined to words) : they defy each other, and meet rapier in hand. Bussy, one of the most expert as well as courageous of the Prince's followers, succeeds in wounding La Ferté so seriously that he is unable to do more than parry the attacks, and appears to be growing more and more faint, and perceiving this, he says to him : "Brother, I see that you have had enough. I know that you would fight to the very last drop of your blood ; but your wound is so severe that it prevents you from defending yourself with your usual generous courage. We should do well to postpone the rest of our combat till another day, and at present the best thing I can do will be to take you home to have your hurt attended to." M. de la Ferté is well pleased to take Bussy at his word, and in recounting the affair to his friends can hardly find words sufficient to praise such courtesy. It need hardly be said that the duel was not renewed, and that the two gentlemen became greater friends than ever.

The Generosity of La Fautrière.

We are at La Rochelle with the Huguenots, and at the Court of Henry of Navarre. Among the company there is a young D'Aubanye, a gentleman of Angoulmois, brave enough, certainly, but inclined to be a swaggerer, with an extraordinary fancy for imitating the famous Bussy d'Amboise, and a very poor copy of him he makes. For all that he is not to be despised ; he had spent five years in Italy, and had not wasted his time, for he had devoted a considerable portion of it to the study of arms, and especially of the "single rapier," under the famous Patenostrier, and at this particular kind of fight he has the reputation of being a hundred times more expert than the gentleman with whom he has chosen to quarrel, a native of Anjou named La Fautrière. What the matter of their disagreement had been history does not relate ; but they meet, as arranged, in an old garden, on the walls of which are seated the seconds, thirds, and fourths, who watch the affair with much interest. Aubanye is armed with his rapier only, while La Fautrière carries, as is customary, his dagger as well, to which the other objects, saying: "I am accustomed only to fight with the rapier single, and think it unfair that you should use your dagger." To which La Fautrière replies by simply throwing the weapon over the garden wall. Aubanye hopes by this to secure an advantage for himself; but the Fates determined otherwise, for the other's good fortune is such that, although he is vastly inferior to him as a swordsman, after a very few passes he leaves him dead on the ground.

The Good Nature of M. de Sourdeval.

Francis I. sent, on a time, his favourite Minister, the Cardinal of Lorraine, into Flanders to arrange a treaty with the Emperor Charles, and he was attended by a goodly company, among whom was a gentleman of Brittany of a somewhat high-handed character, named M. de Sourdeval, and he fell a-quarrelling with another French gentleman whose name does not appear. They decide to settle the matter without troubling their friends in any way, so they repair to a quiet spot outside the walls of Brussels, where the Imperial Court happens to be. They cross swords, and the valiant Sourdeval receives a slight hurt indeed; but fortune favours him, so that he manages to inflict an almost mortal wound on his enemy. It happens that he has come to the rendezvous on horseback, and as it turns out it is lucky that his mount is a strong one, for the other has arrived on foot. Sourdeval proves himself to be as generous as he is brave; he raises up his fallen enemy, places him in the saddle, while he himself mounts on the croup behind him, and, supporting him in his arms and giving him what comfort he is able, conducts him back to the city to the house of a barber-surgeon, where he has him so admirably tended that before long he is completely cured. The Emperor, to whom this exploit is recounted, desires greatly to see the gallant Sourdeval, commands his presence in the great hall of the palace, and before all his Court praises him enthusiastically as much for his valour as for his generous courtesy, and, in order that he may make the braver show, rewards him with a present of a magnificent gold chain.

The Count de Grand-Pré and the Broken Sword.

The Count de Grand-Pré was one of the most courteous and gracious gentlemen ever seen at the French Court, and withal as brave and gallant as the good sword he wore; but this did not save him from a quarrel with a certain M. de Givry. When they meet to settle the affair, fortune deserts Givry, whose sword breaks in half; but he concerns himself so little about it that he continues to fight. The Count lowers his point, exclaiming: "Get another sword; mine cannot touch you with such an advantage." But this courtesy Givry will not accept, and calls out to him: "No, I mean to kill you nicely with this stump." The Count refuses to attack him with such odds in his favour, and after a little persuasion they are brought to an understanding and become friends again.

Captain Leviston refuses a Proffered Courtesy.

A certain Scotch Captain named Leviston, who was in the train of Mary, Queen of Scots, when she was in France, had contrived to obtain a post at Montagut in Auvergne. He was a big, powerful man, and inclined to be boastful; he was also thoroughly unscrupulous, and played his game so persistently, taking bribes from all sides, and having no regard whatever to right or wrong, that in two years he had amassed a fortune of 100,000 crowns. This dishonesty was the cause of his death, as we shall show: it brought him into collision with a person whom he had in some way injured. This gentleman sends him a challenge, but Leviston has so great a contempt for his enemy that he cannot help showing it, although the latter is known to be a brave fellow and "a tall man of his hands," a fact which he quickly gives the Captain cause to recognise. For no sooner have they got to work with their rapiers and their daggers, than he gives him a terrific thrust in the body, exclaiming: "Friend Leviston, that was pretty good for the first hit; does it content you?" The Captain, enraged, replies: "Before you can give me such another I shall have settled you outright." Says the gentleman: "So then, since you have not had enough, parry me this one;" and, suiting the action to the word, he gives him a second, remarking the while: "That is another fine one for you, I fancy; you had really better go home and get yourself looked to." For indeed it is the wish of the Auvergnat to spare the Scotchman's life if he will only allow him to do so.

But Leviston, furious at having been so thoroughly beaten by a man whom he had affected to despise, cries out: "Finish me if you can, or I will have your life." The Auvergnat begins to think the affair serious, and says: "Will you never be content, and will you still brave me thus, you saucy fellow? I'll kill you outright this time." And with two more sound sword-thrusts he stretches him dead on the ground. And who can blame him? Although it might be better treatment for these braggarts, who would play the bully, but lack the courage for it, to disarm them of their weapons, deprive them of the means of doing harm, and leave them to the ridicule they deserve.

The Kindness of Count Claudio.

In the days of the Emperor Charles V., a brave gentleman lived in Milan, whose surname is lost and forgotten; for he was so renowned for his courtesy, his valour, and his skill at arms, and so beloved by all around him, that he came to be spoken of only by his Christian name, Count Claudio. The Count goes out hunting one fine day, and chance leads him to a secluded spot where some peasants have arranged a sheep-pen, and not a too-well-kept one, either; and this sweet place has been chosen as a fighting-ground by four soldiers who have a difference to arrange among themselves.

The party are assembled, they have stripped to their shirts, their weapons are ready, and they are just about to commence, when Claudio approaches and salutes them courteously, saying, "Gentlemen, I pray you for my sake do not throw away such valuable lives but tell me what your quarrel is, that I may bring you to accord." Now, be it understood that when a party of decent people have met together for the purpose of having a pleasant fight, nothing annoys them more than that some meddling interloper should chance to appear and interfere with their gentle pastime. And so it happens now. The four soldiers tell him bluntly that it is no business of his, but that if he likes to look on and judge the hits, they have no great objection. The Count dismounts from his horse, saying that it will be a reproach to him if he permits them to cut each other's throats in his presence, and by way of emphasizing his speech he draws his sword. This is really too much for them; they consult together, and cry out in chorus: "Let us rid ourselves of this tiresome busybody, and then we can resume our business, and have out our fight in peace and quietness." Whereupon they attack him furiously, all of them together. But they have met their match. Claudio covers himself so cunningly against them, and counter-attacks them so bravely, that in less than a minute he has two of them on the ground; he would gladly grant their lives to the remaining pair, but they, seeing that they are still two to one, will have none of it, and being minded to avenge the deaths of their two friends, or enemies as it may be, assail him with more and more fury. He shifts his ground, as rapier men are wont to do, as occasion may demand, parries with skill, and shortly settles the mundane affairs of number three.

He now has leisure to amuse himself with the remaining hero, on whom he finally inflicts a serious wound, but mercifully spares his life, and with all speed sends a surgeon to him; the treatment is skilful, the soldier recovers and proves grateful. He tells everyone the story of the splendid feat of arms performed by Claudio, concealing nothing, praising his generosity, and vowing that he will repay the kindness whenever an opportunity may offer. The Count likes him greatly, receives much good service from him, and only regrets that he was unable to save the lives of the other three.

How M. de Crequi spared the Life of Don Philip of Savoy, and what came of it.

The cause of this quarrel was a very trifling one: it was nothing more than a silken scarf, so at least tells us Vulson de la Colombière. During the years 1597 and 1598 Henry IV. of France was at war with the Duke of Savoy, and his army was commanded by the famous Lesdiguières, who, among other operations, found it necessary to lay siege to a small fort at a place called Chamousset, on the Lisère; which was quickly taken, and everyone in it put to the sword, except a few who escaped by way of the river. Don Philip, a half-brother of the Duke, was among these, and unfortunately he could not swim; but three of his people contrived to save him. They procured two empty wine-casks and fastened them together, the whole party divested themselves of their clothes, Don Philip was placed on the top of the improvised raft, while his friends swam, and so pushed it into a place of safety, and the spoils which they had left behind them fell into the hands of the enemy. Don Philip was greatly chagrined at the loss of his clothes, as it clearly showed that he had saved himself in a somewhat ignominious manner.

The fort was razed to the ground, and M. de Crequi, who commanded the infantry, withdrew his men and rejoined the main army, which was besieging Charbonnières, a much more important place. A day or two afterwards an officer with a flag of truce was sent by the Duke to inquire about a certain Baron de Chanviray, who had been killed in the taking of the fort. Crequi, happening to meet this officer, showed him a silken scarf said to have been part of the costume which the Don had so hurriedly left behind him, and he was courteous enough to say that if that really was so he would gladly return it; this showed positively that the manner of Don Philip's flight was known to others besides himself and his three friends, and he did not take Crequi's civility in the way in which it was intended. The Castle of Charbonnières as well as certain other places fell into the hands of the French General, after which his army encamped at a place called Les Mollettes, not far from that of the enemy, the two forces being only separated by a wide plain, on which took place from time to time a goodly number of combats and skirmishes, and which also served as a battle-ground for various ardent spirits of both sides, who amused themselves with challenging one another.

One fine day, when so much as a thought of Don Philip never entered Crequi's head, a Trumpet arrived and informed him that the Don was waiting on the plain in full armour, to indulge in a shot with a pistol and three strokes of the sword with him, for love of ladies and for knightly honour. He mounted his horse and accompanied the messenger to the field, but to his surprise found no Don Philip. He sent his own Trumpet to the advance guard of the Duke's army to inquire what had become of him, and it turned out that the Duke had heard of the affair, and had refused to allow him to enjoy his interview with Crequi on any account. The latter told the officer who had brought him the information that he was greatly annoyed at having been made a fool of, and hoped that he would convey the same to Don Philip, and as night was coming on he had to return home without having had any adventure whatsoever; but the next day he himself sent a challenge to Don Philip, with the like result: the Duke had set his face resolutely against any encounter between the two.

Peace at last was established, and several gentlemen were sent on either side to try and arrange a meeting, but they were always prevented by the ever-watchful Duke, who was now at Chambéry. On August 20, 1598, however, Philip contrives to slip away, accompanied only by M. de Puygon, one of his brother's esquires. They arrive within half a league of Grenoble, from whence he sends his companion to inform Crequi where he is to be found. Crequi is delighted, and sets forth at once, taking with him his friend M. de la Buisse. They find Don Philip awaiting them at the rendezvous, and offer him the choice of two rapiers and two poniards which they have brought with them. They doff their doublets, each is examined by the second of his adversary to make sure that he wears no secret armour or anything likely to give him an unfair advantage, and they commence action, each of them resolved to put an end to the dispute once and for all. They exchange a few thrusts, here an *imbroccata*, there a *stoccata*, anon a *punta riversa*, all of which are promptly parried or dexterously evaded, when at last Don Philip receives a thrust between his sword and his dagger which penetrates the pap of his right breast. He has clearly had enough of it; he is losing much blood, and is beginning to grow faint; whereon Puygon, his second, explains the case to Crequi, who is perfectly satisfied with his own share in the proceedings, and takes possession of the weapons of the vanquished man, as it had been agreed that the victor should do. He then gives him all the help he can, accompanies him to a place called Gière, where he prefers to stay, sees that he is properly attended to, and, after mutual expressions of goodwill and friendship, bids him adieu. Crequi and Don Philip are now excellent good friends, and would remain so but for the interference of that meddlesome Duke, who, after so often interrupting their arrangements, now veers round exactly the opposite way. He is irritated at the duel having taken place in spite of him, annoyed at the defeat of his relative, and perfectly furious when he is told that Crequi is boasting among his friends of having tasted of the royal blood of Savoy. He sends a message to his brother saying that he will not see his face again until he has repaired all this, and that as soon as he has recovered from his wound he must challenge Crequi again.

Certain preliminary difficulties having been overcome, it is arranged that this second duel shall take place near St. André in Savoy and close to the river Rhone. On the part of M. de Crequi four gentlemen, the Sieurs du Passage, de Morges, d'Auriac, and de Dizimieu, pledge their word that the affair shall be carried out fairly and without interruption, and the Sieurs Marquis de la Chambre, Baron de la Serra, Degey, and de Montferrant undertake the same for Don Philip, who has as his second M. d'Attignac, while M. de la Buisse performs the like office for Crequi. The conditions of the combat are that they shall fight on foot in their shirts with rapier and poniard, that the seconds shall not separate them, but that they shall fight until one is killed, and that twelve gentlemen on each side shall lie in waiting at a considerable distance to bear away the corpse of the vanquished. The seconds of each now approach the opposite principal to make sure that he wears no secret armour. D'Attignac, of course, visits Crequi, and to reach the battle-ground it is necessary for them to cross the river in a boat. Don Philip and La Buisse are awaiting them, and as they land the latter cannot restrain the exclamation: "The day is ours! the day is ours!" Don Philip asks him coldly: "Why have you so poor an opinion of me?" "Oh, I have the very highest opinion of you, only just now you have on your hands the very fiercest blade in all France."

Both parties are now on the ground, and Crequi has if anything a little advantage as regards the light, but Don Philip attacks him with such impetuosity that his success seems almost certain. Crequi, however, is prompt with his parries, and knows so well how to seize on an opening that he gives his man three sword-thrusts and two stabs with his dagger without receiving even a scratch, and at last, passing his rapier clean through his body, lays him prone. He springs upon him, and, threatening him with his dagger, calls upon him to ask his life; but this the brave Don Philip will in no way do, when D'Attignac, his second, cries out to Crequi that he asks it for him. Crequi very willingly grants it, and, aided by La Buisse, attempts to raise him, while a clever surgeon named Lyon, whom they have brought to the field, does what he can, but to no purpose. He is so fearfully hurt that he dies in the course of a few minutes.

The Duke of Savoy repented of having forced his half-brother to renew this quarrel, and sent a special messenger to forbid the combat, but he arrived on the scene two hours after everything was over.

CHAPTER XIII

Of the Dagger.

According to modern ideas, the dagger is looked on as the weapon of the secret assassin only, and certain it is that in those countries where it is still to be met with it is the exclusive property of the most vicious of the lowest classes. But in the sixteenth century and times previous to that it was openly carried by great and small, and was a most useful appanage of their dress. It was not often employed by itself in solemn combat, although a few such instances are on record, but it flashed from its scabbard many and many a time in sudden anger, and the masters of those days did not forget to teach its use, as is proved by the still extant works of several of them, notably the "Fechtbuch" of Talhoffer, a fifteenth-century manuscript, which was reproduced a few years ago at Prague; the "Opera Nuova" of Marozzo, traced back by Gelli to 1517; and a curious work by Joachim Meyer, which was published in Strasburg in 1570.

The practice of the dagger was taught sometimes "single," as was that of the rapier—that is to say, without the accompaniment of any defensive weapon, such as cloak or shield—and in such case it was customary to shift the weapon from one hand to the other, and often to engage the enemy with both hands behind the back, so that he should not know with which hand the blow was about to be delivered. Sometimes it was used "double"—that is, accompanied by defensive apparatus of some kind, such as a cloak, a buckler, or a second poniard carried in the other hand.

The dagger of the period we are in at present had a strong and rather thick blade, roughly speaking about twelve inches in length, with two very sharp edges, and from its shortness it was an extremely dangerous implement to play with in earnest, for the men, when within striking distance, were also near enough to grapple one another, and the fight became of a very rough order, partly wrestling and partly stabbing. One fellow, seeing the hand of his enemy in an advanced position, would deal it a strong blow with his sharp edge, to the end that he might afterwards arrange with his crippled enemy as best it pleased him. Then, again, it would so fall out that in some tavern squabble a man would draw his dagger upon one absolutely unarmed. But our masters were equal to that. They taught their pupils various ways of disarming him, even to the risky trick of seizing the weapon by its blade and wrenching it away, which was easily done with a stoutly-gloved hand, especially if the edges of the dagger were a little dulled, a thing which might easily occur with one of winey qualities and careless as to the keeping of his weapons. But some of our sword cutlers were alive to this. They furnished the edges of the dagger with little saw-like teeth, set backwards like tiny barbs, the effect of which was to cruelly lacerate the hand that seized it. And now the glove-makers came forward with a counter-invention. They lined the palm of the gauntlet with fine mail, which protected the hand and did no little damage to the teeth of the

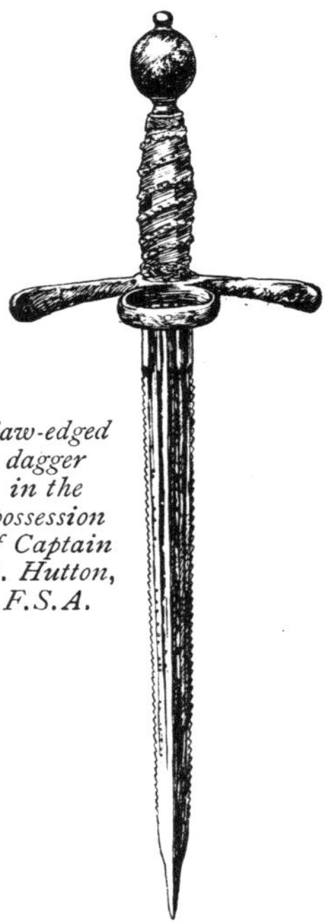

Saw-edged dagger in the possession of Captain A. Hutton, F.S.A.

dagger. It would happen, too, that a fellow having a dagger cunningly made and dexterously balanced would take hold of the blade by the point and so fling it that it would turn in the air, and, striking, penetrate up to the hilt its human target. This trick was a well-known one, and a man who had by accident let fall his sword would resort to it as a threatening feint to gain an opportunity of recovering his lost rapier.

George Silver, the great amateur swordsman of Queen Elizabeth's time, gives in his "Bref Instructions" the following hints on the handling of the dagger, which we reproduce in all its original quaintness :

"Of the Single Dagger fight against the lyke weapon.

"1. First know y^{t} to this weapon ther belongeth no Wards nor gryps, but against such a one as is foolehardy & will suffer himself to have a ful stabb in the face or bodye to hazard the geving of Another, then against him you may use yor left hand in throwinge him asyde, or strike up his heeles after you have stab^{d} him.

"2. In this dagg^{r} fyght, yõ must use cõtynual motion so shal he not be able to put yõ to ye cloze or grype, because yor cõtynuall motion disappointeth him of his true place, and the more ferce he is in runynge in, the sooner he gayneth you the place, wherby he is wounded, and yõ not anything the rather endangered.

"3. The manner of handling yor cõtynuall motion is this, kepe out of distance and strik or thrust at his hand, Arme, face or body, y^{t} shall press upõ yõ, and yf he defend blow or thrust w^{t} his dagger make yõ blow or thrust at his hand.

"4. Yf he com in w^{t} his left legg forewards or w^{t} the right, do you strike at y^{t} prte as soone as it shalbe w^{t}in yor reach, remembring y^{t} yõ use contynual motion in yor progression and regression according to yor twyfold gov̄nors.

"Although the dagg^{r} fyght be thought a verye dangerous fyght by reason of ye shortnes and synglenes therof, yet the fight therof being handled as is aforesaid, is as saf and as defencive as is the fight of any other weapon."

The Dagger Stroke of Benvenuto Cellini.

A lawyer in Rome, by name Ser Benedetto Tobbia, was by way of being a great friend of Benvenuto Cellini, but to a certain Felice, at that time Cellini's partner, he owed money for some rings and such-like trinkets which he had bought of him. Felice wanted his money, and Ser Benedetto preferred keeping it; so they had words together, and as Felice happened to be among a party of his friends at the moment, they all drove the lawyer away, and very angry it made him. Some little while after he betook himself towards Cellini's shop, under the erroneous impression that the matter in dispute was known to the great artist, who, chancing to meet him on the way, saluted him with his usual courtesy, which he returned with very abusive language, to which Cellini replied: "My good Ser Benedetto, why are you so irate with me? I know nothing of this quarrel of yours with Felice. For Heaven's sake go to him and finish it, but do not trouble me any more; for let me tell you, I am not the man to put up with annoyance of this kind." Ser Benedetto, who had by this time thoroughly lost his temper, told Cellini that he knew all about the matter, and that he and his partner were a pair of big blackguards. Meanwhile a crowd had assembled, and was beginning to amuse itself at the expense of the quarrellers, when Cellini, furious at the language used to him, bent down, picked up a large handful of mud, and threw it at Benedetto's face; but the latter stooped suddenly, and received the missile, not in his face, but on the centre of his head. Now, it chanced that, unknown to Cellini, there was in the handful of mud a rough, rugged piece of stone, which not only stunned Benedetto, but cut him severely also, so that he fell to the ground bleeding and insensible. All the bystanders thought that he was killed, and some of them were about to raise him and carry him away, when a jeweller named Pompeo, an ill-conditioned fellow, who entertained a jealous grudge against Cellini, happening to pass that way, inquired what was the matter, who was the injured man, and who had given him the fatal blow. The people replied: "Benvenuto gave it to him, and it served him right!"

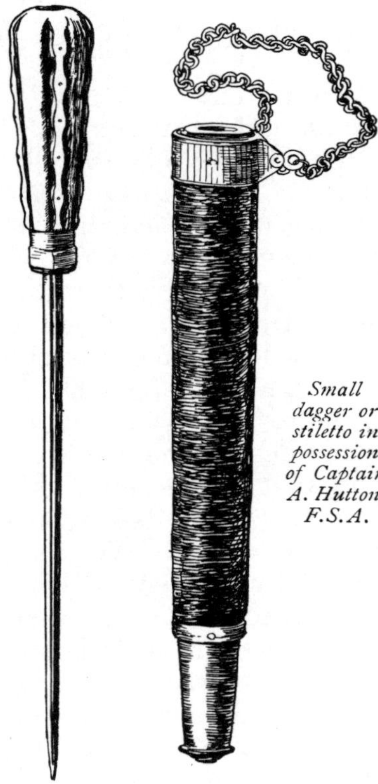

Small dagger or stiletto in possession of Captain A. Hutton, F.S.A.

Pompeo saw here a fine chance of playing a spiteful trick upon a trade rival. He was on his way to the Pope on business in which His Holiness had employed him, and as soon as he reached the presence he said: "Most blessed father, Benvenuto has just now murdered Ser Benedetto Tobbia: with my own eyes I saw him do it." The Pope was extremely angry, and ordered the Governor, who was present, to catch Cellini, and hang him at once on the spot where the murder had been committed; but the latter had received warning, had borrowed a horse from a friend, and had made his escape to Palombara, a place belonging to one of his patrons. Pope Clement sent a Chamberlain to inquire further about Ser Benedetto, who speedily returned with the information that he had found him at work in his office, and that there was nothing at all the matter with him. The Pope, hearing this, turned to Pompeo, and said: "You are a miscreant, and I protest to you that you have stirred up a serpent which will sting you badly, and well do you deserve it."

Things were going so well with Cellini that he quite forgot both the squabble with Benedetto and the wicked trick played upon him by Pompeo, and from this point we will leave him to tell his own story:

"One day," he says, "having put on my shirt of mail, and armed myself as usual with sword and dagger, I betook myself to a certain place where I and my friends were wont to meet and make merry. As we were conversing together, Pompeo arrived on the scene in company with some ten men, all well armed, and when they came opposite to us he stopped suddenly, as if inclined to raise a question with me. My friends, seeing this, signed to me to look to myself. I thought for a moment, and decided that, if I set my hand to my sword, it would cause great trouble to many dear to me who had no real part in my quarrel, and that I had better take all the risk upon myself. Pompeo stood looking at us so long as it might take one to say two Ave Marias; then, laughing at me scornfully, turned on his heel, and, saying something to his companions, moved away, the whole party following him with laughter and insulting gestures. My friends wished to interfere, but I told them that, where I might have such an affair on hand, I was man enough to see it through myself, and I prevailed on them to return to their homes, albeit much against their wills. One, however, Albertaccio del Bene, my greatest friend of all, a splendid young fellow, remained behind, and implored me to let him share my adventure. I replied to him: 'My dear Albertaccio, the time may come, and that perhaps soon, when I may need your help; but at present I pray you leave me, as have done the others: for the affair presses, and I have no time to lose.' Meanwhile, Pompeo and his party having passed on, I followed them, and found that he had entered the shop of a certain apothecary, whence, having finished his business, he came forth, and from the looks of the people there it was plain that he had been boasting of the affront he had put upon me. At this moment his armed friends were somewhat scattered, so that access to him was not so difficult. I drew a little sharp dagger which I wore, charged him, struck at his breast, and aimed another stab at his face, it being my wish to disfigure, but not to kill him. But from fear of me he turned, and, receiving the stroke underneath his ear, fell dead at my feet. I took my dagger in my left hand, and drew my sword to defend my life; but none of Pompeo's bravos took any notice of me: they all rushed towards the fallen man. So I slipped away quietly, and meeting Piloto the goldsmith, a great friend of mine, I told him what had happened. He said: 'Well, what is done cannot be undone. We must find some means to save you.' We went therefore to the house of Albertaccio, who received me with open arms, where shortly afterwards the Cardinal Cornaro sent, for my protection, a guard of thirty men, armed with partisans, pikes, and arquebuses, who conducted me in safety to their master's palace. All this was related to Pope Clement, who remarked: 'I know nothing of the death of Pompeo; but right well do I know what reason Benvenuto had for striking him;' and with that he signed me a safe-conduct with his own hand. A Milanese gentleman, Messer Ambrogio, a well-wisher of the late Pompeo, who was very intimate with the Pope, happening to be present, suggested that his clemency was ill-placed. His Holiness turned to him, saying: 'You do not understand this matter as I do, nor do you know what provocation Benvenuto has received. Besides, to my mind, an artist such as he, who is unique in his profession, stands absolutely above the ordinary laws of the land.'"

The Strange Fight of the Corsican Soldiers.

Brantôme tells the story of these two lusty fellows, how they fell a-quarrelling, and how they agreed to settle the matter in the *champ clos*. The armour they decided to wear consisted of a jacket of chain mail deprived of sleeves, and worn over the simple shirt, without any other body clothing, and on their heads they wore the steel morion. Here the fortunate man who had the choice of arms, from fear of the great strength and skill in wrestling of his enemy, made a peculiar demand: He insisted that the dagger blade of each, having been duly sharpened both in its edges and its point, should be securely set in the front of his morion, and beyond this strange arrangement their only other weapon was to be the sword. They were ushered into the lists with all the usual ceremonies, and fell to work; a number of stout blows were exchanged without result, for they were well-trained swordsmen; seeing which the stronger of the two, who was also the good wrestler, came speedily to close quarters, grappled with his man, and threw him. But he, although the weakest, was a determined fighter, and would not quit his hold, so they fell together; and in the fall the great wrestler had the misfortune to break his arm, which took much of his advantage away from him. They had lost their swords in the struggle, and neither had any weapon of offence left to him than the beaklike dagger in the front of his helmet, but they did their best as they lay locked together on Mother Earth. There could be no possible skill in their fight; but they struggled, and they scrambled, and with those formidable steel beaks they pecked at each other like a pair of angry dickybirds, until their faces and their necks and their unprotected arms were so pierced and gashed and lacerated that they were almost unrecognisable. And thus they struggled and fought on, more like beasts than like Christians, until they were so spent with fatigue, agony and loss of blood that they rolled over side by side, hopelessly exhausted, and unable to move either hand or foot; and in that piteous state their seconds caused them to be carried away, neither being the victor, and neither of them having reaped any credit for valour, skill, or even courtesy. It was sad that such a wild-beastly fight should have been permitted, for it cast something like a slur on the time-honoured knightly combat in the lists.

The Duel of the Sieur de la Rocque and the Vicomte d'Allemagne.

The Sieur de la Rocque, a gentleman over sixty years of age, and the Vicomte d'Allemagne, a young man of about thirty, were near neighbours in the country, and it was by reason of their living so near to one another that they fell to quarrelling. It happened that they were co-lords of certain villages, by which we mean that they had in those places equal rights of seigneurie, and the unpleasantness between them commenced, not with themselves, but with their bailiffs—their servants, in fact.

Shakespeare gives us in "Romeo and Juliet" just such a scene. The retainers of the hostile houses of Capulet and Montagu meet in the street, and start a squabble which they had much better have left to their betters. After a little preliminary snarling and thumb-biting, Gregory says to Samson: "Do you quarrel, sir?" who replies: "If you do, sir, I am for you; I serve as good a man as you." "No better." "Yes, better." And to it they fall right lustily. And so it happened with our two bailiffs: they met on some business matter in one of the villages, and fell out, each claiming that, as his master's representative, he should have the precedence; but seeing that, being common fellows, they were not privileged to wear swords, their affair spent itself in hard words, which they duly reported, each in his own fashion, to their good lords.

Not long afterwards Allemagne chanced to be out hunting in the forest, and he met with La Rocque's man, who was out hunting too. "Why, how now, bailiff?" he said: "I hear that you have thought fit to take the precedence of my fellow. Have a care how you do that again, for if so I will rap your knuckles so soundly that you will not do it a third time." So this worthy bailiff went to his master and told him that M. d'Allemagne had threatened to soundly box, not only his ears, but also those of his revered lord, the great La Rocque himself. The latter part of this Allemagne emphatically denied, averring that he had spoken of no one but the bailiff. This was duly conveyed to La Rocque by certain of his friends, who pointed out that the well-deserved threat to his servant was in no way an injury to himself. But nothing would satisfy him short of sending a challenge to the Vicomte; and thus this unfortunate old gentleman, past the age at which to fight a duel was unavoidable, and within reasonable distance of his natural decease, must needs anticipate it by engaging in an affair which, blinded as he was by passion, he could not conceive would end otherwise than in his favour. He accordingly possessed himself of two poniards, and one day, meeting his man in the streets of Aix, he accosted him with: "Sir, you are a young man, and I an old one: if we fight with rapiers you will have too much the advantage of me; choose, then, one of these daggers, and give me satisfaction for the affront you have put upon me." Allemagne accepts

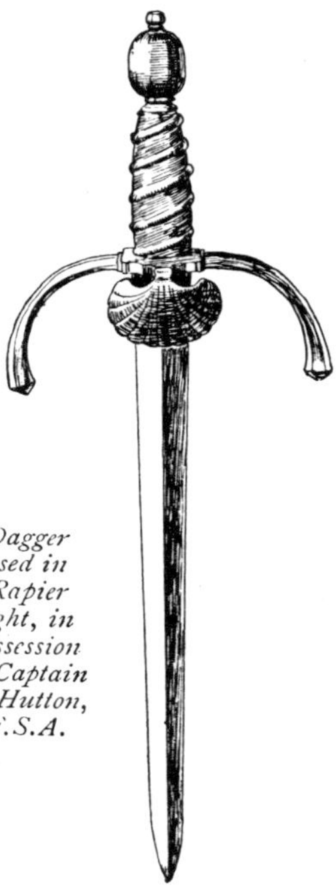

Dagger used in Rapier fight, in possession of Captain A. Hutton, F.S.A.

this pretty invitation. They take with them as seconds the Sieur de Vins for La Rocque, and the young Salernes on the part of Allemagne. They leave the town and proceed to the fosse, which happens to be dry, and then, the seconds having withdrawn a little aside to watch the progress of events, La Rocque exclaims to Allemagne: "Give me your left hand." They join hands, and at once go to work with their daggers; the elder gentleman thrusts his man in the body, and in return receives the weapon of his enemy up to the hilt in his throat, and falls dead at his feet. The other has just life enough left in him to separate the two seconds, who are now amusing themselves by fighting on their own account, and who are both wounded, when he, too, succumbs to his hurt.

The Fight of the Two Daggers.

The dagger, being accounted a knightly weapon, could not be refused as the instrument in a duel; but, seeing that gentlemen were no more in the habit of carrying two of them on their persons than of wearing two swords at the same time, such a curious combination of weapons did not often occur to the imagination; but Brantôme records one instance of it.

The Count of Martinengo was a great fighting man, whose exploits in the wars had undoubtedly done him credit, but, alas! he was also a brutal and unscrupulous bully. He had a disagreement with a gentleman of Brescia, of high estate in that town, and made many attempts to bring him into the field; but the gentleman had no mind for such an encounter, and kept out of the way. The Count, unable to procure a fight with him, made up his mind to kill him anyhow. He hired two soldiers, a pair of as determined ruffians as he was himself; the three presented themselves at the gentleman's house at full mid-day, found him in his chamber, slew him without form or ceremony, got away quietly, mounted their horses, which were in readiness for them, and, before either the authorities or even the relatives of the murdered man could get on their track, made their escape into Piedmont, where the Count offered his services to Henri II. of France, by whom they were joyfully accepted.

After such an escapade as that which we have just described, it is hardly surprising that several people, relatives or otherwise of the deceased Brescian, were anxious to interview the Count. One of them, an Italian Captain, whose name appears to have slipped the memory of M. de Brantôme, was sufficiently fortunate, or, as the event subsequently proved, sufficiently unfortunate, to obtain such an interview, and it took place on a bridge over the river Po, which seems to have been almost consecrated to interviews of this peculiar kind. It happened that the Captain had been in some previous fray somewhat crippled in his left arm, so he stipulated that, in order to give him a reasonable chance of success, they should meet armed with a dagger in each hand, and that on their left arms they should wear *brassards à la Jarnac*—that is to say, a solid covering of plate armour without any joint, which so confined the arm that it could only move from the shoulder. This was a piece not in general use among gentlemen, and, as in the case of Chastaigneraïe, might have been refused ; but, like Chastaigneraïe, the Count was one of those spirits that feared neither man nor devil, and said : "Oh, what matters it ? Let him have his brassard." And it did not matter much—at least, to the Count, who, after a few preliminary passes and volts and *esquivements du corps*, sent one of his two daggers clean through the heart of his enemy, and went his way rejoicing, and, what is more, gained great credit by his exploit.

Now, if we were writing a story, we should, of course, tell how this brutal assassin and wicked duellist came to a bad end, to be hung, drawn, and quartered, or broken on the wheel, or burned at the stake, or put to death in some equally disagreeable manner; but we are quoting from history, and we have to record that, instead of all this, he died gloriously, as every brave soldier should wish to die, bravely fighting in the cause of his royal master at the siege of La Charité.

CHAPTER XIV

A Merrie Pranke of Long Meg of Westminster, and how she vanquished a Spanish Knight with her Sword and Buckler.

"In the time of Henry the eigth of famous memory, there was borne of very honest parents, a Maid called for her excesse in heighth, *Long Meg:* for she did not onely passe all the rest of her Country in the length of her proportion, but every limbe was so fit to her talnesse, that she seemed the picture and shape of some tall man cast in a womans mould. This *Meg* growing to the age of eighteene, would needs come up to London to serve, and to learne City fashions: and although her friends perswaded her to the contrary, yet forsooth she had determined, and up she would. Wherefore she resolved to come up with a Carrier, a neighbour of hers, called Father *Willis*, and so she did, accompanied with three or four Lasses more, who likewise came to London to seek service. After the Carrier had set up his Horse, and dispatcht his lading, hee bethought him how he might place these Maides: with that hee called to minde that the Mistresse at the Eagle in Westminster had spoken divers times to him for a servant, he with his carriage passed over the fields to her house, where he found her sitting and drinking with a Spanish knight called Sir *James of Castille*, Doctor *Skelton* and *Will Somers;* told her how hee had brought up to London three Lancashire Lasses, and seeing she was oft desirous to have a Maid, now she should take her choyce which of them she would have, and *Meg* was entertained into service.

"A great Suter to *Meg's* Mistresse was Sir *James of Castile*, to winne her love, but her affection was set on Doctor *Skelton*, so that Sir James could get no grant of any favour. Whereupon he swore, if hee knew who were her Paramour, hee would runne him thorow with his Rapier. The Mistresse (who had a great delight to bee pleasant) made a match between her and Long *Meg*, that she should goe drest in Gentlemans apparell, and with her sword and buckler goe and meet Sir *James* in Saint *Georges* field, if she beat him, she should for her labour have a new Petticote. Let me alone. quoth *Meg*, the devill take me if I lose a petticote. And with that her Mistris delivered her a suit of white Sattin, that was one of the Guards that lay at her house. *Meg* put it on, and tooke her whinyard by her side, and away she went into Saint *Georges* fields to meet Sir James. Presently after came Sir *James*, and found his Mistris very melancholy, as women have faces that are fit for all fancies. What aile you sweet heart, quoth he, tell me? hath any man wronged you? if he hath, be he the proudest champion in London, Ile have him by the eares, and teach him to know, Sir *James of Castile* can chastise whom he list. Now (quoth she) shall I know if you love me, a squaring long knave in a white Sattin doublet, hath this morning monstrously misused me in words, and I have nobody to revenge it: and in a bravery went out

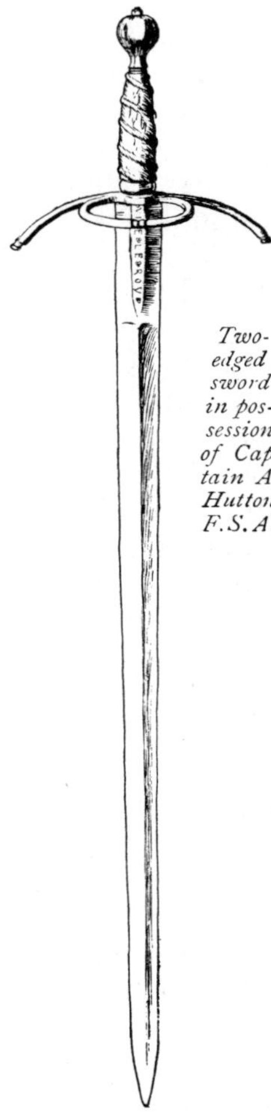

Two-edged sword in possession of Captain A. Hutton, F.S.A.

of doores, and bad the proudest champion I had come into Saint *Georges* fields, and quit my wrong if they durst: now Sir *James* if ever you loved me, learne the knave to know how he hath wronged me, and I will grant whatsoever you will request at my hands. Marry that I will, quoth he, and for that you may see how I will use the knave, goe with me, you and Master Doctor *Skelton*, and be eyewitnesses of my manhood.

"To this they agreed, and all three went into Saint *Georges* fields, where Long *Meg* was walking by the windmills.

"Yonder (quoth she) walkes the villain that abused me. Follow me Hostesse, quoth Sir *James*, Ile goe to him. As soone as hee drew nigh, *Meg* began to settle herselfe, and so did Sir *James*: but *Meg* past on as though she would have gone by. Nay sirrah, stay, quoth Sir James, for I am this Gentlewomans Champion, and flatly for her sake will have you by the eares. Meg replied not a word: but only out with her sword, and to it they went. At the first bout *Meg* hit him on the hand and hurt him a little, but endangered him divers times, and made him give ground, following so hotly, that shee strucke Sir *James'* weapon out of his hand; then when she saw him disarmed, she stept within him, and drawing her Ponyard, swore all the World should not save him. Oh! save mee Sir (quoth hee) I am a knight, and 'tis but for a Womans matter, spill not my blood. Wert thou twenty knights, quoth *Meg*, and were the King himselfe heere, hee should not save thy life, unlesse thou grant mee one thing. Whatsoever it bee, quoth Sir *James*. Marry, quoth shee, that is that this night thou wait on my trencher at Supper at this womans house, and when Supper is done, then confesse me to be thy better at weapon in any ground in England. I will do it Sir, quoth he, as I am a true knight. With this they departed, and Sir *James* went home with his hostesse sorrowfull and ashamed, swearing that his adversary was the stoutest man in England.

"Well, Supper was provided, and Sir *Thomas Moore* and divers other Gentlemen bidden thither by Skeltons means, to make up the Jest: which when Sir James saw invited, hee put a good face on the matter, and thought to make a slight matter of it, and therefore beforehand told Sir *Thomas Moore* what befallen him, how entring in a quarrell of his hostesse, hee fought with a desperate Gentleman of the Court,

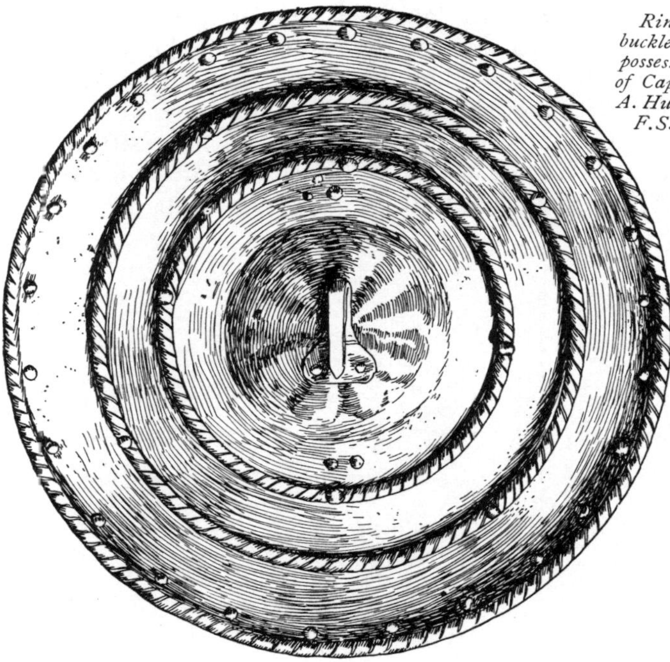

Ring buckler in possession of Captain A. Hutton, F.S.A.

who had foiled him, and given him in charge to wait on his trencher that night. Sir *Thomas Moore* answered Sir *James*, that it was no dishonour to be foyled by a Gentleman, sith *Cæsar* himself was beaten backe by their valour.

"As thus they were discanting of the valour of Englishmen, in came *Meg* marching in her mans attire: even as shee entered in at the doore, This, Sir *Thomas*

Moore (quoth Sir *James*) is that English Gentleman, whose prowesse I so highly commend, and to whom in all valour I account myselfe so inferiour. And Sir, quoth shee, pulling off her Hat, and her haire falling about her eares, hee that so hurt him to-day, is none other but Long *Meg* of *Westminster*, and so you are all welcome. At this all the company fell in a great laughing, and Sir *James* was amazed, that a woman should so wap him in a whinyard : well, hee as the rest was faine to laugh at the matter, and all that supper time to wait on her trencher, who had leave of her Mistris, that shee might be master of the feast : where with a good laughter they made good cheere, Sir *James* playing the proper Page, and *Meg* sitting in her Majesty. Thus was Sir *James* disgraced for his love, and *Meg* after counted for a proper woman."

CHAPTER XV

Of the Two Swords, or the "Case of Rapiers."

It was no more the custom for a sixteenth-century gentleman to wear, in ordinary dress, two swords at the same time, than to carry two daggers in his belt or two walking-staves in his hand; but for more than a hundred years this curious combination of weapons, in their character both offensive and defensive, was regarded as "knightly," and therefore not to be refused in a duel, if selected by the person on whom devolved the choice of arms. They consisted of a pair of straight, double-edged swords, of reasonable and about equal length, furnished on one side only with a shell and protecting rings. They were contained side by side in one scabbard, and hence the name of "case" of swords or rapiers. Such an awkward apparatus clearly could not be worn on the person with any degree of comfort, wherefore when required for use it was carried by an attendant should the affair be *à la mazza*—that is, a private quarrel in some secluded spot—or by the second when the combat took place solemnly in the *champ clos*. From its not being an article of every-day wear, it and its practice escaped the notice of most people, but it did not escape that of the leading professors of fence. They taught it, they preached the cultivation of it, and explained its method in their published works, and they earnestly advised their pupils to take up its study, on account of the advantage which a knowledge of its use would give them if engaged in a serious affair.

Regarded as a game to be played in the *salle d'armes*,

the case of rapiers is more interesting than even the picturesque fight of the rapier and dagger, for in the latter the arms consist of a very long sword and a short dagger, and the player is therefore obliged to fight all through his bout as either a right-handed or as a left-handed man; but when provided with the "case," owing to the two swords being of moderate length and of equal size, he is in a position to change from right hand to left, or left to right, as the need to do so may flash across his mind, and that without the necessity of shifting his weapons, thereby altering instantaneously and radically the scheme of his play, and compelling a similar though unintended change in that of his adversary.

The fence of the case of rapiers, as of all the other Elizabethan weapons, is much in vogue at the present time at the Bartitsu Club, now the headquarters of ancient swordplay in this country, and it was admirably exemplified at the Prince of Wales's Theatre on May 15, 1896, by Mr. W. H. Vernon as Mercutio, and Mr. Frederick Volpé as Tybalt, when the Misses Esmé and Vera Beringer gave their remarkable performance of Romeo and Juliet.

How the Sieurs de Sarzay and de Veniers fought with the Case of Rapiers, and how they fared.

In the year 1537, during the reign of Francis I., there was a pretty quarrel in which were mixed up four gentlemen, namely, the Sieur de Sarzay, the Sieur de la Tour, the Sieur de Gaucourt, and the Sieur de Veniers. Sarzay, in speaking of La Tour, stated bluntly that at the Battle of Pavia, an unfortunate day for King Francis, he had taken to his heels. La Tour called him to account for this in the presence of His Majesty, and asked him plainly if he had made this statement. Sarzay replied, "In good truth I did so, and I had the whole story from M. de Gaucourt," whose attendance was presently commanded, and it might have been expected that La Tour would have promptly called him to account; but before he had time to say a word Sarzay called out to Gaucourt: "Did you not tell me that La Tour had bolted from that battle?" Gaucourt paltered and equivocated, and at last said: "Why, you told me yourself that you had the tale from Veniers," a fact which Sarzay was compelled to admit. On this Gaucourt remonstrated, pointing out that, since Sarzay had confessed that he had derived his information from quite a different person, it was a trifle hard upon him that his name should be dragged into the discussion, and the King, seeing the justice of this, allowed him to depart. M. de Veniers was then summoned, the matter in dispute was explained to him, and he at once plainly told Sarzay that he lied in his throat. This was serious for Sarzay, especially as it was shortly discovered that not a single one of this precious trio, who were amusing themselves by taking away the character of an honest gentleman, had ever been near the Battle of Pavia at all, but had been skulking at home, enjoying themselves at ease on their estates, instead of helping their Sovereign in Italy in his hour of peril, and they were certainly not in a position to say who had fought in the battle and who had run away. King Francis dismissed the accusation against La Tour with absolute contempt, but ordered that Sarzay and Veniers should fight in the lists on account of the lie given between them.

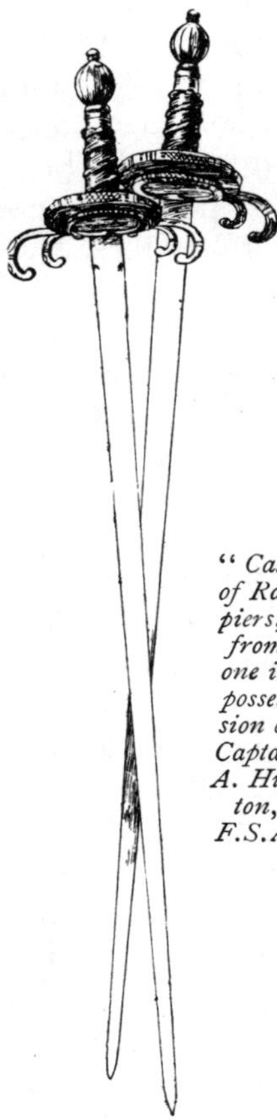

"Case of Rapiers," from one in possession of Captain A. Hutton, F.S.A.

The eventful day has arrived, the lists are duly prepared at the town of Moulins, and His Majesty in person presides at the combat. Veniers seems to have had the choice of weapons, the armour consisting of a corselet with long tassets which well protected the abdomen and the hips, sleeves of chain mail, gauntlets on the hands, and on the head a morion, while the arms were a sharp, double-edged sword in the right hand, and in the left a similar sword a possible inch or two shorter—in fact, a distinct case of rapiers, and of course the usual dagger in its sheath at the side. Thus provided they are ushered into the lists by their respective seconds, the Sieur de Bonneval on the part of Veniers, and the Sieur de Villebon on that of Sarzay. After the administration of the usual oaths and other customary ceremonies, the Heralds cry. "Laissez les aller, laissez les aller, laissez les aller, les bons combattans."

Now, it is a fact well known to our twentieth-century votaries of antique swordplay that a man who has confined his practice to the rapier, with its concomitant dagger or cloak, will be sadly put to his shifts if he is suddenly called upon to fight with the two swords, owing to the difference of size and weight of the sword as compared with the dagger, when used as the parrying weapon. And so it is with our two present champions. Had they been granted, as were Chastaigneraïe and Jarnac, the customary month in which to prepare themselves for the fray, they would no doubt have betaken themselves to masters of repute, to improve their skill in this rather difficult game; but Francis I. had pushed the matter forward with such precipitation that there was no time for anything of the kind, and although they attack each other with some show of resolution, it soon becomes manifest that they are both of them utterly devoid of anything like skill in the management of the weapons they have in their hands, and to no one is this more apparent than to the men themselves, for after a few awkward attempts they throw away their pairs of swords, and draw their daggers with a view of coming to the "close and grype." But the King has had enough of this sorry exhibition, throws his truncheon into the lists, and so ends the encounter. Sarzay and Veniers are charged to become friends, and are sent out of the *champ clos* with more loss than gain of credit, for it is clear to all men that their valour as men-at-arms is only on a par with their veracity as Christians.

La Tour, on the other hand, who has been present during the combat, is completely restored to all his honours, the King affirming in the presence of all his Court that he had himself noticed him, during the battle, fighting like a brave soldier close to his side.

CHAPTER XVI

Of Further Inconvenients which ensued from the Rash Vow of Henri II. of France.

WE have already seen how in the days of chivalry, in the time of Francis I. and his predecessors, it was impossible that a duel, or, rather, a *combat à outrance*, in the lists could take place without the express permission of the monarch himself, or at least of one of his provincial vicegerents; we have seen how from sentimental grief at the death of his favourite Chastaigneraïe King Henri II. registered a solemn vow that he would never again grant the list to any, great or small; and, resulting from this, we have seen how gentlemen having a quarrel together, and being refused the ordeal of the knightly combat in the *champ clos*, with all its attendant regulations to insure fair and honourable conduct, took upon themselves to go out into some quiet field or forest place to void their difference, not clad in knightly armour, but stripped to their shirts, and fighting each other with the deadly rapier and dagger; we have seen how various acts of "supersticerie" arose—how a wicked-minded man, feeling sure that his adversary was honest, would appear on the field with a good strong coat of mail concealed under his shirt, and how another, knowing that his enemy would come unattended, would hire a gang of ruffians to waylay and slay him ere he could arrive at the place appointed; and we have easily seen how needful it became for each man to be accompanied by a number of his friends, for no other reason than to ensure protection from such-like supersticery. And now we arrive at a further development of these evils. In the older time, when seconds were present, it was their recognised duty to bring their principals to accord if that could be done, and if not, to see that the duel should be fought as fairly as possible and without undue advantage to either side; but it became the fashion for the seconds, thirds, fourths, and even larger numbers, to fight as well as their principals, although they had no quarrel to void, and this baneful practice was introduced as we are about to tell.

The Duel of the Mignons.

King Henri III. of France and Poland, of curious memory, had among his courtiers a number of young noblemen whose ideas of morality were of the most elastic kind, and certain of the most prominent of these young sparks were favoured with the most intimate friendship and affection of their royal master. They were known to those who were not members of this precious inner circle by the not very complimentary name of His Majesty's Mignons.

The most favoured of all these was M. de Quelus. He came of a right good stock, being the son of Antoine de Quelus, Seneschal and Governor of Rovergne, and one of the most honoured of the Knights of the Order of the Holy Ghost, but, beyond his courage in fighting, he inherited none of the virtues of his noble father. This Quelus was jealous of the Sieur de Dunes, a younger son of the Seigneur d'Entragues, whence he was known at the Court by the pet name of Entraguet, just as Charlot (or Charlie) is the pet name for Charles. Be it known that this Entraguet was one of the prime favourites of the famous "Balafré," the great Duke of Guise. There were mighty differences between the Houses of Guise and Valois, which somewhat accentuated the feelings of their adherents.

These two young fellows were, or fancied that they were, in love with a certain lady, who was well known as being much more pretty in her person than prudish in her character. One fine evening Quelus caught Entraguet coming out of this lady's apartments, and, finding it a splendid chance for saying something unpleasant to his rival, bantered him with: "Ho! ho! Entraguet, do you think you are the only favoured one? By my faith, there are plenty of others. The fair one is making a fool of you." To which the other replied, in the same light tone: "Oh, that's a silly lie!" Now the trouble begins. The word of the first Mignon of the first King in the Christian world has been impugned, and nothing but blood can obliterate the stain. So Quelus takes into his confidence two other Mignons of his august master—to wit, Maugiron, a very pretty gentleman, and brave withal, and the then notorious Livarot—explains to them how his honour has been attacked by a myrmidon of the Guise, that a challenge will be duly sent to him, and requests their presence simply to guard against any act of supersticery on the other side, and to see that the affair shall be conducted with all possible fairness. The challenge is sent, and is rather joyfully accepted by Entraguet, who relishes the idea of anointing his blade with the blood of a favourite of the hated Valois, to say nothing of the slight squabble in which he is personally concerned, and he elects as his assistants Ribérac and Schomberg. The place of meeting is arranged to be the Parc des Tournelles, used as a market-place for the sale of horses, and the time the following Sunday at four o'clock in the morning (these Mignons seem to have been early birds), when not very many horses or helpers should be about.

The two parties arrive on the ground, and it is evident that the Guises are in a reasonable frame of mind and by no means averse to a reconciliation. Ribérac advances towards Livarot and Maugiron, saying to the latter, "My good sir, it seems to me that the best thing we can do is to try and bring these two gentlemen to a friendly agreement, and not to let them slay one another for so slight a cause," to whom Maugiron insolently replies: "By Heaven, Ribérac! I have not come here to play at stringing pearls; I have come here to fight, and I mean to do it." The other, in much more moderate tone, asks: "Why, Maugiron, who on earth do you want to fight with? You are not personally mixed up in this quarrel, and, what is more, there is not so much as an ill-wisher of yours on the ground." Quoth Maugiron, expressing himself in a manner which we cannot record: "It is you that I mean to fight with." The insolence of this young braggart is too much for the brave Ribérac, who promptly draws his weapons, but holds up his hand, saying: "Stay; since you insist on fighting with me, be it so—my honour forbids me to refuse; but at least let us first say our prayers." And with that he places his dagger athwart his sword in the form of a cross, kneels down, and prays fervently. Maugiron, impatient, and using language of still worse character, says: "You are much too long over those prayers of yours." Ribérac rises, takes his weapons in hand, charges his man, and gives him a sound thrust in his body. He feels himself badly hurt, and recoils step by step, but is vigorously pursued by his antagonist. At last he falls. In falling the point of his rapier is presented to the front, and on to it the unfortunate Ribérac, in his hot haste, rushes, and dead he falls on the ground. The wretched Maugiron expires also with blasphemy on his lips.

Now to see how our principals are faring. Quelus has come to the ground furnished only with his rapier, and, seeing Entraguet armed with a dagger as well, tells him that he ought to throw it away; but the other replies: "The more fool you for leaving yours at home. Rapier and dagger were the weapons agreed upon. We are here to fight, not to discuss punctilios of arms." Quelus attacks him vigorously, and touches him slightly in the arm, but in attempting to parry his fierce ripostes gets his left hand cruelly mangled.

Entraguet, through making use of time thrusts and voltes, and having great advantage from his dagger, succeeds in planting his point several times in his enemy's body, so that at last he staggers and falls, and Entraguet is on the point of finishing him completely, when Quelus, exhausted, implores him to be satisfied with what he has done.

As to the other two seconds, when they see that all their friends are engaging each other, Schomberg remarks, with an idea of separating them: "Why, all four are fighting; what had we better do?" Quoth Livarot, "Let us fight also, for our honour's sake," a strange remark, seeing that up to this time seconds had never been accustomed to fight. "With all my heart," says Schomberg; and they fall to. Schomberg, impelled by his Northern instinct, with a strong "mandritto" completely lays open the left cheek of his opponent; but Livarot more than repays it, for he returns the compliment with a thrust in the chest, which lays the German dead at his feet, and then himself falls fainting from loss of blood.

Henri III. is in despair: of his two prime favourites, Maugiron is slain and Quelus dangerously wounded. He offers a hundred thousand francs to the surgeons if they will but cure him, and a hundred thousand more to Quelus himself to keep up his spirits; but one of his many wounds is absolutely mortal, and their skill is of no avail. At his death the King is beside himself with grief, takes from the ears of his dead favourite the earrings which he had attached to them with his own hands, and, causing his hair to be cut off, preserves it as a relic. He forbids all duelling throughout his dominions on pain of degradation and death; he erects in the Church of St. Pol in Paris most superb marble effigies in honour of both of the departed, and he exhibits his affection for them and his sorrow for their loss in the most extravagant manner conceivable.

The actors in the miserable drama which we have

just described have almost all vanished. Quelus and Maugiron have gone to their long home, and the kindly Ribérac has succumbed to his wound at the Hôtel de Guise, whither he was carried after the affray. Entraguet, with nothing more than a scratch on his arm, has prudently slipped away and saved himself from the displeasure of the King, who would, if he had caught him, most assuredly have made him shorter by a head; and of Schomberg, the German, we hear nothing more after he had received his quietus from the point of Livarot's rapier. Poor Livarot, after the disfiguring slash that his left cheek received from Schomberg, had his beauty so hopelessly spoiled that Henri, who always preferred nice-looking people, did not much care for him, and he had to find amusements for himself, which he did to some purpose; for two years after the terrible triple duel he got himself into trouble with M. le Marquis de Malleraye, and we shall see how this ended.

Exit Livarot.

M. le Marquis de Malleraye, eldest son of M. de Pienne, has just returned from Italy, where he had been sent to put the finishing touches to his education, and where, among other things, he carefully studied the dexterous use of "verie manie weapons," and especially that of the fashionable rapier and dagger, which he has learned to handle with remarkable grace and skill. He forthwith presents himself at Court, where he is received with the cordiality and courtesy which so accomplished a young gentleman may reasonably expect. One evening, during a ball at the palace, he falls out with our old friend, the Seigneur de Livarot, whether from any serious reason or from mere "gaieté de cœur" is not recorded. Livarot, ever since his success in the famous duel of the Mignons, has prided himself greatly on being a "mauvais garçon," a sad dog, and now fancies himself so invincible as regards either sex that he inclines to treat his neighbours with something of disdain. He sets his affections on a certain fair lady of the Court, and will not have it that any gallant but himself should go near her, so jealous does he think himself of her beauty, her honour, and her well-being. The Marquis, a handsome, courageous young gentleman of about twenty years of age, and of courtly manners withal, has perceived this, and ventures to address the lady. Livarot, in his high-handed fashion, replies for her, and in words unpleasing to Malleraye, who, ready to take fire as a stack of straw, speedily comes to an understanding with him, and they agree to meet the next day, without troubling any of their friends, on a small island in the river near the town of Blois.

In the morning they proceed on horseback to the rendezvous, attended only by their grooms. The affair does not last very long, for ere a couple of passes have been exchanged the Marquis, eager to give evidence of his "Italienated" skill, with a cunning thrust which he had learned during his travels, lays low the survivor of the famous fight, never to rise again. But he meets with his punishment at the inglorious hands of Livarot's groom. This man, who, although a common fellow, knew something of the use of a sword, had (either of his own idea or by his master's order) hidden one hard by; he finds his weapon, comes up behind the Marquis, runs him through the body, and leaves him dead on the field. It is satisfactory to know that this act of supersticery was witnessed, that the groom was caught and promptly hanged, and, dying, confessed his crime, saying that he did it to avenge the death of a good master.

CHAPTER XVII

Touching what resulted from the Duel of the Mignons.

In the preceding chapter we have seen how this monarch of curious memory, after the disappearance of Quelus, Maugiron, and the rest of the crew, issued an edict forbidding duelling of any kind throughout the length and breadth of his dominions under pain of death and all sorts of other unpleasantnesses; but he reduced his terrible threats to something like a comedy by erecting statues, and recording on solid marble the valiant deeds and the eminent virtues of men who had brought themselves to their end in an adventure of this very kind, and the honours which were rendered to these Mignons, the affection of their Prince, and the reputation for manly valour which they left behind them, had much more the effect of stimulating His Majesty's liege but light-hearted subjects to follow their example than had the thunder of his edicts to prevent them, for everyone believed that they were quite contrary to the real feelings of him who had issued them.

The young Baron de Biron, who afterwards became, under Henry the Great, a Marshal of France, with many other high dignities, was a pet of the Duke d'Espernon, who had succeeded to the place in his royal master's affections vacated by the late M. de Quelus. Biron conceived a liking for the heiress of Caumont, a young lady who was supremely wealthy, and therefore highly regarded by many young gentlemen; but M. de Carancy, the eldest son of the Count de la Vauguion, was also attracted by this golden loadstone, and seeing that two dogs and one bone do not make pleasant company together, these young sparks fell a-quarrelling over the particularly rich and luscious one that they were both longing for.

Both of our "sad dogs" had got their bristles up, and on an occasion, happening to meet in a narrow passage, they of course quite accidentally jostled one another. Biron, whether it was that he had not his sword about him, or that he had hopelessly lost his temper, wanted to fight it out there and then with his fists; but Carancy, clapping his hand on his rapier hilt, haughtily declined anything so vulgar, so it was decided that they should discuss the matter in a more gentlemanly fashion elsewhere. They have selected, as the place of their encounter, a quiet country spot a little way from Paris, and they slip away from the city secretly, so as not to annoy the King, who dislikes affairs of this kind. Biron takes with him his friends Loignac and Janissac, while Carancy is escorted by Estissac and La Bastide. It is midwinter, the weather is vile, and it is snowing heavily; but our principals are so heated in their tempers that the cold is indifferent to them, and they have managed their arrangements so cleverly that their meeting is witnessed by no one, except perhaps some passing peasant.

Carancy engages Biron, and sends him a thrust which slips off the hilt of his dagger, glides up his left arm, and inflicts a trifling wound in his shoulder. Biron counters this with a vigorous thrust in the body, which stretches his enemy dead on the snowy ground. He now turns to the assistance of his friends, for which act Brantôme extols him, saying that in addition to his valour he shows judgment and forethought, although he is very young and has not the experience in arms which he afterwards acquired. As this is proceeding, Loignac and Janissac pair off with Estissac and La Bastide, and are as fortunate as their principal. Estissac and his man are longer about their business than are their friends, when at last Estissac drops, and his enemy rushes upon him and brutally stabs him several times as he lies on the ground. But the unhappy man does not die outright, and the victor, although his party have already left the ground, remains on horseback alone for a considerable time to gratify himself by witnessing the end.

After all, we do not find it recorded that the heiress married Biron.

M. de la Garde Valon.

M. de la Garde Valon: La Garde was his real name, and Valon that of the château where he lived, and where his mother kept house for him. He was a young man, he never became an old one, and he was a bachelor; which was perhaps fortunate, considering his numerous escapades and the violent end to which they ultimately brought him, for any possible young lady who might have been rash enough to have married him. He was one of the most advanced examples of the turbulent young nobleman type of the days of Henry the Great; he was brave to a fault; he had an absolute disregard for life, whether his own or that of another; he was kind and ever loyal to his friends and servants, high or low, so much so that it was commonly believed that every rapscallion in the district, if he had anything of courage for fight in him, was more or less La Garde's man, and therefore not to be lightly meddled with. But to his enemies he was bloody, cruel and vindictive; in fact, he was a splendid specimen of the boisterous society in which he lived. Now we shall see one of his kindly performances.

A poor soldier, one of his friends of lesser degree, named Jonas, has fallen into misfortune, has been arrested for some crime or other, has been imprisoned in a strong place named La Baleine, in the town of Figeac, and arrangements have been made for the hanging of him shortly. This news comes to the ears of La Garde, who promptly determines that such a brave fellow and such a splendid fighting man deserves a better death, and that rescued he must be, and very cleverly does La Garde effect it.

One day when the gaoler happens to be absent, he goes to the prison and asks those who remain in charge to permit him to comfort the poor fellow with a glass of wine, a request which is readily granted. So he packs off one man to fetch the wine, another to buy some fruit, and a third after something else, till he has sufficiently diminished their numbers, when he draws his rapier, drives away the few who remain, forces the door and gets safe out of the building, when they are joined by another soldier and a servant of La Garde's, who are ready waiting for them. They cross the town and come to the house of the Chief of the Police, who with his wife is seated at a window. This worthy official, catching sight of our little party, is on the point of issuing forth with some of his men to arrest them, for the rescue has been reported to him, but his wife clings to him and will not let him go. This little domestic episode tickles amazingly the fancy of La Garde, who has witnessed the whole of it: he raises his hat, and addresses her with, "Fair lady, I pray you let him come, and I promise to rid you of a burden which so beautiful a creature does not deserve to be saddled with." With this he turns away, takes his soldier safely through the gates of Figeac and home to his château, where there is much joking about how he drew Jonah from the belly of the whale.

The Treachery of Marrel.

Not very long after the above-mentioned exploit, our friend La Garde found himself in the neighbourhood of a place called Villefranche, where three unhappy soldiers, humble friends of his, had been condemned to be hanged. This town of Villefranche was a strong place and well guarded, and La Garde knew that he could not play there the lively pranks to which he had treated the good people of Figeac. So he temporized: he rode up all alone (so like him) to the gate, and told the guard that he wished to see a shopkeeper named Dardene. Likely enough there was no such person in the place.

Now, La Garde and his adherents were a perfect terror to the district, or at any rate to those in it who were not of his following, and the Commandant, one Marrel, to whom his presence had been reported, saw here a fine chance of capturing him, and if he had done so he would have given him very short shrift indeed. He issued forth from the gate followed by some dozen of his soldiers, and entertained him by addressing him courteously. While the men were quietly surrounding him, he said: "Dear sir, will you not come into our town? we shall be so happy to receive you." La Garde replied: "Oh, thank you, I have no particular business with your town. I only want to see a tradesman who can come out to meet me." "Ho, ho!" said Marrel, "that's it, is it? but my good town has business with you To your work, men!" And with that they fall to work; one drags his sword from its carriages, another tears his pistol from its holster, a third takes his horse by the bridle, while a few others threaten him with their arquebuses. The brave La Garde, taken completely unawares, starts like a man awakened from a deep sleep, perceives at once the peril he is in, seizes the sword by both scabbard and hilt, tears it from the grasp of the man who holds it, sets spurs to his great strong horse, forcing it upon the others, when the man who has hold of the bridle lets go at once, thinking that La Garde must be the devil himself. He lays about him lustily with his sword, scattering his enemies right and left, most of whom run as fast as they can back into the city, and canters gaily away, with his doublet positively smoking from the arquebusades they have vainly fired at him at close quarters, but with no hurt whatever beyond a slight scratch on the thumb which he gave to himself in wrenching back his rapier, and he rides away to the town of Naiac, of which a friend of his is Governor.

The people of Villefranche are now in absolute terror of La Garde, and if ever they meet a horseman on the road who asks them where they come from, they invariably answer from Naiac; but he contrives to get hold of some of them, and holds them as hostages for the safety of his three soldiers. Terms are agreed upon, but as soon as these men are released Marrel breaks faith with him, hangs the unlucky trio, and offers a price for the capture of La Garde himself, as a disturber of the public peace. This act of supersticery goads our hero into a fury which otherwise was foreign to his nature; but he first of all goes out at night, attended only by a lackey, removes the bodies of the three victims from the gibbet where they were left hanging, and sees them decently interred. He vows vengeance upon all and sundry of the town of Villefranche, and especially upon Marrel and all belonging to him, and he writes to him as follows: "Ta maison en cendres, ta femme violée, tes enfans pendus. Ton ennemy mortelle La Garde." The children only just escaped being caught, and if he had got hold of them there is no doubt that the Lord of Valon would have kept his word better than did Governor Marrel. Another member of the family, however, does fall into his clutches, but seeing that he is only a distant relative, La Garde lets him off more easily, and contents himself with cutting off his nose and one of his ears, and then turning him loose, from which exploit our hero receives the nickname of Coupe-le-Nez.

The Duel of Bazanez: the End of La Garde.

M. de la Garde, in addition to his other accomplishments, was a bit of a poet; that is to say, he was in the habit of writing verses, mainly for the amusement of his lady friends; but his verses, such as they were, always had a sarcastic vein in them, and these poetic proclivities of his brought him into collision with a gentleman whom he had never set eyes on in his life, and eventually brought about the end of his career. One day an intimate friend of his, the Baron de Merville, being at a party, happened to recite some verses in which the name of a M. de Linerac of Auvergne was rather freely mentioned ; unfortunately, a brother of Linerac, M. de Bazanez, was present, and, seeing who it was that recited the verses, he began to think that they smacked very much of the style of La Garde. Bazanez, well aware of that gentleman's fighting reputation, conceived it possible to gain some laurels for himself by an encounter with him ; so he told Merville that if he could manage to show him the author of the verses with a rapier in his hand he would very greatly please him. Merville replied that he would do so with all his heart, and that this sarcastic poetaster was a man to go a good deal further than only very greatly pleasing him. Bazanez was delighted, and, uncovering, presented his hat to Merville, saying : "Give this to your poet, and tell him that I will not take it back again unless I take his life with it." It was a great big gray hat, with an enormous plume attached to it by a magnificent golden cord. This was something like the gage of battle thrown down by the knights of old ; how the Baron looked at it we do not know, but he duly delivered both the hat and the message to La Garde, who viewed them both very favourably indeed, put the hat on his head, and set forth from Valon at once to try and find his man. But although he searched for him in several places in Auvergne where he was always welcome, he failed in his quest, for Bazanez was laid up ill ; so La Garde was compelled to return home adventureless, and still wearing his great hat.

A month afterwards Bazanez was on his feet again, and no sooner was he on them than he was on his horse also ; he provided himself with two rapiers and two daggers of equal size and weight, and, accompanied by a young cousin of his named Fermontez, a country-bred boy, who had never yet seen anything of Court life, he took the road to Quercy to look for La Garde. They arrived one evening, in nice time for supper, at the house of a friend who lived about a league from Valon, and then and there despatched a note for La Garde by the hand of a young servant lad. This youth went straight to Valon and asked for La Garde, who had gone to sleep in his room (it was summer time and the weather very hot) with a book in his hand, and no one dared wake him; so he was sent to Mme. de Valon, who, aware that they were looking for her son on account of Bazanez, said that he was not at home, and bade the messenger go away. But the young fellow made up his mind to wait outside the gates, at least until supper-time, when at last Mirabel, the youngest of the family, returned from hunting, found him there, inquired who he was and what he wanted, and, learning the story, said: "Oh, you won't find my brother; he is not here." "But, sir," said the lad, "they tell me in the village that he is here; anyhow, my master has ordered me, if I cannot find him, to address myself to his brother." "That same am I," replied Mirabel; "have you any letter for us?" The little note was handed to him; he read it, and said: "Boy, go home to your master and bid him send a gentleman to explain this to us"; upon which he turned on his heel and entered the house. During supper Mme. de Valon, who was a talkative lady, contrived to find out what had happened, and remarked to her son: "This is nice behaviour of M. de Bazanez, to send a lackey to you on such business, after you have in person searched for him in so many places." La Garde made no reply, but shortly after left the room with Mirabel, who suggested that they should not wait for the gentleman, but should start at once and interview Bazanez himself. Mme. de Valon, on her part, perceived that she had been a little too loquacious, and, fearing the consequences, ordered all the doors of the château to be locked and the keys delivered to her. So our two brothers were obliged to get out through a window, with the help of a ladder. They went first to the house of the village priest, and made him get out of bed and say midnight Mass for them, after which they started for the house where Bazanez was staying. When they had arrived near enough, La Garde dismounted, remained beneath a tree, and sent his brother to reconnoitre the enemy. It was broad daylight when he arrived, and he found Bazanez, Fermontez and the master of the house all three together. After the usual greetings, he said to Bazanez : "Sir, my brother is close by, and he is anxious to restore to you your hat, on the conditions under which you have undertaken to recover it ; bring a friend with you, and I will conduct you to him." Fermontez and the master of the house came very nearly to a quarrel as to which of them should have the honour of being this friend, but the post of second had already been promised to the young cousin.

Bazanez now presents to Mirabel the two sets of weapons which he has provided, requesting him to go and offer the choice of them to his brother, which done he returns and conducts the pair to the place where La Garde is waiting for them. As soon as they appear in sight, the two principals salute each other smiling, approach with their hats in their hands, and embrace one another with as many compliments and courtesies as if they had been the best friends in the world. Then they lock up their servants in a barn, and carry away the keys to the ground which they have selected for their field of fight.

La Garde, having told Mirabel to keep Fermontez amused with a bout of rapier and dagger, withdraws some fifty paces to arrange matters with his principal. They engage. La Garde is a splendid swordsman, and lands a thrust right in the centre of Bazanez's forehead ; but the skull is a strong one, and the point does not penetrate. Presently he is more successful, for the second takes effect in the body, and he exclaims: "There, that is for the hat!" They begin again, and he lands the third also in the body, adding: "And that is for the plume." They charge each other a fourth time, La Garde crying out: "And now to pay for the beautiful gold cord. Really, sir, your hat fits me to perfection"; and he promptly pays for the said cord in precisely similar coin. Bazanez, badly wounded and thinking of anything rather than hats, shrieks out: "Look to it, or you are a dead man!" then, actuated more by despair than by judgment, throws away his sword, and, taking his dagger in his right hand, rushes upon La Garde and stabs him in the neck. In the struggle they both fall, but Bazanez, being uppermost, redoubles his energy and gives him no less than fourteen wounds from his neck to his waist; but in his death agony La Garde bites off a good half of Bazanez's chin.

While all this is going on, Master Mirabel, the young brother, is amusing himself at rapier and dagger with Bazanez's cousin, and receives from him several thrusts which pass between his shirt and his body without hurting him, but at last sends him back a real one. Fermontez stops, calls out to him: "Are you wounded?" and at the same instant rushes at him, closes, and attempts to wrestle; but the unwounded Mirabel, fresh and vigorous, holds him tight, when the injured lad shrieks out to his principal, who is busy finishing off La Garde: "Cousin, cousin! look to yourself; I am killed." On this Mirabel relaxes his hold, and poor young Fermontez sinks down dead on the ground. Mirabel is a brave boy, and he is excited, too; he calls to Bazanez, who is retiring from the scene: 'Ho, you! you have killed my brother, and I your cousin; let us finish the affair together." But Bazanez, who has regained his sword and also the famous hat, though minus that large piece of his chin which his enemy has swallowed, is already on horseback, and, bowing, says: "My dear boy, your brother was such a splendid swordsman that he has not left anything in me for a fresh fight; I am going to see my doctor"; and away he canters.

The plucky young Mirabel is left master of the field, the proud possessor of three rapiers, four daggers, and two corpses, which latter he causes to be carried away; but the poor boy is so overcome with grief at the death of his brother that it is a long time before he can persuade himself to return to Valon.

Adieu, and a long fair sleep to you, brave La Garde!

CHAPTER XVIII

George Silver, Gentleman.

THE fashion for those elegant and highly ornate weapons, the Italian rapier and dagger, with their deadly method of "poking" fight, had found its way into England, and it was promptly followed by the arrival on our shores of one or two Italian adventurers, who seem to have been men accustomed to arms, but not in any sense masters of the art they pretended to teach; had they been really great masters, what need could there have been for them to travel so far, when travelling was so slow, so difficult, and so costly, when they ought to have been able to gain a handsome living in their own country?

Until almost quite recently, people of those nations on the Continent which still uphold the duel have had the idea that, because an Englishman is not permitted by the laws and customs of his country to engage in private fight, he is therefore altogether innocent of the art of fence. And this brings to our mind how, within the last twenty years, a certain noble Marchese, whose name we purposely omit, condescended to come to London with the kindly intention of teaching us ignorant Englishmen something of the real art of self-defence. The very name of this noble swordsman was—hear it, ye gods and little fishes!—absolutely unknown to unfencerlike England, and to get an introduction of any sort he had to betake himself to a professional musician, to some of whose belongings a relative of his had elsewhere been kind. This musician numbered among his pupils a gentleman who proved to be a sort of George Silver junior. He was an ardent lover of weapons of all kinds, and reasonably skilful in the use of them, so the musician asked this pupil of his to take lessons from his friend. The gentleman replied, "Well! but I must know what he can teach me: if he can beat me, it will certainly be worth my while to learn from him how he has done it." Quoth the musician: "That will be very easy, as he intends to set up a school somewhere near Leicester Square, where he will fence with anyone who likes to cross blades with him for a guinea a bout." The gentleman said that he subscribed to several fencing schools, where he could play assaults with various good swordsmen at not quite so high a price, but that he would be well pleased to find out what kind of stuff the Marchese was made of. An introduction was arranged. The gentleman obtained permission from a certain master of fence to bring the stranger to his school, and, wishing to show him kindness and hospitality, invited him to lunch, entertained him well, and when they had finished their cigars and coffee took him to the fencing-master's house, where were assembled a fair number of his scholars. The pair engaged first with the foils, and the great Marchese did not acquit himself in any way as his host had expected; in fact, he was well beaten; but he explained that the foil was not his favourite plaything—that with which he excelled was the sabre. He produced a pair, one of which, very much worn and bent, he offered to his opponent, and the other, practically new, he kept for himself. But even with that advantage he fared no better than he had with the foils. He played afterwards with several members of the school, who were not all of them of the first rank, but he got the better of none of them.

The establishment near Leicester Square never came to exist, and the sojourn of the Marchese in London came to an end much sooner than he had intended.

But we digress. The Italians who came to England

in Queen Elizabeth's time were more fortunate than their modern prototype, in that they were provided with good introductions; moreover, they professed to teach the art of rapier and dagger play, for which there was then such a craze, especially among the Court people. They were therefore well received, and so much employed by the young sparks of the town that they were soon able to present a very brave appearance. We have said something about one of them, Rocco by name, in Chapter VI., and there were also "Jeronimo, that was Signior Rocko, his boy that taught gentlemen in the Blacke-Fryers, as usher to his maister in steed of a man." And the third was Vincentio Saviolo, who has made his name a lasting one by the treatise he wrote on rapier play.

It must not be supposed that the English were such utter barbarians as to possess no skill at arms whatever, but their favourite weapons were the broadsword and buckler, and sometimes the "long sword," and it is a historical fact that King Henry VIII. formed the leading professors of the art into a corporation, which unfortunately lasted only a short time. There were plenty of sound teachers in the country who, together with the bulk of their pupils, had a hearty dislike for the new-fangled "Italienated" style of fighting; these men were clearly but little educated in anything except their own special art: they have left us no written records of their work. But it is fortunate for posterity that there lived among them two brothers, gentlemen by birth and scholars by education, by name George and Toby Silver. These two were ardent devotees of the art dimicatory, thorough Englishmen, and bitterly hostile to the fence tricks of the fifth-rate Italians who had been taken up by the society of the day, and whose false teachings seemed likely to oust the good old English custom of fighting with sword and buckler, where honest downright blows, and not "frog-pricking" thrusts, were concerned.

Of these two brothers, George, the elder, is the one

who most appeals to us, for he has left his name in history by his valuable writings. He published in 1599 his "Paradoxes of Defence," mainly a fierce attack upon the unsound teachings of the then fashionable Italians, and he fully justified the production of this work by writing a sequel to it under the title of "Bref Instructions upon my Paradoxes of Defence." This the most valuable portion of his work never saw the light in his own time, but remained only in a manuscript form, which fortunately came into the possession of the British Museum. The reason for this was most probably the death of Silver, very shortly after its completion; he certainly seems to have been dead some seventeen years later when Joseph Swetnam brought out "The Schoole of Defence," and even his name was but imperfectly remembered, as Swetnam remarks that "George Giller hath most highly commended the short sword and dagger," which George Silver most certainly did, both in his "Paradoxes" and in his "Bref Instructions." Swetnam appears to have been apt to make mistakes in the matter of names, for in the same chapter he recommends his readers to "aske Augustin Badger, who speaketh highly in praise and commendation of the short sword, for hee hath tried that weapon in the field so often, and made as many tall fraies as any man that ever I heard of or knew since my time." The description of this Badger tallies completely with the character and ideas of that Austin Bagger who a few years before had relegated Signior Rocco to private life, and, from the manner in which Swetnam mentions the two, it is clear that at the time when he wrote Austin Bagger was still alive and amusing himself with making his "tall fraies," while it appears equally so that George Silver had paid the debt of Nature.

Those who take the trouble to read his works, now completely brought to light by Captain Matthey, must recognise in George Silver the father of English swordsmen, although he claims for himself no such honour, but professes only to record what he himself has learned. He was the first genuine English author who ever put before the public anything in the way of printed lessons of fence, and he was the first author in any country to lay down distinct instructions for the parry and riposte. In his chapter "Of divers advantages y[t] you may take by strykinge from your warde at y[e] sword fyght," he gives the ripostes in great variety, teaching no less than six of them from the parry now known as high tierce, three from high seconde, five from high prime, eight from tierce, and eight again from quarte; while his chapter on "The manner of certaine Gryps and Clozes to be used at the syngle short sword fyght" is replete with useful instruction as to how a man should behave when *corps à corps* with his enemy.

George Silver and his brother Toby were as good in their practice as they were in their preaching. The former tells an amusing story of a challenge they sent to the Italians Vincentio and Jeronimo. Signior Rocco evidently retired from public life after his unpleasant experience with Austin Bagger, and his place was taken by "his boy," who went into partnership with Saviolo. "Then," says George, "came in Vincentio and Jeronimo, they taught Rapier-fight at the Court, at London, and in the countrey, by the space of seaven or eight yeares or thereabouts. These two Italian fencers, especially Vincentio, said that Englishmen were strong men, but had no cunning, and they would go backe too much in their fight, which was great disgrace unto them. Upon these words of disgrace against Englishmen, my brother Toby Silver and myself made challenge against them both, to play with them at the single Rapier, Rapier and Dagger, the single Dagger, the single Sword, the Sword and Target, the Sword and Buckler, and two hand Sword, the Staffe, Battell Axe, and Morris Pike, to be played at the Bell Sauvage upon the Scaffold, where he that went in his fight faster backe than he ought, of Englishman or

Italian, shold be in danger to breake his necke off the Scaffold. We caused to that effect five or six score Bils of challenge to be printed, and set up from Southwarke to the Tower, and from thence through London unto Westminster, we were at the place with all these weapons at the time apointed, within a bow shot of their Fence school: many gentlemen of good accompt, caried manie of the bils of chalenge unto them, telling them that now the Silvers were at the place appointed, with all their weapons, looking for them, and a multitude of people there to behold the fight, saying unto them, now come and go with us (you shall take no wrong) or else you are shamed for ever. Do the gentlemen what they could, these gallants would not come to the place of triall."

The Last of Jeronimo.

"Jeronimo this gallant was valiant, and would fight indeed, and did, as you shall heare. He being in a Coch with a wench that he loved well, there was one Cheese, a verie tall man, in his fight naturall English, for he fought with his Sword and Dagger, and in Rapier fight had no skill at all. This Cheese having a quarrel to Jeronimo, overtooke him upon the way, himselfe being on horsebacke, did call to Jeronimo, and bad him come forth of the Coch or he would fetch him, for he was come to fight with him. Jeronimo presently went forth of the Coch and drew his Rapier and dagger, put himself into his best ward or stocata, which ward was taught by himselfe and Vincentio, and by them best allowed of, to be the best ward to stand upon in fight for life, either to assault the enemie, or stand and watch his comming, which ward it should seeme he ventured his life upon, but howsoever with all the fine Italienated skill Jeronimo had, Cheese within two thrusts ran him into the body and slue him."

Throughout his writings George Silver manifests no personal rancour against these rapier masters, but explains carefully his disapproval of, and hostility to, their false teaching, and the faulty weapon which they introduced. And he was justified. The long rapier was eminently the arm of the private duellist, and not of the soldier, and it went out of fashion some fifty years after the time when we lose sight of our author. From the wise teachings in his "Bref Instructions" Silver has won for himself the indisputable right to be for ever regarded as the father of the art of swordsmanship in these realms.

CHAPTER XIX

The Reign of Richelieu.

THE reign of Henry the Great was prolific in sanguinary encounters of private fight; to call such meetings by the name of "duel" is almost absurd, a duel being a combat between two men only, whereas in these affairs seldom less than four, and often a larger number, met in deadly conflict about a matter which in reality only affected two of them. It is said that during the reign of this monarch a larger number of French gentlemen came to their end in personal quarrels than had been slain in the terrible civil wars which preceded his advent to the throne. It is not our intention to compile a history of duels, because that has often been done already, but merely to draw attention to the various types of sword used in various periods, and to describe historical, not fictional, examples of how these swords were employed in real earnest. We fear that we have told more than enough of the private fights of the sixteenth century, so we will pass on to the next, when the man who was King of France was Louis XIII., but the man who reigned over France was his great Minister, Armand du Plessis, the terrible Cardinal de Richelieu. At this time the rage for duelling was more virulent than ever, but the customs of the duel had altered, and that very much for the worse. In the older time the gentlemen who engaged had at least some idea of what the quarrel was about, but "autres temps autres mœurs." Now it had become the fashion for a party who were on their way to keep their appointment, and found themselves short-handed, to stop the first gentleman they met in the street, and invite him to join them, whether they knew him or not, and the etiquette of the day precluded him from refusing, but compelled him to take up a quarrel with which he had nothing to do, on account of people he was utterly unacquainted with, and to fight to the death with a man he had never heard of before. Of a duel of this kind there is a remarkable instance in the early career of M. d'Artagnan, the details of which we take from his memoirs, and not from the fictitious description given by Dumas in the "Three Musketeers." It should be noted that the real D'Artagnan, at the time when he first arrived in Paris, was a mere boy of not more than sixteen years of age, and a very brave, pugnacious boy he was, too.

The Musketeers.

The plucky, hardy little Bearnais, the sixteen-year-old D'Artagnan, arrives in Paris, and presents himself at the hotel of the King's Musketeers, where presides the great M. de Treville. M. de Treville is also from Bearn, and some years before had come to Paris, no better off than our brave little lad, and by his indomitable courage and fidelity in the service of the King, to say nothing of his cleverness with his weapons in certain other affairs in which His Gracious Majesty had no personal concern, had made his name so respected that he had arrived at the great honour of being appointed Captain of the King's Musketeers, the highly-trusted royal body-guard. M. de Treville was in old days an intimate friend of the elder D'Artagnan, the boy's father, so the youngster is fairly sure of a kindly reception.

In the antechamber there are a number of musketeers awaiting an audience, among whom are three brothers, named Athos, Portos, and Aramis. They are inseparable. If one is in want of a breakfast, and the other two have one, there is enough for the three. If another has a clandestine love affair, he has two friends ready to help him up to the lady's window, and if any interfering relative of hers should chance to make himself obnoxious, their two rapiers are there ready to bring him to reason. While if a third happens to have a serious matter in hand, there is no occasion for him to ask the first gentleman he meets in the street to lend him his aid. These three had made for themselves a considerable reputation in Bearn by their fighting propensities, on which account M. de Treville had brought them to Paris and enrolled them in his company. It was politic on his part, as the King's Musketeers were constantly quarrelling with the guards of Cardinal de Richelieu, who had agents all over France charged to find out for him the greatest "cutters" in the country. Young D'Artagnan addresses himself to Portos, who asks him who he is, when did he arrive, and what has he come to Paris for, and his curiosity being satisfied, he remarks, "Oh, I recognise the name very well. My father has often told me that he has known some very brave men of your family. You must do your best to imitate them, or else go back at once to the paternal cabbage-garden." The boy is extremely sensitive on all matters touching the point of honour, and, indeed, that he should be so was part of the advice given to him by his father on quitting his home. He begins to look sour on Portos, and asks him sharply: "Why do you address such language to me? If you doubt my courage, I will soon put your mind at ease, and if you will come down into the street with me I will give you an example of it at once." Portos is a great big, powerful man, but good-natured withal, and not by any means the sort of person to engage in a quarrel with a boy of sixteen; he laughs, and advises the lad that, though he must be brave, there is no need that he should be so quarrelsome; tells him too that, since he is not only a fellow-countryman, but a near neighbour at home also, he will be much more pleased to take him under his wing and give him a hand, than to draw his sword upon him; but if his mind is so bent on having a tussle with somebody, he will provide him with an opportunity sooner than he thinks for. They leave the house together, young D'Artagnan expecting to have to draw his rapier the moment he finds himself in the street. But on reaching the door Portos says, "Please follow me at a little distance without seeming to have anything to do with me," which the boy does, feeling not a little puzzled at the proceedings of his supposed enemy. Portos passes along the Rue de Vaugirard until he arrives at the Hôtel D'Aiguillon, where he finds a gentleman named Jussac standing at the door, and they greet each other in such a fashion as to make D'Artagnan think that they are the dearest friends in the world. The latter has passed on a few paces, when, on turning his head to see if his man is following him, he perceives that Portos and Jussac have left the door and have come into the middle of the street, in order to be out of earshot of the porter of the house, and that their friendly attitude has changed altogether. They are talking with some heat, and neither of them seems particularly well pleased, while during the course of the conversation Portos points out D'Artagnan, a thing which puzzles that young gentleman still more, and not a little disquiets him.

The discussion is at last over. Portos rejoins his young friend, and says: "I have had a nice altercation with that fellow, and all for love of you. In an hour's time we are going to fight in the Pré aux Clercs, three against three, and, since you are so anxious to christen your rapier, I made up my mind that you should be one of our party; but I did not tell you so, lest difficulties might arise and you might be disappointed, so I have come here to warn M. de Jussac that we shall be four instead of three, and to request him to bring another gentleman for the purpose of entertaining you. And now perhaps I had better explain what our quarrel is about. It is none of mine; it is between my eldest brother Athos and M. de Jussac, who is one of the Cardinal's people. In company the other day my brother happened to remark that the King's Musketeers had had the best of His Eminence's guards whenever they had crossed swords with them, and Jussac declared that it was not so. There, that is what we are going to fight about."

Young D'Artagnan is immensely pleased, thanks Portos most heartily for the honour he has done him in allowing him to make his maiden effort in the cause of the musketeers, and promises to do his best to deserve the good opinion he has formed of his courage. So they proceed together to the Pré aux Clercs, where Athos and Aramis have already arrived. They, seeing the chubby face and youthful appearance of the new-comer, take Portos aside and ask what it all means. He explains everything to them, when Athos expostulates with : "Why on earth have you done this? Look at the position in which you have placed us. Jussac has seen this little friend of yours, and, just like him, will bring some great swashing bully from the Cardinal's Guard, who will wipe out the poor little thing at the very first thrust, and then where shall we be? There will be four of them against three of us." However, as Portos has arranged the affair, there is no getting out of it, so they put on a good face, receive the lad very courteously, and, with most extravagant compliments, thank him for his kindness in coming to the assistance of three gentlemen whom he has never met before ; but it is pretty clear that all these high-flown compliments of theirs are considerably less than half-hearted.

Now we must return to M. de Jussac. The poor gentleman is sorely perplexed. He is in the position of having to find at less than an hour's notice an opponent qualified to cross blades with Master d'Artagnan, and being a soldier, and something even more than that—for he is a captain of experience to boot—is not in the habit of mixing in the society of small boys, and he cannot bring to his mind any small boy whom he can decently invite to the merry meeting he has in prospect. So he betakes himself at once to the brothers Biscarat and Cahusac, two creatures of the Cardinal whom he has secured as his seconds, and explains his trouble to them. They immediately refer the matter to a third brother of theirs named Rotondis, a gentleman whose inclinations are towards the Church. In point of fact, he is on the eve of taking Holy Orders, but when the difficulty is explained to him he professes himself willing to waive his religious prejudices provided no other person will take his place; but, luckily for him, a friend of Biscarat happens by chance to drop in, and is at once introduced to Jussac. His name is Bernajoux. He is a gentleman of some distinction, being a Captain in the regiment of Navarre, and he is a tall, handsome, soldier-like man. Jussac briefly tells him of the strait that he is in, and implores his assistance. Bernajoux, rather pleased than otherwise, instantly offers him his hand and his sword, so off they go together, to the infinite relief of the clerically-minded Rotondis.

All is now comfortably settled. They arrive on the ground, where the other gentlemen are waiting for them, when Jussac, Cahusac, and Biscarat immediately commence pairing off with our three musketeers, leaving the great Bernajoux face to face with a mere scrap of a lad. He looks the lad up and down, twisting his large moustache, and turns haughtily to Jussac with, "How now? If you are playing a joke upon me, I tell you I don't like it! Have you brought me here to give a lesson in fencing to a child like this, or is it your intention to send me home with the reputation of an ogre, a creature that delights itself by gobbling up wretched little boys?" The word "wretched little boy" fires the heart of Master d'Artagnan to boiling-point. He whips out his rapier, crying: "I'll soon show you what wretched little boys where I come from can do when people talk about them in that way."

Bernajoux is compelled to draw and defend himself, for the angry boy, whose father has by no means neglected his son's fencing education, attacks him furiously, and the big Captain, intending the lad to see that he is serious, replies with several strong thrusts. These D'Artagnan luckily parries, and sends a riposte home to him in his right side. He staggers back a few paces and falls. The boy, grieved at having hurt so severely a man whom he has never seen before, approaches with the idea of assisting him; but Bernajoux mistakes his meaning, and presents the point of his sword, in the hope that he may rush upon it. D'Artagnan calls out to him that he is not such a fool as to kill himself in that way, but if he will only throw away his sword he will do his best to help him, which, judging the youngster to be honest, he promptly does, whereon the other, taking a pair of scissors from his pocket, cuts off as much of the wounded man's shirt as is necessary, and binds up his wound with it.

This act of courtesy, however, is very near costing his life to Athos, and perhaps even to his brothers also: for Jussac, having wounded him in the sword arm, is pressing him hard, and he has but his left hand to defend with. D'Artagnan, perceiving this, springs forward, calling to Jussac, "To me, sir, to me: I have no heart to kill you from behind," and engages him at once. Athos, meanwhile, having recovered somewhat, is not the man to allow his young preserver to fight so dangerous an enemy single-handed. He comes forward again, when Jussac, seeing that the odds are against him, attempts to edge away towards Biscarat in order that at least they may be two against three; but D'Artagnan, understanding the move, slips round and intercepts him, on which he is obliged to deliver up his sword, and so to set both his opponents free to help Portos and Aramis, whose partners are quickly deprived of further means of doing any harm, and are packed off home feeling very much disconcerted. The whole of them now turn their attention to Bernajoux, who, weakened by loss of blood, has again fallen. The musketeers tend him to the best of their power, while D'Artagnan, having the youngest legs of the party, runs off to find the carriage of M. de Jussac, in which the wounded man is placed. He is taken home, and it is six weeks before he can rise from his bed; but he appreciates the courage and generosity of the young Bearnais so thoroughly that the fight between them proves to be the commencement of a life-long friendship.

How Monsieur de Treville told the Story to the King.

Louis XIII., under the advice of Richelieu, issued many edicts against duelling, but the threatened punishments contained in them were of such an extravagantly cruel nature that it came to be believed that they were little better than paper threats, especially when it was the talk of the town that the sanguinary squabbles, of almost daily occurrence, between His Majesty's Musketeers and the guards of His Eminence passed off quite quietly, the participators in them receiving nothing more than a problematical scolding for their breach of discipline, while it was equally well known that the august masters of these two companies made the exploits of their men a matter of more or less friendly banter between themselves; and of this the affair which we have just described is a typical instance.

Immediately after the affray, Athos, Portos, and Aramis, taking their young friend with them—not a bad introduction for him to their great chief—reported themselves to M. de Treville, and told him frankly and honestly the whole story. Treville says: "This is a dangerous business, seeing what are the King's edicts, to say nothing of the Cardinal, who must be highly annoyed at the defeat of his bravos. Leave it to me; I'll see to it." So he went at once to His Majesty, before the Cardinal had time to arrive, and told him how there had been a most unfortunate occurrence : that the three very bravest and best of his musketeers, to wit, Athos, Portos and Aramis, had, accompanied by a young friend of Portos, a lad only just arrived from the country, gone for an innocent walk outside the city, and they happened to stroll into the Pré aux Clercs, where, as ill-luck would have it, they encountered a party of three or four of the Cardinal's chiefest "cutters"; that His Majesty was cognizant of the unhappy tension of feeling between the members of the two companies, and—well, it was difficult to ascertain exactly how the affair began, but it was certain that somebody said something disagreeable to somebody else, words ensued, and somebody's rapier came out of its scabbard, and then a rapier belonging to someone on the other side got loose too, then there were more words, on which all the rapiers flashed out, and there was a regular hurly-burly. But it all ended fairly well ; it was true that poor Athos received an ugly wound in his sword-arm, and he would have been sorely put to his shifts had it not been for the timely intervention of the brave little country boy who had come with Portos. He told His Majesty that this boy was evidently something out of the common ; that he had found himself opposed to one Bernajoux, a great strong fellow and a highly experienced swordsman ; that he stood bravely up to him, parried all his fierce attacks, and finally succeeded in running him through the shoulder, after which exploit he found himself free to go to the assistance of Athos just in the very nick of time. He recounted, too, how, on being defeated and deprived of their swords, the Cardinal's men had taken to their heels, leaving the unfortunate Bernajoux bleeding on the ground, when the musketeers took pity on him, and attended as well as they could to his wound, while the youngster ran off to find a carriage, in which they conveyed the injured man to his lodgings, and never left him until they had seen him safe in the hands of a surgeon. Treville added too that, as regards the boy, he knew all about him, and that the elder D'Artagnan, the lad's father, was one of his oldest friends. From this recital the King was perfectly satisfied that the affair had been merely a rencontre, a chance collision, with nothing whatever of a prearranged duel about it; he sent especially for our young hero, complimented him highly on his conduct, gave him a handsome present, and commended him to the care of M. de Treville.

François de Montmorency, Comte de Boutteville: his Deeds and his Death.

The mind of Cardinal de Richelieu was permeated with one great idea, as had been, many years before he lived, the mind of King Louis XI. The old-time King was actuated merely by personal selfish motives, to make himself all-powerful. Richelieu, on the other hand, was impelled by feelings of a grander nature, his absolute and unswerving loyalty to his royal master, and his determination to make the King of France, be he who he might, a monarch absolute. He adopted a similar plan to that used by old Louis, of utterly crushing the great nobles of the realm, or at any rate all those who did not readily fall in with his views; and it must be said of him that he reaped but little for himself, for, by his rigorous and often cruel prosecution of the programme he had laid down, he earned the reputation of being the best-hated and worst-feared personage throughout the length and breadth of his country. Among those whom he struck down was François de Montmorency, Comte de Boutteville, a rabid duellist and a notorious bully, of whom they said that whenever he chanced to hear it remarked that such and such a gentleman was a brave man, he would, although quite unacquainted with him, march up and accost him with, "Sir, they say you are brave; I have a mind to prove you: what are your weapons?" And the poor gentleman had to fight and be killed simply to gratify the mad vanity of a man with whom he had no quarrel at all. Boutteville, thanks to his own misconduct, fell into the clutches of Richelieu and never escaped them ; but the fatal blow was directed, not against the duellist, but against the Montmorency.

Boutteville was the king of the fencing world of his day ; he had in his house a great hall well stocked with foils and a variety of weapons, both blunt and sharp, with which practice could be obtained ; it was well provided, too, with refreshments for his visitors—he was a hospitable man. Here the young bloods, the "raffinés d'honneur," as they pleased to call themselves, were wont to assemble every morning to enjoy the excitement of a fencing bout or to arrange some meeting of a less innocent character. The foil existed in the rapier period, although most of our theatrical managers seem to be under the impression that it did not, seeing that they invariably arm poor Hamlet and Laertes in the fencing scene with foils of the present day, which represent a weapon, and require a method of fence, which did not come into being until long after Shakespeare was dead. However, as the public does not hiss them for their ignorance, we suppose it does not matter very much. The foils which adorned the walls of Boutteville's great hall were undeniably of the rapier pattern, a very fine specimen of which we have already illustrated.

The exploits of M. de Boutteville in the field of honour would fill a fairly sized volume of themselves, so we will only touch upon one or two which occurred towards the end of his career. On one occasion, when he had a quarrel with the Count de Pont-Gibaut, it happened to be Easter Sunday, and the Count was at church ; but Boutteville thought nothing of disturbing him at his devotions and compelling him to come out and fight. Pont-Gibaut escaped with his life on this occasion, but only to fall two years afterwards by the hand of the Prince de Chalais. In 1626 Boutteville was again successful in an affair with the Count de

Thorigny, whom he killed, and this victory helped greatly to bring about his downfall.

It was sad for M. de Boutteville that he was so thoroughly successful in his affair with Thorigny, for it raised up for him an implacable enemy in the person of the Marquis de Beuvron, a near relative of the deceased, who vowed that he would avenge his death. It was difficult, however, to arrange a meeting, for the adventures of Boutteville had made him so many enemies, and had caused the issue of so many decrees of Parliament against him, that France was a country in which it was scarcely safe for him to appear in public; so the two betook themselves to Brussels, that they might be able to fight the matter out in peace and quietness. Richelieu, however, had got wind of the arrangement, so Louis XIII. wrote a letter to the Archduchess, the Sovereign of the Low Countries, asking her not to permit two of his subjects to cut each other's throats in her dominions, to which request the Princess, who, womanlike, was averse to bloodshed, readily acceded, and she commanded the Marquis de Spinola to bring the two gentlemen to reason. The good Marquis saw at once that the way to accomplish his task was to invite them to dinner, and when their souls were made warm and genial with good wine, to bring them to friendly accord. And so he did. He entertained them superbly, and he brought them together; but during the protestations, the handshakings, the embracings, and the oaths of eternal friendship, that passed between them, Beuvron found the opportunity of whispering into the ear of Boutteville: "Mind, I owe you something on account of my poor Thorigny. I am his executor, and I shall never be satisfied until I have you opposite to me sword in hand." Fight in Brussels Boutteville would not, for he had pledged his word to the Archduchess not to do so, and he meant to keep it. Besides, he had prevailed upon her to request Louis to permit him to return to

France. His Majesty's reply was that all he could do to oblige her would be to let Boutteville alone, but that he must be very careful not on any consideration to make his appearance at Court.

The Marquis de Beuvron, not being under the royal ban, returned immediately to Paris, whence he despatched quite a number of letters to Boutteville to persuade him to arrange a meeting. The latter set out for Paris, and immediately on his arrival went to Beuvron's house, who was glad enough to see him, but, having no wish to drag any of his friends into a fatal encounter, suggested that they should pursue their affair by themselves, to which Boutteville replied: "You may do as you will, but two of my friends are anxious to have a hand in the matter, so if you come alone you will have to fight all three of us at once."

The rendezvous was fixed for three o'clock in the afternoon the next day, for Boutteville insisted on fighting, as he put it, "au grand soleil," and such was his impudence that, in further defiance of the edicts of the King, he demanded that their battle-ground should be the Place Royale itself. The seconds of Boutteville were the Count de Rosmadec des Chapelles, his relative and habitual companion in his escapades, and a certain Sieur de la Berthe, while Beuvron brought with him his esquire, Choquet by name, and the Marquis de Bussy d'Amboise, famous for his feats with the sword, who, although laid up ill, had risen from his sick bed to do this service for his friend.

They get rid of their upper garments and make ready for the fray. Boutteville and Beuvron attack each other so furiously that they soon come to such close quarters that their long rapiers are useless. They throw them aside, and, grappling with one another, attempt to bring their daggers into play; but they are so equally matched, and both are in such imminent peril, that they mutually beg for life, and thus their part of the encounter ends. Bussy, meanwhile, is engaged with Rosmadec, but he is weak from his illness, and in poor state for such a business, and he speedily succumbs to a thrust from his opponent which pierces the jugular vein. He is carried to the house of the Count de Maugiron, where he shortly expires without having uttered a word. La Berthe is also wounded, and is taken to the Hôtel de Mayenne, while Beuvron and Choquet make at once for their carriage and escape to England. Boutteville and Rosmadec, on the other hand, take things much more coolly. They go first to the house of a barber named Guillemin, where they refresh themselves, and where they are advised to save themselves as soon as possible, since the King is in Paris, to which they reply that they knew that perfectly well before their fight took place, and, their repast finished, they proceed to the Hôtel de Mayenne to inquire after La Berthe, after which they mount their horses and leisurely take the road towards Meaux. They arrive at Vitry without any mishap, when a quaint incident occurs, which has the effect of marring all their plans. The breath was scarcely out of the body of the unfortunate Bussy, when his sister, Mme. de Mesmes, determining to be first in the field, despatched two of her confidants to take possession of the castles, lands, and effects of the defunct Marquis before his aunt, the Countess de Vignory, who might try to claim a share in the heritage, could manage to move in the matter. These men, on arriving at Meaux, heard that two horsemen had just passed that way, and made after them, judging them to be emissaries of the Countess, but on coming closer they recognised the fugitives. They rode on, and gave information at once to the Provost, telling him how the Marquis de Bussy, who was Governor of the district, had been killed by one of the pair. The Provost immediately ordered the arrest of Boutteville and Rosmadec, who had retired to an inn, where, after a plentiful supper, they had gone comfortably to bed.

They were taken to Paris and lodged in the Bastille. The King, furious at their insolent contempt for his edicts, ordered their trial at once. They were duly condemned, and on June 22, 1627, they both perished, not in the field by the sword of honour, but ignominiously on the scaffold by the blade of justice.

CHAPTER XX

The Sword of Justice.

WE have just seen Boutteville and Rosmadec perish by the sword of the executioner, an arm more swift and more certain than those of which we have already said so much, the estoc of the knight and the rapier of the Mignon. Its object was decapitation, and nothing else, and it was fashioned in such a manner as to make its work sudden and complete. It was a heavy sword, with a blade some thirty-three inches in length and two and a half in breadth, having both its edges very sharp, but with no point, while its hilt consisted of a simple crossguard, a handle long enough to be grasped with both hands, but not so long as that of the fighting two-hander, and a pommel sufficiently heavy to make it balance well for its work. Such was the headsman's sword. And now what of him who wielded it? Of the mode of life, both public and private, of such men we learn much from the memoirs of the Sansons, who for seven generations were the hereditary executioners of France. The first of them, Charles Sanson de Longval, by birth a gentleman, was compelled by circumstances over which he ought to have had better control to marry Marguerite Jouanne, the only daughter of the executioner of Rouen, and, since Maître Jouanne had no male offspring, the law compelled his son-in-law to inherit the fell office at his death. This office was the only one held under the Crown which carried with it no honour. It is true that it was confirmed by letters patent, but when granted these documents were not formally presented to the recipient. They were flung on a table and he was ordered to take them away.

The previous life of Charles Sanson, as we must now know him, had been, through no fault of his own, an embittered one, and, to add to his troubles, his beloved Marguerite, for whose sake he had sacrificed all his prospects, was taken from him in less than a year after their marriage, leaving behind her a son, sole heir to this terrible heritage. This final blow deeply affected the mind of the bereaved man, and gave to it a sombre, morose tone which was much in accord with the sinister profession to which he had been obliged to devote himself. He had grown aged before his time, and his appearance was such that the good people of Rouen, recognising him from afar, shuddered at his approach, and as he passed them drew aside. The greater part of them were ignorant of the past events of his wrecked life, but the result of it, the very aspect of the man, conveyed at once to their minds *the headsman*, and all of them—men, women and children—recoiled from him in terror. At this juncture the executioner of Paris happened to die, and it was a

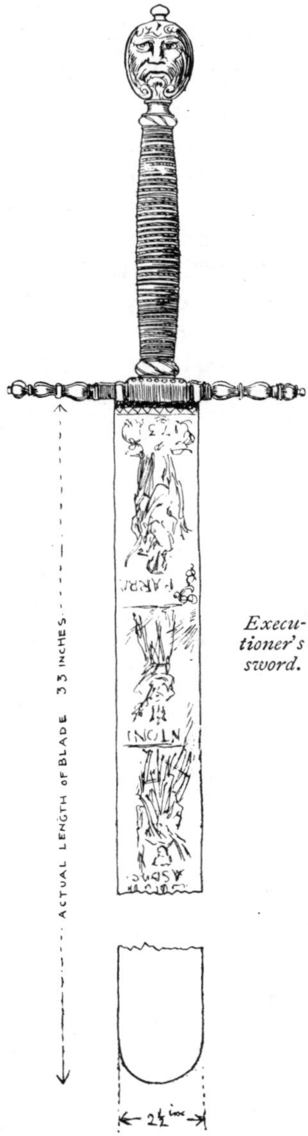

Executioner's sword.

relief to the mind of Sanson when the authorities of that city offered him the vacant post. His official residence in Paris was known among the people as the Pilori des Halles, and it was scarcely a place to dissipate the profound melancholy of its new tenant. It was a sombre-looking building of octagonal form, surmounted by a wooden cage revolving on a pivot, in which was fastened any person who might have been condemned to the degrading punishment of exposure in the pillory; but the headsman was not actually compelled to live in this place, so Charles Sanson contrived to let it for a very respectable sum, and fixed his abode in a then almost deserted quarter known by the name of La Nouvelle France, and here continued to dwell the seven generations of the Sanson family.

Mme. Tiquet.

Mdlle. Angélique Carlier was born in 1657. Her father was a rich bourgeois of Metz, where he had amassed a fortune of over a million of money, to which his daughter and a son some years her senior were the sole heirs. When she was fifteen her father died, and her brother, her sole guardian, placed her in a convent school to finish her education, and this achieved she came out into the world young, rich, accomplished and singularly beautiful. She speedily attracted a host of admirers, among whom were several highly eligible young gentlemen, but whether it was that she had too many strings to her bow, or that her heart was not yet in any way touched, she took a very long time to make up her mind, and her procrastination lent itself to the projects of a certain M. Pierre Tiquet, a man old enough to be her father, and whose plebeian name showed that he was of anything but gentle birth; but by his merits alone he had risen to the respectable position of Councillor of Parliament, which flattered the vanity of the young lady, although it by no means won her affection. The middle-aged swain was actuated not so much by the dictates of his heart, for he was a long way past the age of romance, as by the attractions of her banking account. The worthy man contrived to bring over to his side two very valuable auxiliaries—the brother who had been the guardian of Angélique, and a maternal aunt who had considerable influence with her—so that what with the counsels of these two relatives, and the prospect of becoming the wife of so important a person as a Councillor of the Parliament of Paris, an honour of which, but for her money, she would never have dared to dream, she overcame the secret repugnance which she felt for the man, and made up her mind to accept the Councillor. Besides this, the latter, although by nature a fearfully stingy old fellow, had screwed up his courage to purchase a magnificent bouquet of flowers intermingled with diamonds and other precious stones, which he presented to her on her birthday. So he married the lady, and the honeymoon was quite a romantic affair It lasted nearly three years, during which time a son and a daughter were born to them.

Mme. Tiquet began to develop extravagant tastes. Her household, with her carriages and her numerous servants, was very costly, and to add to this she had recently inaugurated a salon, in which foregathered a society brilliant undoubtedly, but, as might be expected, a trifle mixed. Tiquet, who possessed on his side nothing but his salary, and who had run into debt in the matter of the famous bouquet and other things connected with his courtship, became uneasy on account of all this expenditure, and mildly expostulated with his wife, of which thing she took no notice whatever, whereon the expostulations, from being at first mild almost to timidity, waxed strong, and even imperious, while the feelings of the lady towards him changed gradually from esteem to indifference, from indifference to annoyance, and at last to absolute aversion.

Among the frequenters of Madame's salon was a

Captain de Montgeorges, an officer in the army. He was young, handsome, of soldierlike appearance, of courtly manners, and in every way the complete opposite to the disagreeable, surly, stingy old hunks to whom she was tied for life, so it was hardly surprising that she should take a violent fancy to so fine a fellow, and, indeed, there was not a single thing that she could find it in her heart to refuse him. She became quite foolish about her admirer, and forgot herself so completely that she very soon made the pair of them the talk of Paris, and rumours of her goings on at last reached the ears of M. Tiquet. The astonished old man, who had been entirely blind to the state of affairs, was perfectly furious, and commenced operations by turning Montgeorges out of the house and suppressing his wife's receptions—stern measures which did not tend to improve the relations of their home life, and Angélique made up her mind that somehow or other she would rid herself of the yoke which galled her, a thing which seemed fairly possible, seeing that she had brought the old gentleman a very large dowry; and, unfortunately for her, she found a pair of devoted assistants in the brother and the aunt who had urged her to make this ill-assorted match, and, thanks to their intervention, a whole swarm of creditors swooped down upon the unlucky man, set their lawyers to work, and gained case after case against him, so that at last there was nothing left for him to do but to sell his house, and his wife took this opportunity of demanding a judicial separation in the matter of worldly goods. Meanwhile old Tiquet was far from being idle. He went about complaining to his friends and colleagues of the scandalous intrigues of his wife, evoked their sympathy, and finished by obtaining a *lettre de cachet* against her. He now thought himself master of the situation, and treated her more harshly than ever, ordering her, if she wished to retain her liberty, to be more submissive for the future, and never again to see her beloved Captain. The lady turned upon him and, among other things, accused him of having bribed the servants to spy upon her. They had a terrible scene, and Tiquet, driven into a corner, shook his *lettre de cachet* in her face, and took his oath that he would set it in motion; but Angélique, active as a cat, sprang upon him, snatched the paper from his hand, and popped it in the fire.

The old fellow, defeated and disappointed, fairly foamed at the mouth with rage and vexation; he approached all sorts of great people with a view of obtaining a second letter, but he met with nothing but point-blank refusals and ill-concealed merriment, and he shortly became the laughing-stock of all Paris, and of the Court as well; while, to crown his woes, his wife succeeded in obtaining her judicial separation, and with this, although they still continued to inhabit the same house, she should have been satisfied. Unfortunately, however, her success had whetted her appetite, and she conceived the idea of ridding herself of Tiquet altogether, and putting in his place the attractive Captain, with whom she still continued to have clandestine meetings. She waited until one day the old gentleman, happening to be unwell, was confined to his room: she made some nice soup for him with her own fair hands, and put into it something of a stronger nature than the herbs which are generally used for flavouring purposes, and gave it to his valet to take to him. The man, fancying that there was a trifle not altogether right, pretended to trip against the carpet, stumbled, and down he fell: the bowl was broken, the soup spilled, and the servant, scrambling to his feet, picked up the bits of broken china, made what excuses he could, and took himself out of the room. But he mentioned nothing about his suspicions, and old Tiquet never knew what a narrow escape he had had.

Mme. Angélique now turned her attention to other means of accomplishing her wicked end. She contrived to gain the sympathy and services of her porter and of some dozen others as well. Everything was arranged, and on a certain evening an ambush was placed in a narrow lane leading to Tiquet's house, through which he would have to pass ; but he escaped a second time, for at the last moment Madame's heart failed her, she suddenly countermanded all her arrangements, and sent the intended assassins home, no doubt paying them well to keep quiet. Old Tiquet, although he knew nothing of either of his escapes, made himself more objectionable than ever. He suspected the porter, and not without reason, of infidelity, sent him about his business, and took to watching at the gate himself, through which he would scarcely allow any of his wife's friends to pass, which exasperated the lady more than ever, and one fine evening, after visiting a friend, he set out for home, but he had hardly got into the street when some half-dozen shots were fired at him from close quarters, and he fell to the ground badly peppered. But, luckily, none of his hurts were mortal ; assistance was soon forthcoming, and the people were for carrying him home : he would, however, in no way have it so, but directed them to take him to the house of the friend he had just left. The night was dark, the attack had been sudden, and M. Tiquet was unable to recognise any of his assailants, but his conduct in refusing to go home, where he would have enjoyed the tender care of his wife and children, was looked upon as strange, and tongues began to wag about what the relations might be between him and the lady of that house, and they were not silenced when it became known that Mme. Tiquet had rushed there as soon as she heard of the accident and had been refused admittance. After the surgeon had dressed M. Tiquet's wounds, a magistrate paid him a visit with a view to commencing an inquiry about the matter. But to all his questions as to what the reason of the attempt might be, the only answer the old gentleman gave was that he was quite sure that he had no possible enemy in the world but his wife. This looked ominous, and many friends of the lady advised her strongly to make good her escape while yet there was time; but she was overconfident from the fact that no witnesses were forthcoming, and besides, being of a credulous nature, she had paid a visit to a palmist, or some such other person having dealings with the devil, who had told her that in a very short time she would be in such a position that her enemies could never harm her more; and so it fell out, though not in the manner she had anticipated.

The attack upon M. Tiquet, and the statements he made, rendered an inquiry necessary, and eventually Mme. Tiquet was arrested and lodged in the prison of the Grand Châtelet. Her trial commenced, but no evidence against her could be produced, had not an officious fellow, who had been mixed up in the first ambush—the abortive one—come forward voluntarily, and declared that on that occasion she had sent him money by the hand of her porter, as a bribe for the assassination of her husband. The ex-porter and the man who had made the disclosure were both arrested, and confronted several times with the prisoner; but although the names of quite a dozen conspirators in the first affair were discovered, that of not a single participator in the second and more successful attack came to light at all. The wretched woman was tried for the former, and condemned to lose her head on the Place de Grève; the porter was sentenced to be hanged; and the informer got penal servitude for life.

It was the custom in those days, between the conviction and the execution of a criminal, that he should be put to the torture in order to elicit the names of his accomplices, if there were any, so Mme. Tiquet was taken to the terrible chamber, where she was adjured to confess her crime and to reveal the names of the persons concerned in it with her. This she flatly refused to do, so the "question" of water was applied. It was effected as follows: The culprit was thrown on his back, and fastened down upon a sort of wooden bed, near which were standing eight pots of water, containing about a pint each. A cow's horn was then forced into the mouth of the patient, and the water poured down his throat. The "question ordinary" consisted of four of these pots, and the "question extraordinary" of eight, and it sometimes happened that the unhappy wretch expired before the full number was accomplished. To this treatment Mme. Tiquet was subjected, but by the time she had swallowed the first potful her mind was made up to confess everything. She was asked if Montgeorges had had any hand in the crime, and she replied: "Oh, heavens, no! If I had even mentioned it to him, I should have lost his affection for ever, which was dearer to me than life itself."

She was now conveyed in the usual cart to the scene of the execution, where Sanson and his satellites were awaiting her. Charles Sanson had always more than a repugnance for the duties of his office, and his mind had been much exercised about this particular case, the proceedings of which he had followed minutely, feeling certain all the time that they would have to be ended by himself, and when the condemned woman appeared on the scaffold a strange fancy seized him. He thought that the figure before him resembled his lost Marguerite, and it unmanned him completely. Having disposed the criminal in a manner suitable for the purpose, he raised his great sword. It whistled through the air and struck the neck of the victim. But the head did not fall. There was only a great gaping wound, from which the blood flowed freely. He struck a second time, but with no better success, and the blood from the severed arteries spurted in all directions, the mob all the while hooting the executioner, who, half frantic at the yells of the spectators and at his own bungled work, delivered a third blow, when the head of the would-be murderess rolled at his feet.

A Master-stroke of the Headsman.

M. Duval de Soicourt was Lieutenant Criminel of the town of Abbeville. He was an individual of peculiar aspect, with an overtall, lean, angular figure, a low forehead suggestive of a brutish nature, a long, sharp, ill-formed nose, thin, compressed lips, which, when they wore a smile at all, wore a malignant one, and disagreeable greenish eyes peering out from beneath a pair of stiff, bushy, grizzled eyebrows. The man's face was the index of his mind. We can picture to ourselves the evil spirit of the story we are about to relate. Strange to say, this remarkably unprepossessing person had found someone to marry him, for at the time we make his acquaintance we find him possessed of a son who seems to have been very much a chip of the old block. The amiable father had been left guardian of a little girl, a very rich heiress, and he placed her for her education in the Convent of Villancourt, whose Abbess was a venerable lady of high lineage, beloved and respected by all who knew her. When the young lady came to be nearly of marriageable age, M. de Soicourt, for mercenary reasons alone, determined to compel her to become the wife of his son; but she evinced such absolute repugnance to the match that the Abbess, whose influence was very great, managed to get the guardianship of the girl taken away from him. At this he was furious, and, fancying that the old lady destined this rich morsel for a young cousin of her own, the Chevalier de la Barre, swore that he would be revenged.

A few years before this there had been erected on the new bridge at Abbeville a sort of Calvary surmounted by a crucifix, and now an event happened which played into the hands of M. de Soicourt. A gross act of sacrilege was committed. Some evil-disposed person had come in the night, had broken off an arm of the central figure, had removed the crown of thorns, and had soiled the visage of the venerated statue with mud. Just then party religious feeling ran very high. The philosophers and freethinkers were attempting to bring sacred subjects into contempt, and a royal edict had just been issued against the Jesuits. Nor did the necessary reconsecration, which was performed by the Bishop with much pomp and ceremony, in any way allay the excitement. But the true culprits were never discovered.

Acting under the orders of the Bishop, the Lieutenant Criminel commenced investigations, and many witnesses were examined, but, as none of them had seen anything done, the inquiry was fruitless. A few days afterwards, however, another event occurred which gave Soicourt an opportunity for arranging his wicked scheme of revenge. The Chevalier de la Barre was walking in the streets with a friend, when a procession of monks passed by, and they positively neglected to take off their hats, an omission fairly excusable, as at that particular moment it happened to be pouring with rain. Soicourt saw here a means of realizing his object. He mixed up this trivial matter with the affair of the crucifix, and brought charges of blasphemy, sacrilege, and Heaven knows what besides against several young gentlemen belonging to the most important families in the neighbourhood. Most of these managed to evade his clutches, but the Chevalier de la Barre was arrested, and after a very short trial was condemned to be beheaded, and his remains burned. He appealed against the conviction, but his appeal was dismissed. The sentence was ordered to be carried out, and the chief headsman from Paris was sent to Abbeville to effect it.

On the fateful morning the Chevalier, placed in a tumbrel and seated between his confessor and the headsman, is conveyed first to the porch of the cathedral, where it was usual to compel malefactors to make the *amende honorable* (a confession of their crime and an acknowledgment of the justice of their punishment), when he definitely refuses to repeat the required formula, saying that he is innocent, and that he will not die with a lie upon his lips. The mournful procession now approaches the scaffold. All is prepared. The headsman requests the Chevalier to kneel, as that is the custom. The Chevalier replies that this time the custom must be in abeyance, that it is for criminals to kneel, that he is no criminal, and that he will meet death standing. The executioner, much troubled, asks: "What, then, am I to do?" To which La Barre replies, "Your duty. I shall give you no trouble." The headsman gathers himself together, and delivers a mighty circular cut, which seems to have passed clean through the neck of the victim, but with no apparent effect when, a second later, the knees give way, the body falls, and the head rolls on the scaffold.

BOOK III

THE PERIOD OF TRANSITION

CHAPTER XXI

The Flamberge and the Early Small Sword.

About the middle of the seventeenth century there came, more or less gradually, a radical change in the fashion both of the sword itself and of the manner of using it—at least, among the nations of Western Europe, always excepting hyperconservative Spain. The long rapier, whose hilt had assumed the form of the cup, came to be considerably shortened, and therefore lightened, so that it was possible to effect certain *simple* parries with the sword itself, whereas in its former state it was so unwieldy that something of a defensive nature in the left hand was absolutely necessary. Then, again, the "lunge," much as we know it nowadays, began by degrees to be recognised; of this we shall have something special to say further on. A new kind of sword, which formed a connecting-link between the big rapier and the small sword, came into somewhat ephemeral fashion—the flamberge—whose blade was long and slender; it was, in point of fact, nothing more than a very light rapier. The blade of the specimen which we illustrate is "flamboyant"—an eccentricity, most certainly—while its hilt, deprived of the counter-guards of the long rapier, and having its quillons curled up, as being no longer required for anything but ornament, still possesses the *pas d'âne.* It has a shell delicately perforated, a fairly long grip, and a pommel of great length, admirably formed as a counterpoise to the rest of the weapon. It is a sword of graceful form, most certainly, but hardly strong enough for practical work.

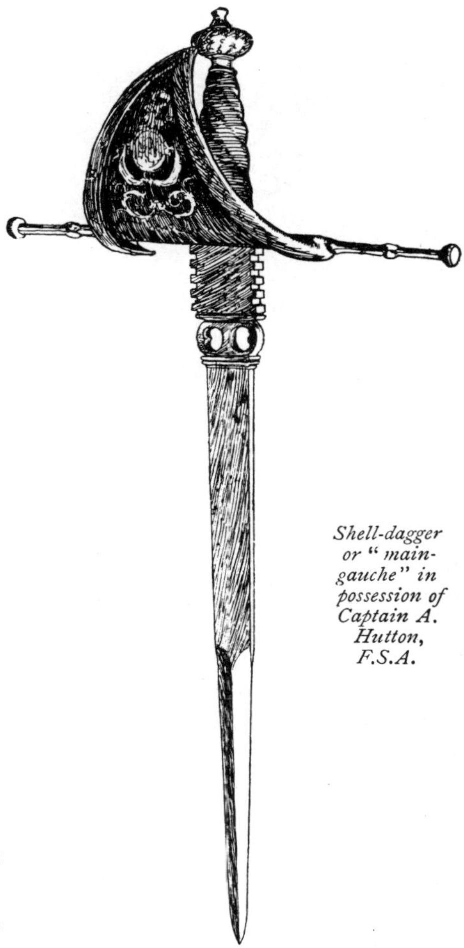

Shell-dagger or "main-gauche" in possession of Captain A. Hutton, F.S.A.

During the third quarter of the century the small sword in its earliest shape made its appearance. Its blade was flat and double-edged, something over thirty inches in length, but so light that it could in no way have been used for cutting purposes. Its object was the thrust, and that alone, and for this the flat blade proved too supple to be trustworthy. Its section, therefore, was altered into the "diamond" form, which made it much more stiff and solid, but caused it to be so uncomfortably heavy in the hand that the masters, Philibert de la Touche among them, taught their pupils to occasionally relieve themselves by taking hold of the blade just above the shell

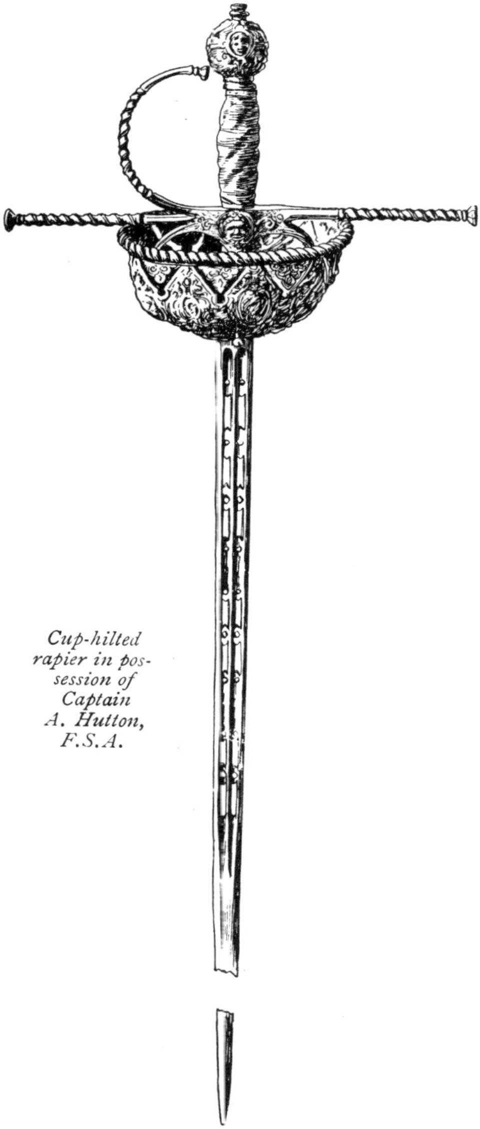

Cup-hilted rapier in possession of Captain A. Hutton, F.S.A.

with the left hand. In fighting, the dagger, being no longer worn openly on the person, entirely disappeared; but the left hand, protected by a stout gauntlet, was so posed as to be in readiness to parry a thrust, while the seizure with it of the sword or person of the enemy was still adhered to. Another form of parrying gauntlet — a very large one, completely covering the left hand and arm above the elbow — had been used since the days of good Queen Bess; but this seems to have been employed mainly as a protection during a nocturnal expedition, although in 1738 Captain James Miller recognises it as still in occasional use among the "gladiating" prize-fighters of the stage. The movements of the early small sword were much the same as those of the foil of to-day, the "quarte" and "tierce" parries for the upper lines, and the "cercle," or "quarte with a sloping point," and the "seconde" for the lower. But we must not diverge into technicalities, save, perhaps, in tracing the origin of what we now know as

The Lunge.

This movement, the complete development of the attack, was not the result of a sudden happy thought on the part of some particular master, but appears to have been a gradual growth, emanating at first from Italian sources.

The first suggestion of a forward movement of the leading foot is given, so far as we can make out, by Di Grassi in 1570, whose work so retained its repute that in 1594 it was Englished by an enthusiastic amateur, known to us only as "J. G., Gentleman." At this period the movements of the feet were passes, or steps forwards, backwards, or to either side, with voltes and demivoltes as occasion required, to effect which it was necessary to keep the knees as nearly straight as possible. J. G., with the help of Grassi, gains an addition to his reach by "somewhat encreasing his forefoot more forwardes, to the end the thrust may reach the farther. But if he chance to increase the fore foot a little too much, so that the breadth thereof be painfull unto him, then for the avoiding of inconveniences, he shall draw his hinderfoot so much after as he did before increase with the forefoote." Grassi advises this "increase of the foote forwards" in many parts of his work. Vincentio Saviolo appears also to have been acquainted with it, although in his "Practise" he makes no mention of it whatever, but seems to have kept it mainly for his private use. With regard to him, however, and his doings, George Silver tells us something in

"The Story of the Blacke Jacke.

"Upon a time at *Wels* in Somersetshire, as he (Vincentio) was in great braverie amongst manie gentlemen of good accompt, with great boldnesse he gave out speeches, that he had bene thus manie yeares in *England*, and since the time of his first comming, there was not yet one Englishman that could once touch him at the single Rapier or Rapier and Dagger. A valiant gentleman being there amongst the rest, his English hart did rise to heare this proude boaster, secretly sent a messenger to one *Bartholomew Bramble* a friend of his, a verie tall man both of his hands and person, who kept a schoole of Defence in the towne, the messenger by the way made the maister of Defence acquainted with the mind of the gentleman that sent for him, and of all what *Vincentio* had said, this maister of Defence presently came, and amongst all the gentlemen with his cap off, prayed maister *Vincentio* that he would be pleased to take a quart of wine with him. *Vincentio* verie scornefully looking at him, said unto him, Wherefore should you give me a quart of wine? Marie Sir, said he, because I heare you are a famous man at your weapon. Then presently said the gentleman that sent for the maister of Defence: Maister *Vincentio*, I pray you bid him welcome, he is a man of your profession. My profession, said *Vincentio;* what is my profession? Then said the gentleman, he is a maister of the noble science of Defence. Why, said maister *Vincentio*, God make him a good man. But the maister of Defence would not thus leave him, but prayed him againe he would be pleased to take a quart of wine of him. Then said *Vincentio*, I have no need of thy wine. Then said the maister of Defence: Sir I have a schoole of Defence in the Towne, will it please you to go thither: Thy schoole, said maister *Vincentio;* what shall I do at thy schoole? Play with me (said the maister) at the Rapier and dagger, if it please you. Play with thee, said maister *Vincentio;*

if I play with thee, I will hit thee 1 . 2 . 3 . 4 . thrustes in the eie together. Then said the maister of Defence, if you can do so, it is the better for you, and the worse for me, but surely I can hardly beleeve that you can hit me; but yet once againe, I hartily pray you good Sir, that you will go to my schoole and play with me. Play with thee, said maister Vincentio (verie scornfully), by God me scorne to play with thee. With that word scorne, the maister of Defence was verie much moved, and up with his great English fist, and stroke maister Vincentio such a boxe on the eare that he fell over and over, his legges just against a Butterie hatch whereon stood a great blacke Jacke; the maister of Defence fearing the worst, against *Vincentio* his rising, catcht the blacke Jacke into his hand, being more than halfe full of Beere. *Vincentio* lustily start up, laying his hand upon his dagger, & with the other hand pointed with his finger, saying, very well: I will cause to lie in the Gaile for this geare, 1 . 2 . 3 . 4 . yeares. And well, said the maister of Defence, since you will drinke no wine, will you pledge me in Beere? I drinke to all the cowardly knaves in *England*, and I think thee to be the veriest coward of them all: with that he cast all the Beere upon him; notwithstanding, *Vincentio*, having nothing but his guilt Rapier and Dagger about him, and the other for his defence the blacke Jacke, would not at that time fight it out; but the next day met with the maister of Defence in the streete, and said unto him, you remember how misused a me yesterday, you were to blame, me be an excellent man, me teach you how to thrust two foote further than anie Englishman."

Here, again, we have something in the form of a lunge, which, although known to the Italians, was evidently unknown to English fencers, seeing that the father of them, the famous George Silver himself, says nothing more than the above about it, even in his highly practical "Bref Instructions."

Joseph Swetnam, our first English professional writer, in his book "The Schoole of the noble and worthy Science of Defence," published in 1617, distinctly advocates what we now know as the "lunge," although he does not give it that name. On p. 74 he tells us: "to observe distance, by which is meant that thou shouldest stand so far off from thine enemy as thou canst, but reach him when thou dost step foorth with thy blow or thrust, and thy foremost foote and hand must goe together, and yet thy left foot, which should be the hindermost foot of a right-handed man, should be mored fast and keep his standing without mooving an inch, for then he will be the readier to draw back thy fore foot and body into the right place and distance again; whereas if in stepping foorth with thy fore-foot, thou suffer thy hinder foot to dregge in after the other, then thou breakest thy distance." And on p. 88 he says: "And standing thus in thy guard, looke for thy advantage, I meane where thine enemie lieth most ungarded; then thou must steppe foorth with thy forefoot and hand together, to offend thine enemie in such a place as thou findest unguarded; but so soone as thou hast presented thy thrust, whether thou hit or miss, fall back againe to recover thy guard and distance so soone as thou canst, but stand always fast on thine hindermost foote, I mean whether thou strike or thrust, and then thou shalt recover thy guard." Here we have both the "lunge" and the "recovery," a distinct improvement on the "increase of the foote forwards" suggested by Grassi and J. G.

In 1639 there appeared a curious little book, "Pallas Armata," by an enthusiastic amateur, who was clearly a scholar, for he is equally admired by members of both of the great Universities, and men, too, of respectable position in them, but the initials "G. A." are the only signature to be found in his work. Here, again, the lunge appears to be gaining in the matter of recognition. His words about it are:

"When thou wilt make a thrust, then stretch out thy right arme, and step forward with thy right foot, and let them both goe together at one and the self-same time, and when thou steppest forward with thy right foot doe not stir thy left foot."

During this period of about forty years we find that the Italian masters, to whom is due the first inception of the lunge, are no further advanced than our own. To Philibert de la Touche, the great French professor at the Court of Louis XIV., whom we must hail as the father of small-sword fencing, belongs seemingly the honour of having completely developed the movement; in fact, he and his contemporaries, Liancourt and Le Perche, somewhat overdeveloped it, as they caused their pupils to allow the left foot to roll over on to its side, with the view of gaining a trifle more reach, and Liancourt commits a further error in causing the trunk to fall violently forward with similar intent. In the following century, when fencing had reached its perfection of stateliness and grace, these errors were completely corrected. Witness the beautiful engravings in the famous work of Angelo in 1763.

The Chalais-La Frette Affair.

In the year 1663 there lived in Paris a certain lady of the frolicsome sort, who by chance succeeded in being the more or less innocent cause of a fight which in some way resembled the famous one of the musketeers, which we have already described, in that two gentlemen who had nothing whatever to do with the original quarrel were drawn into it, and in this instance very much to their subsequent inconvenience. This fair lady had attracted the admiration of Prince de Chalais, and also that of the elder La Frette, who, with his brother Ovarti, was regarded as being one of the most quarrelsome bullies in the French King's dominions. Consequently the two gentlemen looked

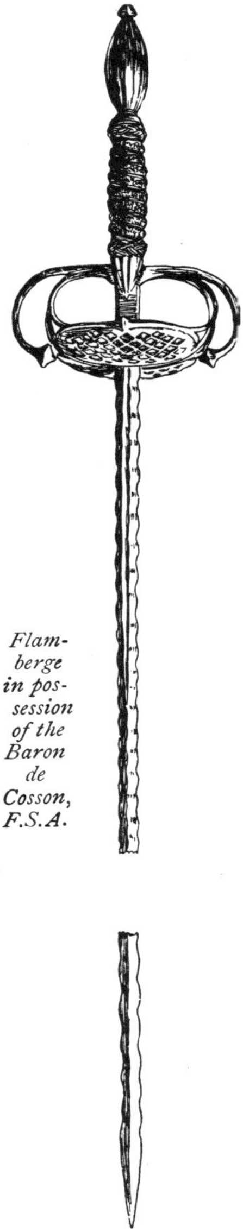

Flamberge in possession of the Baron de Cosson, F.S.A.

askance at one another, and either was quite of a mind to play some rough trick upon his rival. There happened one night to be a ball at the Palais Royal, which passed off with all the éclat usual in royal entertainments; but on leaving the palace La Frette, seeing his opportunity, pushed viciously against Chalais. The fat was in the fire at once, and had they been armed there would have been trouble on the instant: but, being dressed for dancing, and not for fighting, they had left their swords at home, and had to content themselves with arranging a pleasant little party of six for the next day. The fracas—for it had practically come to that—was reported to the King, who speedily discerned which of the two quarrellers was really to blame. In such matters Louis XIV. was a man of prompt action, and he commanded the Chevalier de Saint-Aignan to go at once to La Frette to distinctly forbid any act of violence, and to inform him that, if the affair went any further, his head would answer for it. His Majesty thought that he had selected quite the right man to be his messenger, as La Frette and Saint-Aignan were first cousins; but for once he had made a mistake. The Chevalier found his cousin at home, and told him everything that the King had said; but La Frette laughed at it, and replied, "Oh, come, Saint-Aignan! you are far too good a friend to me to break up such a nice little party as this which we have arranged. Never mind the King and his message; you had far better join us. I will send word to Chalais, and he will soon find a partner for you." The Chevalier, forgetful of his duty to his Sovereign, accepted the invitation, very much as young D'Artagnan did when he made his début as a duellist in the company of the three famous musketeers, and a message was sent to Chalais to bring a fourth friend with him. The parties accordingly met, those on the side of La Frette being, of course, his younger brother Ovarti, the Marquis de Flammarens, and the Chevalier de Saint-Aignan, while the Prince de Chalais was supported by the Marquis de Noirmoutiers, the Marquis d'Antin, and the Vicomte d'Argenlieu. The seconds, thirds, and fourths, after seeing Chalais and La Frette settled to their work, paired off and engaged on their own account. The combat was of short duration, for after the exchange of a very few thrusts the Marquis d'Antin was run through the body, and fell dead on the spot, and the rest of the party, although unhurt, had to think of saving themselves from the royal wrath, and they took shelter with all possible speed in foreign countries.

The King, when he heard of the duel, was perfectly furious, especially—and with good reason, too—against the Chevalier, who had not only disobeyed His Majesty's commands, but had broken his confidence also; while the young gentleman's father, the old Duc de Saint-Aignan, was as angry as the King himself, and declared that whatever ill-fortune might happen to his son, he would only get his deserts.

Louis Quatorze, although the determined enemy of the duellist, was the most generous patron that the world ever saw of the very man who trained that duellist to do his deadly work—the fencing-master.

Since the days of Charles IX. there had existed in France a society of teachers known as the Académie d'Armes, which consisted of the most accomplished masters of the art of killing. This society had always been more or less recognised, but it remained for the Roi Soleil to confer upon it its greatest and final glory. It was a somewhat exclusive society; consisted of only some twenty individuals, and the Grand Monarque conferred upon it the right that the six senior members, provided that they had been on its books for twenty years, could claim a patent of nobility; so that a hard-working teacher who had been all his life known as simple "Chose," when he entered the sacred circle of the six, immediately blossomed forth into the "Sieur de la Chose." Could royal encouragement of the art dimicatory go much further? Such of these fortunate gentlemen who possessed skill in writing seem to have deferred the publication of their works until they should have achieved the coveted honour, and then they must have been men of at least middle age. Note especially the Sieur Philibert de la Touche, that father of small-sword fighting whom we have mentioned before. It was in 1670 that he published "Les vrays Principes de l'Espée seule," so it may reasonably be assumed that the weapon of which he treated had come into vogue some dozen years previously. It was the recognised Court sword in France in 1660, and in that year, when our Merry Monarch King Charles II. came into his own again, he and his adherents brought it with them, and from its lightness and its convenience as an article of dress it very speedily ousted the long rapier from fashionable circles.

The Encounter between Sir Henry Bellasses and Mr. Thomas Porter.

This unfortunate affair, which occurred in 1667, was not a prearranged duel, which, as the fashion then was, might have cost the lives of half a dozen people, but a sudden quarrel, and, moreover, a foolish one.

Old Samuel Pepys "did tell us the story of the duel last night in Covent Garden between Sir H. Bellasses and Tom Porter. It is worth remembering the silliness of the quarrel, and is a kind of emblem of the general complexion of this whole kingdom at present. They two dined yesterday at Sir Robert Carr's, where it seems people do drink high, all that come. It happened that these two, the greatest friends in the world, were talking together; and Sir H. Bellasses talked a little louder than ordinary to Tom Porter, giving of him some advice. Some of the company standing by said, 'What! are they quarrelling, that they talk so high?' Sir H. Bellasses hearing it said, 'No!' says he: 'I would have you know I never quarrel, but I strike; and take that as a rule of mine!' 'How?' says Tom Porter, 'strike! I would I could see the man in England that durst give me a blow!' With that Sir H. Bellasses did give him a box on the eare, and so they were going to fight there, but were hindered. And by and by Tom Porter went out; and meeting Dryden the poet, told him of the business, and that he was resolved to fight Sir H.

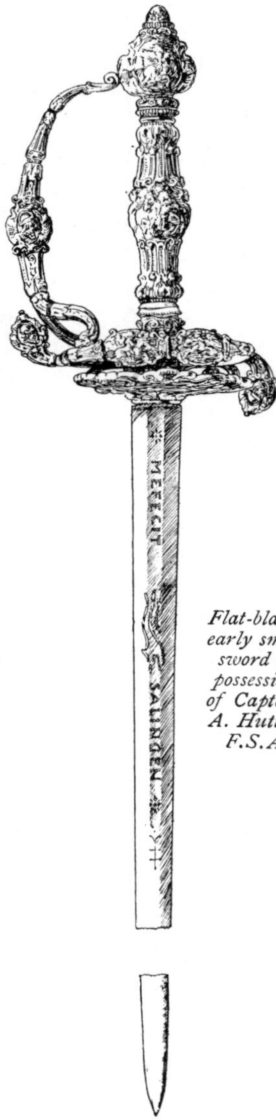

Flat-bladed early small sword in possession of Captain A. Hutton, F.S.A.

Bellasses presently; for he knew, if he did not, they should be friends to-morrow, and then the blow would rest upon him; which he would prevent, and desired Dryden to let him have his boy to bring him notice which way Sir H. Bellasses goes. By and by he is informed that Sir H. Bellasses' coach was coming: so Tom Porter went down out of the Coffee-house where he stayed for the tidings, and stopped the coach, and bade Sir H. Bellasses come out. 'Why,' says H. Bellasses, 'you will not hurt me coming out—will you?'—'No,' says Tom Porter. So out he went, and both drew: and H. Bellasses having drawn and flung away his scabbard, Tom Porter asked him whether he was ready? The other answering that he was, they fell to fight, some of their acquaintance by. They wounded one another, and H. Bellasses so much that it is feared he will die: and finding himself severely wounded, he called to Tom Porter, and kissed him, and bade him shift for himself; 'for,' says he, 'Tom, thou hast hurt me; but I will make shift to stand upon my legs till thou mayest withdraw, and the world not take notice of you, for I would not have thee troubled for what thou hast done.' And so whether he did fly or no I cannot tell; but Tom Porter showed H. Bellasses that he was wounded too: and they are both ill, but H. Bellasses to fear of life. And this is a fine example; and H. Bellasses a Parliament-man too, and both of them extraordinary friends."

"Sir Henry Bellasses is dead of the duell he fought about ten days ago with Tom Porter; and it is pretty to see how the world talk about them as of a couple of fools that killed one another out of love."

Another affair is related by Pepys, how "Mr. Pierce, the chyrurgeon, told me how Mr. Edward Montagu hath lately had a duell with Mr. Cholmely, that is first gentleman usher to the Queene, and was a messenger to her from the King of Portugal, and is a fine gentleman; but had many affronts from Mr. Montagu, and some unkindness from my Lord, upon his score (for which I am sorry). He proved too hard for Montagu, and drove him so far backward that he fell into a ditch and dropt his sword, but with honour would take no advantage over him, but did give him his life: and the world says Mr. Montagu did carry himself very poorly in the business, and hath lost his honour for ever with all people in it." This was certainly the case, for Pepys further remarks: "My Lord (Sandwich) told me he expected a challenge from him, but told me there was no great fear of him, for there was no man lies under such an imputation as he do in the business of Mr. Cholmely, who, though a simple sorry fellow, do brave him and struts before him with the Queene, to the sport and observation of the whole Court."

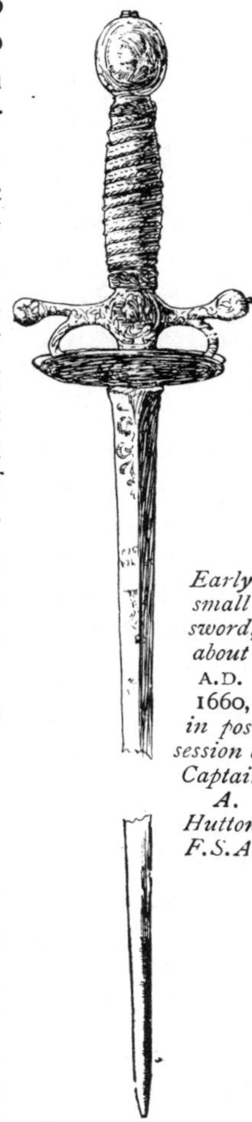

Early small sword, about A.D. 1660, *in possession of Captain A. Hutton, F.S.A.*

The Mischief made by Lady Shrewsbury.

The Countess of Shrewsbury was a lady, with many friends—at least, among the gentlemen of her acquaintance. Two of them were young Mr. Jermyn, a great favourite among the sex, and the Honourable Thomas Howard. This latter, although a man of modest carriage and pacific manners, was in reality "as moody to be moved" as anyone in England. The fair lady secretly favoured the other, but, liking to have more beaux to her string than one, managed to keep on pleasant terms with Howard, and accepted an invitation from him to a party at Spring Garden, a sort of aristocratic Rosherville, to which he naturally did not invite his rival. The lady, however, managed to convey the information to him, and he found himself in the garden as if by chance. He had no sooner shown himself on the principal walk when the Countess encouraged him by appearing on the balcony, whereupon he promptly joined the party uninvited, and contrived to monopolize the dame so completely that her host was perfectly furious. It was all that he could do to restrain himself, and avoid a quarrel on the spot; perceiving which, Jermyn redoubled his attentions, and did not leave Lady Shrewsbury's side until the repast was finished.

Jermyn went to bed not a little pleased at his exploit; but the next morning he received a visit from a Mr. Dillon, who brought him a challenge from Howard. Jermyn selected as his second a certain Rawlings, who happened unfortunately to be a great friend of Dillon's; so, as the custom then was, these two friends were obliged to fight about a matter which did not concern them in the least. The parties met. Dillon, who was a brave man and a clever swordsman (as, indeed, his principal also proved himself to be), engaged Rawlings, and after a pass or two ran him through the body, and laid him out dead on the field; while Jermyn, who had been the wilful cause of all the trouble, was severely handled by Howard, who gave him no less than three awkward wounds, and so injured him that he had to be carried to the house of an uncle of his in a very pitiable condition, and he certainly deserved his punishment.

Lady Shrewsbury as a Page.

Mr. Thomas Killegrew was a gentleman well known at Court for his amorous disposition; but it happened on a time that his heart, or whatever it was that did duty for it, was for the moment disengaged, so he amused it by handing it over to the keeping of Lady Shrewsbury, and she, being in want of some excitement. gave it hospitality; in fact, the pair became very friendly indeed. He was a very witty young gentleman, and capable, especially after dinner, of telling excellent good stories. He was, moreover, on intimate terms with the Duke of Buckingham, one of the very least strait-laced of Charles II.'s courtiers, at whose table he was a frequent guest, where he was wont to boast of his success, and to describe the charms of the lady with more zest than discretion. This awoke the curiosity of the Duke, who made up his mind that he would test the accuracy of Killegrew's assertions, and he did this in a manner so satisfactory both to the fair one and to himself that the poor young man's nose was put completely out of joint, and the Countess went so far as to pretend that she was not even acquainted with him. He was frantic, wrote lampoons about her, exposed her private character, and made fun of those hidden charms which only a few days before he had praised so eloquently.

He really carried things too far, and one fine evening he received a very practical hint to that effect. He was returning home in his Sedan-chair from the house of a friend, when he was set upon by three or four ruffians, who drove their swords through the chair several times, inflicting a rather severe wound upon its occupant; and being under the impression that they had completely finished their business, they took themselves off, and were never heard of again. The satirist, after this, thought it wise to discontinue his witticisms, and to say as little as possible about the episode of the Sedan-chair. Indeed, had he made any attempt to bring the would-be assassins to justice, it was more than likely that they would have silenced him once and for all with a second attack more skilfully arranged than had been the first one, and he left the Duke and the Countess to enjoy each other's society in peace and quietness.

But another actor appeared upon the scene, and one on whom they had not reckoned. There happened to be an Earl of Shrewsbury as well as a Countess, who, good easy man, had hitherto been blind to the vagaries of her ladyship; but this time he was awakened to a sense of the situation by the public manner in which the pair were talked about. He well knew that anything in the shape of expostulation with his wife would be absolutely futile, so he turned his attention to the Duke, and sent his friends, Sir John Talbot and the Honourable Bernard Howard (a son of the Earl of Arundel), to demand satisfaction from him, on which they were referred to Sir J. Jenkins and Mr. Holmes, who were selected to act for His Grace. King Charles got wind of the affair, and was determined to prevent it, and commanded "My Lord Generall" Albemarle to post guards over Buckingham and to keep him at home; but Albemarle seems to have taken a leaf out of the book of the Chevalier de Saint-Aignan, for, although he abstained from going quite so far as did that worthy in actually taking part in the affray, he neglected the commands of his royal master altogether.

So the meeting took place, as Pepys tells us, in a close near Barne Elms on January 16, 1667. This encounter was almost as sanguinary as the first of its kind, the famous one of the Mignons; the seconds and thirds were engaged as well as the principals, and all the six fought with the utmost ferocity. Buckingham at last succeeded in planting his point in the right breast of Lord Shrewsbury, the sword blade coming out at his back just below the shoulder. Sir John Talbot's right arm was put out of action by a thrust which entered near the wrist and came out at the elbow—a very difficult wound to heal—and the unhappy Jenkins was left dead on the ground. Lord Shrewsbury was carried home, and everything possible was done for him, but he succumbed to his wounds exactly two months after the date of the duel. There seems to have been some idea on the part of the friends of Sir J. Jenkins to commence proceedings against the survivors for the killing of him, but the King crushed it in the bud by issuing a proclamation in which he gave a free pardon to everyone concerned.

It was common talk that Lady Shrewsbury was present when the affair was going on, and that, disguised in the costume of a page, she was actually holding the Duke of Buckingham's horse.

CHAPTER XXII

The "Colichemarde."

THANK Heaven! we have done with Lady Shrewsbury and the like of her, at any rate for the present, so we will cross the Channel and see what our friends in Paris are about. To our surprise, we find that, while we in England have been poking sanguinary fun at each other to our hearts' content, in that gay city, erstwhile the happy hunting-ground of the duellist, such a thing as a duel has not been so much as heard of for—"hear it, ye gods and little fishes!"—seventeen long years—so, at least, Campigneulles tells us—to such an extent had the salutary but merciless firmness of Louis XIV. succeeded in crushing down the mania for private fighting. But he had not crushed it out; the serpent was not killed: it was only scotched. His severity towards those who took part in a prearranged duel had one good result. Theretofore not only the principal quarrellers, but their friends also, had their share in the encounter, and the victors went home, were admired by their male friends, and made much of by their fair ones. It became a different thing, however, when, after returning home in triumph, they were arrested by the officers of the law, consigned to an ignominious prison, put on their trial, and shortly afterwards hanged like common thieves. The glory of the duel had departed, and one can appreciate the cynical remark of Philippe of Orleans, "Les duels étaient un peu trop passés de mode."

The duel on its old-fashioned lines of necessity fell into disuse, the seconds ceased to take part in the fray, and, indeed, in many instances their presence was dispensed with as being too dangerous; their appearance on the field would at once suggest premeditation. But it must not be supposed that gentlemen ceased altogether to settle their differences in a manner so dear to them. Even the terrible Sun-King could hardly forbid a man, if suddenly attacked, to defend his "innocent life" with the sword he wore at his side. The private meeting assumed a more private form, and was known by another name. A gentleman having a difference with his neighbour would not go home and send him a challenge, but would say to him, "Sir, we have had some words together, it is true; but that will not prevent me from going about as is my wont, and to-morrow morning I propose to take the air in such-and-such a park." The next day it turned out, curiously enough, that the other found himself strolling in the very same place at the very same time, and it often occurred that only one of those two gentlemen went home again. Such an affair was known as a "rencontre," or chance collision.

But these single-handed clandestine combats opened the door to many acts of supersticery. One man would come to the ground wearing a shirt of mail beneath his clothes; another would carry in his pocket snuff, or even dust, which he would throw into the eyes of his unsuspecting enemy; while a third would make use of some cry or remark with which to divert his attention, and would then stab him unawares, and seeing that the men were alone together, such an act of wickedness could be perpetrated with very little chance of discovery. Again, in those days men drank deep and played high, two forms of excess which often led to the sudden appearance of those light, elegant, naughty little small swords; for "when the wine is in, the wit is out." It did happen, though, sometimes that the least hot-headed of such a pair was of no mind to have the death of the other on his conscience, and here the fencing-masters came to his assistance.

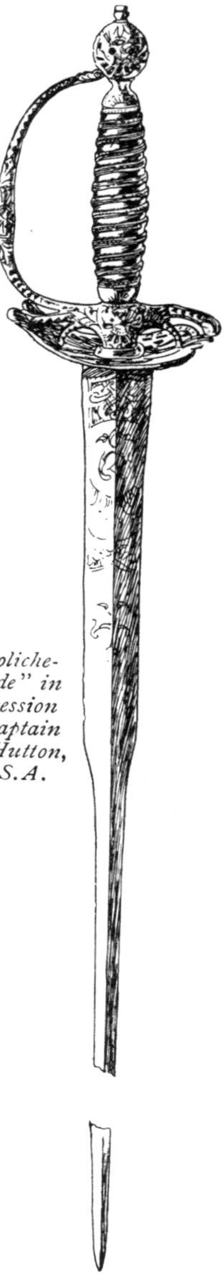

"*Colichemarde*" *in possession of Captain A. Hutton, F.S.A.*

They invented a series of clever movements by which to deprive the enemy of his weapon, and so render him harmless. These were advocated at great length by Girard, and were brought to their perfection in 1763 by the famous Angelo.

Though the manners of gentlemen of the early eighteenth century had by no means improved, an advance had been made in the fashion of their weapons. The flat and the diamond-shaped blades had disappeared, and their place had been taken by one of triangular form, which increased at once both its lightness and its rigidity. In length about the same, it possessed a very broad forte, perhaps intended to augment facility in defending, for at that time apparently only "simple" parries were used; this was continued about eight inches up the blade, where it suddenly narrowed. This type of small sword was known as the "colichemarde"; it was in vogue until past the middle of the century, and serious was the work which it often performed.

"Le Roi est Mort! Vive le Roi!"

The great monarch, the Sun-King, as he loved to be called—his sun was setting. His military glory, which was his greatest pride, had departed, his armies had been defeated in the field, and he himself, infirm and old, was paying that debt to Nature which is the lot of all, whether royal or "roturier." "Le Roi est mort! Vive le Roi!" But what is it that is to take up the reins of government which have just slipped from his strong masterful hand? A little child! And who is the chief preceptor of this child? And who is it that governs the kingdom in his name? Philippe of Orleans, whom, according to Campigneulles, the old King had described as a "fanfaron des vices," a man who was so proud of his excesses that he openly bragged about them, and, if the stories contained in the memoirs of the Chevalier de Ravanne are in any part true, he had more than enough to brag about. Brave reader (not *gentle* one), if you come across this queer little work, peruse it if you will; but if you are a married man do not let it lie inadvertently on the drawing-room table, and if you are a bachelor do not leave it among your effects, lest that, when you have "shuffled off this mortal coil," your executors may find it; it might give your surviving relatives a disagreeable impression of you.

When this era commenced, says Campigneulles, the souls of men had become degenerate from a long despotism; they were weary of constraint, satiated with magnificence, surfeited with glories, and inclined for nothing but complete relaxation and for pleasures of the grossest kind. The evil example of Philippe drew with him the entire Court along this baleful downward path, and he left nothing undone to show that he fully merited the unpleasant term by which his illustrious predecessor had described him. The majestic and courtly gallantry of the ancient régime had given place to mere cynical debauchery; licentiousness was no longer deemed a matter for scandal: it was the fashion of the day; men, and women, too, prided themselves on an evil reputation, and only blushed when found guilty of some virtuous action.

By nature heedless, and by rule of life, if he could be said to have one, a voluptuary, the Regent lived for the joys of the present without a thought for the future. The mere shadow of a King, the mere depositary of regal power, what cared he that the foundation of that power grew rotten in his hands, so long as he preserved the outward show of it? He habitually shut his eyes to anything which did not come into collision with his authority or interfere with his pleasures. So, with regard to the duel, we see him divest himself of all prejudice against it, and of even the semblance of that severity which Louis XIV. had affected as a matter of principle. No wonder, then, that the mania for private fighting became almost as pronounced as in the days of Henry the Great. One heard daily of young people being killed or injured in these affairs, and every family of note lived in a constant state of disquiet or desolation. Be it observed that the laws against duelling were not annulled; they were only ignored, and could be, and were sometimes, appealed to, not for justice, but for the gratification of private spite.

The Story of Bouton, the Banker's Clerk.

The Duchesse de Berri was the daughter of Philippe d'Orléans, and she took after her father. Besides being a Princess, she was a very handsome woman, and as free and easy as most of the ladies who helped to form the Court of the Regent; naturally she had many admirers, one of whom, the Abbé d Aydie, she especially favoured. This precious son of the Church had nothing of the Churchman about him beyond his clothes and a couple of priories, the emoluments of which he did not devote entirely to works of charity. He was very much of a ladies' man, and he did not confine his attentions by any means to his Duchess. There was a certain little operatic songstress at whose house he often found himself, and one fine evening he came into collision there with a certain Bouton, a banker's clerk. Angry words passed between them, they whipped out their colichemardes, and the clerk, who had not only contrived to possess himself of a sword, but also to learn how to use one, after a pass or two, gave the Abbé a thrust in the thigh which kept him out of mischief for a day or two. The Duchess heard of the adventure, and contrived to make her cleric exchange the "petit collet" for the Cross of Malta, so henceforth we recognise him as the Chevalier d'Aydie. The clerk was still madly jealous about the opera-girl, and pursued his rival with such pertinacity that they actually fought with each other four or five times, not in any way to the advantage of the ex-Abbé, till at last the Duchess grew anxious for the safety of her lover, and reported the state of affairs to the Connétablie. This court, which was composed of the Marshals of France, held jurisdiction over all matters affecting the point of honour; but its authority extended only to those who by birth were privileged to wear the sword, the nobility and gentry, by whom its members were addressed as "My Lords," and they would not suffer themselves to be so addressed by persons of meaner rank, the very existence of whom on the face of the earth they hardly condescended to recognise.

The two quarrellers were summoned to appear before this court of honour, and great was the wrath of the Maréchal de Chamilly, its president, when he was informed that one of the pair was not a gentleman.

"What the devil," cried he, "is he doing here? And why the devil does he dare to address us as 'My Lords'? I—I won't be called My Lord by a fellow like you! You—you—you are laughing at the Marshals of France! And you have the unparalleled audacity to tell us that your name is Bouton!"

The thing which really put the president into such a temper was, that he got into his head that someone was making a fool of him, his own name happening to be Bouton de Chamilly. The court was malicious enough to recommend the Regent to imprison the lover of his daughter in the fortress of Ham, in order to teach him to respect the royal edicts, and, moreover, to keep him there for a good two years, seeing that he had disgraced himself by accepting a challenge from a common fellow. As for the clerk, he was simply bundled out into the street; the court took no further notice of him, such low persons did not come within its jurisdiction. But the Duchesse de Berri, spiteful as she was vicious, set herself to wake up the dormant machinery of the laws against the duel; she caused the wretched man to be persecuted, hunted down, and imprisoned by the courts, and she gave herself no rest until she finally procured his execution.

"The Cat did it!"

Yes! all the trouble we are about to relate was caused by a cat—a beautiful cat, a lovely cat, a perfect cat, the most exquisite cat in all the realm of France; but, after all, she was but a cat.

The splendid funeral procession of the great monarch had passed by, and the strong man's sceptre lay for the time in the hand of Philippe the Regent. His character was so very well known that all men felt that, so long as his enjoyments were not interfered with, and his semi-regal authority not absolutely braved, they might kiss or they might quarrel as best pleased them. So it was hardly a matter for surprise when two young officers of the Gardes Françaises fell foul of one another: their names were Ferrand and Girardin; they were scions of families of the "long robe." Their difference, although jealousy was at the bottom of it, was rather a sudden one. They drew upon each other, not in a back-street after a lively supper-party: they had the impudence to do it in broad daylight, in the very middle of a summer's day, and in an almost sacred place, too, the Quai des Tuileries, under the very shadow of the royal palace, under the very nose of the

Regent himself; a place where, if the little child-King had happened to be looking out of the window, he might have been an eye-witness of the whole of the pretty performance.

A real good fight they made of it; neither of them had neglected his opportunities of placing himself under the instruction of a good fencing-master. Both of them were well trained in the use of their weapons, but in the end M. Girardin received a serious wound, which put a stop to their encounter. The affair got wind, and was reported to the Connétablie; but the great court of honour promptly decided that the two combatants were not of sufficient social rank to bring them within the jurisdiction of so august a body. Still, they were officers, and something had to be done. The Regent summoned them to appear before himself, and, seeing that when two gentlemen quarrelled there was usually a lady in the case, he commanded that she should attend also At the time appointed the two officers presented themselves, and so did the fair cause of their jealousy; she was not a lady, however: she was nothing more than a remarkably attractive Angora cat!

The Regent was too much amused to take the matter seriously; he contented himself with ordering each of them a fortnight's arrest, transferring them to other regiments, and advising them, when next they might have a like affair on hand, to settle it with their claws, and not with their "colichemardes."

A Little Jaunt of Philippe d'Orléans.

The Abbé Dubois occupied a peculiar post in the entourage of Philippe d'Orléans: he was nothing more or less than purveyor-in-chief of His Highness's pleasures, while the Chevalier de Ravanne, then a mere stripling, was the favourite page, and with this curious specimen of a Churchman young Ravanne, from his own confession, acted entirely in concert. It is from the memoirs of the Chevalier that we derive our story, and we feel sure that any of our readers who may have perused that remarkable little work will pardon us for slightly bowdlerizing the anecdote.

The Regent was somewhat exacting towards these two faithful followers of his. He was always athirst for some novel excitement, and if he could not get it at home, he would go out at night to seek for it, chancing what might happen to him; but the astute Abbé always took care to warn the Lieutenant of Police beforehand, so that the place they had selected for their diversions was carefully watched by a party of constables in plain clothes. The Prince had been extremely fortunate in his nocturnal rambles, no kind of unpleasant experience having ever presented itself to him; but on a certain special occasion the precautions of that holy man Dubois were a failure, and there happened an incident in which both Prince and parson owed their lives to the courage of the young page, who shall tell the story himself:

"One evening the Prince, the Abbé, and myself, having disguised ourselves in the sober colours worn by the ordinary citizen, but keeping our swords by our sides, slipped quietly out of a side-door of the palace and made for the Porte Saint Roche, near which was a house of entertainment, well known to our clerical friend; but it happened that this freak had struck the fancy of His Highness so suddenly that Dubois had no time to send notice to his friend the policeman. However, there we were. We found the good folks of the house ready to receive us with open arms, and although it was a place of public entertainment, the worthy landlady, more than satisfied at being called upon to provide for the requirements of so august a party, closed her doors to all comers, and we settled down to enjoy ourselves. When, behold, an interruption! Three officers, bent on a frolic much the same as we were, and well acquainted with the place, approached it, and finding the door shut knocked thereat. There was no answer; they knocked again—no response; they became angry; they positively swore, and hammered again right lustily; still the house seemed as silent as the tomb; they banged away again, and, oh! the words they made use of! [Good reader, we cannot chronicle that; remember we have bowdlerized our story.] What with the violence of their blows and the force of their language the door at last gave way, and in they all three marched.

"They were furious at having been locked out in the cold, and when they found nothing better than three very ordinary-looking people (for the Prince had taken care to leave every vestige of his exalted rank at home) keeping all to themselves a feast of dainties which would have been more than enough for both parties, they drew their swords, and were for settling with us there and then. The Prince and I drew ours, the worthy landlady and her maids fell a-screaming frantically, and the miserable poltroon of an Abbé, instead of clapping his hand upon his colichemarde, went on his knees and shrieked for mercy louder than all the women put together. We two, however, stood on the defensive, when the danger in which I saw my master placed, and the example of his royal courage, heartened me so much that, with the very first sword-thrust I ever delivered in my life, I stretched the enemy nearest to me flat on the floor. The two remaining worthies, either from admiration of my handiwork or from fear of having a like operation performed upon themselves, sheathed their swords and offered me their hands. But I, fired with my success, cried out: 'No, no, gentlemen! the sides are equal now. Either you take yourselves off, and carry your friend along with you, or stay and see what will happen next;' and with that I placed myself a pace or two in front of the Prince so as to cover him; but he took hold of my arm, saying: 'No, not that! We must always grant quarter to an enemy when he asks for it.' He was my master, so I had to obey, though with much reluctance.

"Peace was thus proclaimed, and a surgeon was sent for, who, on examining the injured man, pronounced that, although his wound was not a mortal one, he had had a very narrow escape. Having satisfied himself on this point, the Prince withdrew, we two of course following him.

"The next morning, while I was dressing, someone came and said that His Highness required me immediately; so, wondering what it could be about, I hastened to his apartments. On entering, I was saluted by two gentlemen, in whom I recognised my officers of the evening before. After our departure they were informed who the people were with whom they had attempted to meddle, and on reflection thought it wise to present themselves in order to make their excuses and to ask forgiveness. This the Prince at once told me, adding: 'Here are your friends of yesterday: what would you like to do with them?' To which I replied: 'Only, sir, to show them what they have seen already: that I know how to be true to my master, and how to profit by the example of his courage.' 'Gentlemen,' exclaimed the Prince, 'what think you of this page of mine? Is he not as generous as he is brave?' 'Indeed, yes, sir,' replied they. 'Well, well!' rejoined His Highness, 'since he bears you no ill-will, neither do I; but mark you, keep your counsel about last night's adventure. Your part in it would do you but little credit if it got into the mouths of some of our scandal-mongers. Stay a moment,' added he. 'Take this purse, my boy, as a reward for your gallantry; and observe, gentlemen, that I know how to recompense valour. Go, then, and when you meet the enemies of your country, see that you earn your own reward.' And with that he motioned them to withdraw. The purse contained two hundred golden louis."

How the Chevalier de Ravanne gave Satisfaction to an Insolent.

Whatever his other failings may have been, the Chevalier de Ravanne was evidently no quarreller. In all his life he only fought two duels, at a period when such meetings were matters of everyday occurrence, and he fought those under circumstances of very great provocation.

The Chevalier had been seriously ill of a fever at his father's house, but was at last, to the great joy of his family, convalescent. So jubilant were they, indeed, that they determined to celebrate the event with a solemn festival, and for this they only awaited the arrival from Paris of the Chevalier d'Arcis, the bosom friend of Ravanne, who at length appeared, bringing with him letters from the Abbé Dubois, and kindly messages from the Prince himself. The entertainment, which lasted an entire week, passed off with complete success, and the guests departed, leaving behind them only the family party. But two gentlemen, one of whom was betrothed to the eldest daughter of the house, and the other, who, from being a comrade of Ravanne's since the days of their childhood, frequented the house a great deal, were invited to remain. Our hero naturally believed that the visits of this latter were paid out of affection for himself; but he was mistaken: the real attraction turned out to be Mdlle. Ferdinande de ——, Ravanne's betrothed, whom the treacherous rogue designed to take away from him. One evening this man, excited perhaps by the wine he had taken, made himself so insolently obnoxious to the young lady that she boxed his ears, and from this point let the Chevalier speak for himself:

"A slap on the noble cheek of a gentleman, as we all know, is a thing not to be forgiven—in this life, at any rate—and although everybody declared that the rebuke which had been administered to our gentleman was richly deserved, it rankled in his mind.

"He was discreet enough to retire, and I, regarding the incident as closed, accompanied him to the door, when he took me by the hand in such a manner as to let me plainly see that something was to follow; had he taken time to reflect, he would have saved himself from a disastrous fate, and me from a thousand regrets and many a disagreeable embarrassment. However, I kept my counsel, and none of the family party had the least idea that I had been in any way menaced. I did not mention the matter even to D'Arcis until the next morning, when I received a challenge.

"My gentleman, without considering that he had played an insolent part and had brought upon himself the punishment he had received, must needs fix a quarrel upon me, and accuse me of having been the sole cause of what had happened, and therefore the sole person whom he could call to account. He had, moreover, the audacity to dictate the time, the place, and the weapons. This greatly provoked me, and I only regretted that I had not been beforehand with him in demanding satisfaction for his rudeness to Ferdinande. Yes! I said, he shall have presently something in addition to his box on the ear, as he seems so much to wish for it.

"D'Arcis did everything he could to dissuade me; he offered to go to the gentleman and try to bring him to reason; he offered to fight him himself, alleging that I was too weak from my illness to go into the field; he even talked about informing everyone in the house, Ferdinande herself included, in order that they might take measures to keep me at home; but I would have none of all this. I only asked him to assist me like a brother; for whether I should fall or not, it would require all his cunning to quiet the storm that would be raised. 'Then, at least,' said he, 'permit me to accompany you.' 'That cannot be,' I replied, 'for the challenge requires that we shall be attended only by our servants.' 'Strange,' said he; 'but that need not prevent me from looking from a little distance.' This idea of his seemed a good one; for had I set out alone suspicion might have been aroused, but with a companion I might reach the ground and terminate the affair without anyone being the wiser. So we mounted our horses, and rode off under the pretext of merely taking the air.

"The gentleman had already arrived, and, less scrupulous than I, had brought a second with him who, as he explained, was to be only a spectator, and was not to take any part in the encounter. Taking him at his word, I refrained from asking the Chevalier to come forward; but he, perceiving that there were three people on the ground instead of only two, dismounted from his horse, and, fearing treachery, approached near enough to be able to prevent it. My enemy and I stripped to our shirts and engaged each other. When men are in earnest, combats of this kind do not usually last long, and with my second thrust I stretched him on the grass. 'I am a dead man!' he cried. 'That is bad,' said I. 'I only wish I could give your life back to you as easily as I have taken it. By the way, are you satisfied?' 'Yes,' murmured he, 'adieu.' I requested his second to take all due care of him, and, accompanied by my own, I made my escape as quickly as possible."

How Mdlle. Ferdinande changed her Dress, and what came of it.

"Ferdinande and I, with D'Arcis and a sister of mine who had been recently married, decided to pay a visit to Paris, we gentlemen travelling, as was the custom, on horseback, and the ladies by the stage-coach. On arrival, we established ourselves in comfortable apartments, and I myself went at once to pay my respects to His Highness, who, seeing that I was now too old to remain among his pages, did me the kindness to procure for me the casaque of a musketeer. Nor was it long before I met my friend the Abbé Dubois, who gave me much news of the Court, and mentioned casually, among other things, that he had heard of the arrival, the day before, of a very beautiful young lady, who had travelled from Rheims in the diligence, and there was no doubt of it that the Prince would wish to make her acquaintance. This piece of information greatly disconcerted me. No other ladies but Ferdinande and my sister had travelled by that conveyance, and handsomely as His Highness had always treated me, I knew his character so well that he was the very last person in whose company I should care to find my darling betrothed. I sought for D'Arcis and told him everything, when he advised that we should leave our lodging and take up our residence in the Marais, a part of the town less frequented by country-folk, where he fancied we should be safe from intrusion ; but the spies of Dubois were everywhere : Ferdinande was the sole object of their quest. They soon discovered her whereabouts, and the very landlady of the house turned out to be in collusion with them.

"I had been to the palace, and returned home highly pleased with the generosity of my royal patron, who had not only made me a musketeer, but had sent me away with my purse filled with gold, and had promised to refill it whenever it should be empty. There was, however, trouble awaiting me. Ferdinande commenced reproaching me for having told the Prince about her, saying : 'Knowing as you do what a character he has, you ought to have held your tongue had you been pressed ever so much. You must no longer care for me, since you expose me to such a peril.'

"I showed her that she was mistaken, protesting that I had said nothing to the Prince, but that the Abbé, on my first entering the palace, had told me of a new beauty just arrived by the Rheims coach ; that

I had a presentiment that it was of her he spoke, but that I had kept it from her for fear of alarming her unnecessarily, and that after consulting with the Chevalier d'Arcis we had decided to change our lodgings in order to avoid annoyance. 'But,' I asked her, 'how did you find this out? Have no fear: we will quit this place, and will so arrange matters that, although you remain in Paris, you shall be for ever lost to the sight of these people.' Ferdinande then told her story: 'Only this very morning the woman of the house had the audacity to come to me to compliment me on my beauty, and to inform me that I had made a conquest of the greatest and most generous Prince in the realm of France; that she would bring the Abbé Dubois to me, who, in his turn, would present me to His Highness, and the wretch added, "I hope, madame, that afterwards you will extend your patronage and protection to poor little modest me!"'

"'This matter is important,' I replied; 'but we must first warn my sister and her husband, in order that we may act in concert to ensure your safety.' Accordingly we held a council. Ferdinande at first was for returning to the country again; but my sister, in despair at the thought of losing her, hit upon a feasible plan. 'My advice,' said she, 'is that Ferdinande should disguise her sex until such time as these people shall have forgotten her. This place we must of course leave, and all we shall have to do will be to take two separate apartments in different houses, contiguous if possible: you two gentlemen will take one of them, and Ferdinande and I will establish ourselves in the other.' The idea seemed a very good one: Ferdinande was highly amused at it, and we commenced operations at once. She was a rather tall girl, and a suit of D'Arcis' clothes fitted her very fairly well; so he and I went out together to a large ready-made clothes shop, where we bought everything we required, and carried the parcel to the house of a friend of mine, to whose care we entrusted it. We then went to look for apartments, and found two suites in the Rue Quinquempois. The houses were exactly opposite one another, and the street was narrow enough to admit of our speaking across it and of seeing everything that took place in either set of rooms. In matters like this one should act with promptness. Accordingly we were not long over dinner, and we set out at once on foot to hire a fiacre, in which we drove to the house of my friend, where everything—under-linen, stockings, shoes, perruque, hat, and sword—was awaiting Ferdinande, who immediately arrayed herself in her new costume. A very handsome cavalier she looked, and on seeing herself in the glass very nearly fell in love with herself. We drove off to our new lodgings, where we duly installed ourselves, and there was nothing left to be done than to pay the bill at the old one, and take away our baggage, which we conveyed to a house in the Rue Aumère, where we dismissed the vehicle, the better to put Dubois and his men off the scent, and half an hour afterwards carried off our belongings in another carriage to our new apartments. After so many precautions, who on earth would have recognised Mdlle. Ferdinande de —— under the habit and title of the Chevalier du Conseil?

"We spent the rest of the day and all the evening in imparting to our new young gentleman the airs and graces needful for his character. He was so delighted at the metamorphosis that he learned his part without any difficulty; we did not, however, discontinue our rehearsals, but gave him a lesson every day for more than a month. The ready-made suit fitted so well that we sent it to a tailor as a pattern for another, telling him that it was for a gentleman who lived a long distance off in the country. The Chevalier du Conseil was highly delighted: he enjoyed a great deal more freedom than Mdlle. Ferdinande ever had in all her life. I took him about with me with as little ceremony as if he had really been what he seemed, and on one occasion I even went so far as to make him talk to no less a person than the Abbé Dubois himself, whom we happened to meet in the new gallery of the Palais Royal.

"One day, on returning home from the palace, I found Ferdinande and my sister in tears. My sudden appearance took them by surprise, and they had no time to dry their eyes, which made me think that they must have been in some way insulted, and I had much ado to persuade them to explain it to me.

"M. le Chevalier du Conseil and his lady friend had thought fit to go to the Church of St. Sauveur, and there happened to be present a young buck of a fellow who was sharp enough to penetrate the disguise of the said Chevalier. He naturally inferred that the pair belonged to a class of lady whom one may safely address without the necessity of a formal introduction, and as they were going out he did so address them. The sham Chevalier told him with some asperity that he had made a mistake; that the lady he was escorting was the wife of a gentleman of quality, who would make him repent of his rudeness. To which he answered, 'Since you take so much interest in his belongings, you had better take his place, and if you do not, you are nothing better than a coward.' And he continued to treat them to extremely coarse and abusive language.

"'What was the fellow like?' I asked. 'Would you recognise him if you were to see him again?' 'Most certainly,' replied Ferdinande. 'He was of middle height, with rather handsome eyes and a fresh complexion.' 'Well,' I said, 'that is not much to go by; half the young fellows in Paris might be described in such terms.' In point of fact, I was not at all sorry that I was unable to call the brute to mind, for I felt that anything like a hostile encounter just at that time might damage my prospects beyond redemption.

Shortly afterwards the ladies thought it better to return to the country.

"A few months later I happened to be at the Café de Procope with two friends, when there entered a certain musketeer of the First Company, by name the Count de Bre——, whom I had never before seen. My friends pointed him out to me, saying that he was a young man who did very little credit to his name and family, and they narrated how they had actually witnessed a gross insult which he had offered to a very modest young lady in the Rue St. Sauveur, who was being escorted by a remarkably good-looking young gentleman, apparently from the country. At this I was furious, for I recognised the description given me by Ferdinande, and I had just made up my mind to address myself to him, when he slipped away, and I lost sight of him altogether. I went ten or twelve times to that café in hopes of finding him, but without success.

"Some little time afterwards there was a card-party at the Maréchal d'Estrée's. We sat up all night gambling, and the next morning I left the house minus every franc I had taken with me, and in debt, to boot, ten golden louis to another gentleman. I was thoroughly out of temper, when, as ill-luck would have it, the very first person I stumbled against was *my man.* I asked him brusquely, 'Are you the Count de Bre——?' 'I have that honour,' he replied. 'Then I have something serious to say to you. I have been looking for you for a long time, to call you to account for your brutal behaviour to my sister and a relative of mine who was escorting her. You are a musketeer, as I am; therefore we are on equal terms. Let us go to a quiet place behind the Chartreux Convent, where I propose, if I can, to wash out the insult with your blood, not one drop of which, to my thinking, ever ran in the veins of those illustrious ancestors whose scion you pretend to be.' My speech thoroughly nettled him, as I had purposed. He replied: 'You shall see whether or no I preserve the courage of my forefathers.' 'You will need it all,' I rejoined. Accordingly, we departed at once for our rendezvous—he by the Porte Saint Jacques, and I by that of Saint Michel. We arrived simultaneously, and rested a moment to recover our breath, when he exclaimed in the brutal manner peculiar to him: 'There! that will do. Why defer your vengeance any longer?' 'You are right,' quoth I; 'I am impatient for the satisfaction it will give me.'

"We stripped to our shirts and placed ourselves on guard. We had never met before, so it was natural that each should play the other for some time in order to discover any fault that there might be in his method. And this caused the Count's overthrow; for in making a movement which I did not follow up, his blade was deceived, and he gave me a great opening. But I was too cautious to attempt an attack upon his weak point at once. I kept him amused for a little time by merely parrying his furious thrusts, when at last, playing my feint successfully, I disengaged and ran him clean through the body. I disentangled my sword as quickly as I could, when he fell prone in the dust. I approached him to ascertain what state he was in. The Count de Bre—— had insulted a lady for the last time!"

The Fatal Quarrel between the Duke of Hamilton and Lord Mohun.

During some years previous to 1712 a lawsuit was going on between these two noblemen, which ended at last in a terrible personal quarrel. The story has been told by several writers. It appears in the Newgate Calendar, and in addition to this the depositions at the coroner's inquest have been preserved for us by E. Curll, a well-known publisher of that period.

At the inquest Price Williams, my Lord Mohun's footman, swore "That on Thursday November 13th his Lord went to Mr. Orlebar, a Master of Chancery's Chambers, where he met Duke Hamilton; he heard them talk angrily, the door at which he waited being open; he farther heard the Duke, at the reading (as he supposed) of Mr. Whitworth's evidence, say that the evidence he had given had neither truth nor justice in it; to which His Lordship replied, He knew Mr. Whitworth to be an Honest Man, and had as much Honour and Justice in him as His Grace: then the door was shut."

So much for the cause of the quarrel, and now we have an interesting story.

"John Pennington, Hackney-coachman, swore, That on Saturday morning (November 15) about Seven a Clock he was called from Bow Street in Covent Garden to the Bagnio in Long Acre, where he took up my Lord Mohun and another Gentleman. My Lord Mohun bid him drive to Kensington, but when he came near Hide Park he ordered him to drive in there: They were stopped at the Gate, but telling the Keeper they were going to Price's Lodge, he let them in. My Lord then asked the Coachman if he knew where they could get anything good, it being a cold morning? He said at the House near the Ring. When they came near the House they both got out of the coach, and bid the coachman get some burnt wine while they took a little walk. He went into the House, and told the Drawer he brought two Gentlemen, who bid him get some burnt wine against they came back; the Drawer said he would not, for very few came thither so soon in the morning but to Fight: The Coachman said he believed they were very civil gentlemen, but however he'd dog them. A Groom rode up to him and told him, there were two Gentlemen at his coach who, he supposed, wanted him; he ran back and found Duke Hamilton and another gentleman there; the Duke asked him whom he had brought? He answered, My Lord Mohun and another gentleman; he asked him which way they were gone? He shewed them, and ran into the House, telling the man that Duke Hamilton and a gentleman followed my Lord Mohun and the other gentleman, and that he feared they were going to fight; he desired the man to make all the haste he could, and bring anybody he could get with staves to prevent them, for he feared there would be Murther, and he'd run before. He got behind a tree within fifty yards of them, from whence he saw the Duke throw off his cloak, and my Lord Mohun his coat, and both drew their swords, making violent passes at each other; upon which they both fell, he being then within thirty yards of them. He was asked, *Whether the two other Gentlemen drew their swords? And how far they were from the Lords when they fell? And whether they fought or not?* He answered, They drew their swords, but did not fight; and that they were some yards distant from the Lords when they drew, and continued so till they fell: He was asked again *if the seconds fought?* He answered *they did not*, but ran to the Lords when they fell. Two men who followed him from the house with staves were not more than four yards behind the seconds; which two men demanded their swords, which they readily delivered. He being asked which of the Lords was uppermost? He said he could not tell; he then ran for his Coach: My Lord Mohun's footman and the two men put my Lord into this Pennington's Coach; my Lord being almost dead, his Second bid him carry him to his Lodgings in Marlbro' Street: The coachman asked him who must pay him? He said, The footman; the coachman took him by the sleeve and said, He brought him as well as my Lord, and that he should pay him; then he gave him half a crown. He was asked if he knew who the gentleman was? He said 'twas General Maccartney, the Footman having told him so as they were carrying my Lord Mohun to Marlbro' Street.

"Colonel Hamilton's Examination before the Council, viz. That on Saturday morning, the 15th instant, Duke Hamilton sent his servant to Colonel Hamilton, desiring him to get up and dress immediately, but before he was half ready the Duke himself came and hurried him into his chariot so soon that he finished buttoning his waistcoat there. By that time they had got into Pall Mall, the Duke observed that the Colonel had left his sword behind him; whereupon he stopt his chariot, and gave his footman a bunch of keys, with orders to fetch a mourning sword out of such a closet. At the return of the footman they drove to Hyde Park, where the Coachman stopt, and the Duke ordered him to drive to Kensington; when they came to the lodge they saw a Hackney coach at a distance in which, his Grace said, there was somebody he must speak with; but driving up to it and seeing nobody, he asked the coachman, Where the gentlemen were whom he brought? He answered, A little before. The Duke and the Colonel got out in the Bottom, and walked over the Pond's head, where they saw the Lord Mohun and Colonel Maccartney before them. As soon as the Duke came within hearing he said, He hoped he was come time enough; and Maccartney answered, In very good time, my Lord. After this they all jumped over the ditch into the nursery, and the Duke turned to Maccartney and told him, Sir! you are the cause of this, let the event be what it will; Maccartney answered, My Lord, I have a commission for it. Then my Lord Mohun said these gentlemen shall have nothing to do here; at which Maccartney said, We'll have our share: Then the Duke answered, There is my friend then, he will take a share in my dance. They all drew immediately, and Maccartney made a full pass at Hamilton, which he parrying down with great Force, wounded himself in his instep; however he took that opportunity to close with and disarm Maccartney, and said, Your life is in my power. After which he turned his head, and seeing my Lord Mohun fall, and the Duke upon him, he ran to the Duke's assistance, and that he might with the more ease help him, he flung down both the swords: And as he was raising my Lord Duke up he says, *That he saw Maccartney make a push at his Grace; that he immediately looked to see if he had wounded him, but seeing no blood, he took up his sword, expecting that Maccartney would attack him again, but he walked off.* Just as he was gone the keepers came up and others, to the number of nine or ten, among the rest Ferguson, my Lord Duke's gentleman, who had brought Buissière's man with him; who on opening his Grace's breast, soon discovered a wound on his left side, which came in between the left shoulder and pap, and went slantingly down thro' the midriff into his belly."

Further evidence was given by various people, but it is not worth while to reproduce it in these pages.

The coroner's inquest brought in a verdict of wilful murder against all of the four gentlemen who were concerned in this duel.

The Particular Wounds of the above Two Peers, Saturday, November 15, 1712.

"Dr. Ronjat, Sergeant Surgeon to his late Majesty, was sent for to the Duke of Hamilton's, he came about eight a Clock in the morning, and found his Grace dead upon the bed in his cloathes, which he presently cut off, and upon searching the body carefully, observed that the artery of the right arm was cut in two, which he judged to be the immediate occasion of his death: He found likewise another wound on the left side of his breast, three inches above the nipple, two inches broad, running obliquely from the left to the right, and above eight inches deep; besides those a third wound in the right leg, about three inches broad, running from the outside of the shin bone obliquely under the calf.

"When the Lord Mohun's body was brought home,

his chaplain went to Mr la Fage, an able surgeon, who, upon his coming, found three wounds, one on the right side, penetrating obliquely the whole body, and coming out on the left above his hip; another very large one in the right groin, cutting the great artery, which he took to be the principal cause of his death; and, according to the Newgate Calendar, he had in addition three fingers of his left hand almost cut off."

These details are not devoid of interest. The nature of the wounds on both sides suggests that they must have been inflicted with weapons edged as well as pointed, and that the two noblemen were armed, not with the triangular "colichemarde," but with the more antiquated, flat, double-edged small sword. In both cases they were very broad wounds, which would not have been caused by a simple puncture, and in both cases there was complete severance of an artery; while the mangling of Lord Mohun's left hand (as in the affair of Quelus) was the evident result of his attempting either to parry or to seize his enemy's sword with it, a thing which was successfully done by one of the seconds, Colonel Hamilton, who, on the furious "full pass" of Maccartney, parried the thrust with a quarte, and, effecting the necessary seizure of the sword with his left hand, instantly tore it from his opponent's grasp. This was one of a series of movements which were regularly taught in those days for the purpose of ending a rencontre without bloodshed.

This Lord Mohun, fortunately the last of his race, was a man of, to say the least of it, a decidedly turbulent character, as is clearly shown by the part he chose to take in

The Murder of Mountford.

Steinmetz in his "Romance of Duelling," and Millingen, to whom he often refers, have both given what seems to be a fairly accurate description of this atrocious affair.

Lord Mohun, a thorough-going profligate, was surrounded by almost a petty court of spirits even worse than himself, among whom was a certain Captain Hall, who felt himself attracted, partly by her personal charms, but a good deal more by her earnings on the stage, to Mrs. Bracegirdle, a then popular actress. This lady, from her professional intercourse with him, was on terms of strictly friendly nature with a Mr. Mountford, a young actor of considerable repute; he was a married man and lived at home peaceably with his family, but this Hall chose to translate him into a rival to himself, and, unprincipled scoundrel as he was, made up his mind to effect two strokes at the same time—to forcibly abduct the lady and to rid himself of his self-created rival by any means that might come to his hand. He took his friend and patron Mohun into his confidence, and as the latter was only too ready to have a share in any act of violence, he promptly acquiesced.

For the furtherance of their project they hired a two-horse coach, with relays of horses posted in convenient places, and ordered the driver to be in readiness in Drury Lane near the theatre, at nine o'clock on a certain particular evening. They entered the house and went behind the scenes, where, to their disgust, they found that the name of Mrs. Bracegirdle was not in the bills that evening; but they ascertained that she was to sup with some friends of hers at the house of a Mr. and Mrs. Page. They accordingly lay in wait in the neighbourhood, attended by a gang of ruffians engaged by Hall. The supper being over, Mrs. Bracegirdle and her mother, accompanied by her brother and Mr. Page, were quietly returning home, when this precious pair, assisted by the rascals they had with them, seized the lady and attempted to force her into the carriage, whereupon there was a mighty hubbub. Mr. Page attacked Hall and gave him a good deal of trouble, his lordship had the lady's brother on his hands, while Mrs. Bracegirdle senior clung to her daughter and shrieked lustily for help. All this uproar drew such a goodly number of people together that the two pretty gentlemen thought it wise to dismiss their attendants and to take themselves off. But they were by no means satisfied: they still wanted Mountford, who, on his return from the theatre, unluckily fell in with them. Lord Mohun advanced and addressed him in a most friendly and cordial manner, when Mountford asked him jokingly what he was doing in the streets at that time of night. Mohun replied, "I suppose you have heard about the lady." Mountford innocently said, "I hope my wife has given your lordship no cause of offence." "Oh dear no!" said Mohun: "it's not your wife, it is Mrs. Bracegirdle, I am talking about." "Mrs. Bracegirdle!" replied Mountford; "she has nothing whatever to do with me. I hope, however, that your lordship does not countenance the behaviour of Hall towards her." On this the scoundrel Hall, who had his sword ready drawn, stepped forward, and without more ado passed it through the body of the unfortunate actor, laid him dead on the pavement, and instantly took to his heels. There were cries of murder, a crowd assembled, the watch made its appearance, and Mohun had to surrender; on giving up his sword he remarked that he hoped Hall had escaped, and he had the additional impudence to boast of having changed coats with him in order to enable him the easier to do so.

The End of Major Oneby.

This was a bad business. It occurred in 1726, and was fatal to both of the gentlemen concerned in it.

Major Oneby, Mr. Gower, Mr. Rich, and two other gentlemen, had supper together one evening at a tavern the name of which has slipped our memory, and, as was usual in those days, the bottle circulated freely. The meal finished, they settled down to amuse themselves with a game of hazard; and now the trouble began, all owing to a very silly and decidedly vulgar practical joke on the part of Mr. Gower. Mr. Rich asked if any of the party would set him three half-crowns, whereupon Mr. Gower impertinently placed on the table three halfpence, saying to Rich, "Here you are; I set you three pieces." At the same time Major Oneby set him the three half-crowns, and lost them. Now, if anyone had a right to take umbrage at Mr. Gower's stupid behaviour, it certainly was Mr. Rich, who, like a wise man, treated it with the contempt it deserved. But Major Oneby, more or less in his cups, and irritated at having had the worst of the game, although in so small a matter as seven and sixpence (sometimes the buzz of a mosquito is more annoying than that of a bumble-bee, and, alas! when the wine is in the wit is out), turned round angrily to Gower, and said something to the effect that it was an ungentlemanly trick to put down coppers, and that only an impertinent puppy would do it. Mr. Gower replied hotly, "Whoever says that is a rascal." The Major, now well heated, capped the remark by throwing a bottle at Mr. Gower's head, but failed to hit him, the missile doing no more harm than knocking some of the powder out of his wig. (Young and old, they all wore wigs in those days. Wasn't it a funny fashion!) Mr. Gower returned the compliment with a candlestick, which happened to be even still more innocent in its effect. It seems to us that these gentlemen must have been very far gone indeed to have made such execrably bad shots at such short range as the breadth of a supper-table. Both men were now thoroughly angry, and rushed to get hold of their swords, which were hanging up on the wall. Mr. Gower drew his, and Major Oneby was about to do the same, but was prevented by his friends, upon which Mr. Gower threw his weapon away into a corner. A certain amount of judicious argument was used, the two quarrellers were apparently pacified, and the party resumed their seats for another hour or so of play. The "flowing bowl," of course, continued to "flow," and still more inflamed the temper of the irascible Major.

When the game was finished, Mr. Gower, forgetful of the fact that his own impertinent behaviour had been the cause of the misunderstanding, advanced to Major Oneby, extending his hand, and saying, "We have had hot words together, and you were the aggressor; but I think we may pass it over." To which the angry Major replied, "No, d——n you! I'll have your blood!"

The party then broke up, and all but Major Oneby were in the act of descending the stairs, when he looked over the banisters and called out to Mr. Gower, "Young man, come back; I have something to say to you." Mr. Gower returned, and entered the room again; the door was shut and locked; the click, click, click of the wicked little colichemardes was distinctly heard, then a groan and a heavy fall. The remainder of the party, who were on the point of leaving the house, returned, and, anxious to prevent a catastrophe, forced an entrance, when they found Major Oneby, who had received three slight wounds, standing erect with his greatcoat thrown over his shoulders, and Mr. Gower, with his body pierced through and through, extended on the floor in a dying condition. He was asked if he had received his wounds in fair fight; he replied, "Yes, I think so," and fell back insensible.

Major Oneby was arrested and tried for wilful murder. It was contested that after the original fracas the entire party had resumed their seats at the table, and for the space of a whole hour had continued to gamble together in an apparently friendly spirit, and that, whatever the provocation might have been, the Major had had time to cool down; that the fact of his waiting till the party broke up, and then addressing Mr. Gower with the irritating words, "Young man," etc., showed that he had acted deliberately, and had forced Mr. Gower to draw and defend himself.

The jury found Major Oneby guilty, and he was accordingly condemned to death, but he contrived to anticipate that fate by making away with himself.

Young gentlemen of the twentieth century, take warning from this history, and avoid the stupid, senseless amusement of practical joking.

CHAPTER XXIII

The Small Sword.

Introductory.

WHILE the eighteenth-century sword-users, in their capacity of duellists, were creating a demand for an improvement in their weapon, the eighteenth-century sword-makers were doing their best to supply the want, and, roughly speaking, about the year 1760 they succeeded in changing the somewhat lumpy colichemarde into the slender feather-weight arm which is now recognised *par excellence* as the "small sword." This improvement in the weapon was the immediate cause of a vast corresponding improvement in the management of it. A circular parry was understood as a possibility even when the early form of the sword had not disappeared—witness the "counter-caveating parade" of Sir William Hope. But those swords were of such clumsy build as to almost entirely preclude their dexterous use, so the parries then in vogue were mostly simple ones, and to assist them the colichemarde, with its abnormally broad forte, was introduced.

Girard (1736), the most prominent French author of the period, was evidently still dissatisfied as to the handiness of the sword then in fashion. He advises, as did La Touche, Liancourt, and others also before him, the occasional holding of it with both hands, although his manner of doing so differs from theirs. He, too, records the elementary circular parry under the name of the "contredegagement"; be it understood that "caveating" and "disengaging" were synonymous terms. Subsequently to the publication of his work the improvement in the sword seems to have taken place. As the utility of the circular or counter-parry became more manifest, the shape of the blade was altered to assist it; the abnormally broad forte was fined down, and the blade, now somewhat lengthened, tapered gradually from its setting in the hilt up to the point, and the walking-sword of 1760 was as light and manageable as the most up-to-date fencing foil of this our twentieth century.

Silver-hilted small sword in possession of Captain A. Hutton, F.S.A.

The elegant, wicked little weapon had reached the climax of its perfection, and we have under our hand several charming specimens handsomely mounted in silver. The father of the great house of Angelo, in his splendid work which first saw the light in 1763, presents to us the circular parry as the "parade with a counter-disengagement"; and later on Olivier, another famous master, whose work (1780) was published simultaneously in English and in French, terms it simply, much as we do now, the "counter in quarte" and the "counter in tierce," and he makes these an integral portion of the education of the small-sword fencer.

We shall now see how the sword-wearing gentlemen employed their improved weapons; their manners and customs were very much those of their immediate predecessors.

The Encounter between Lord Byron and Mr. Chaworth.

This unfortunate affair bears a very strong resemblance to that of Major Oneby and Mr. Gower. In both cases the cause of the quarrel was an absurdly slight one, in both cases the misunderstanding occurred after a convivial meal at which much wine was consumed, and, again, in both cases the fatal affray took place without seconds or any kind of witness in a room with closed doors.

In the year 1765 the then Lord Byron and Mr. Chaworth were large landed proprietors and near neighbours in the county of Nottingham, and had always been on friendly terms. Whenever they repaired to London, it was their custom to dine or sup in company with other county friends at the Star and Garter Tavern in Pall Mall, where they had established what was known among themselves as the "Nottinghamshire Club." There was a very wide difference between the simple but select club of the last century but one and the palatial building of this present period. In the eighteenth century it was the habit of gentlemen of similar tastes or occupations to form a little social circle of their own. They agreed with the proprietor of some fashionable or at least respectable inn or tavern (the then tavern was something analogous to the restaurant of to-day, and, curiously enough, in Belgium at the present time such an establishment is known by the name of "taverne") to reserve a special room for their use, from which the ordinary customer was, of course, excluded. The members of the little society *clubbed together* for their meals and other requirements, by which means they insured better service and attention than if they had dined separately elsewhere. Such was the origin of the club as we ourselves know it.

On January 26, 1765, Lord Byron and Mr. Chaworth dined at their club with a party of some ten or twelve county friends, when, being all of them landed proprietors and sportsmen, the conversation naturally came round to the subject of game and the preservation thereof. Mr. Chaworth was of opinion that such a sinner as a poacher should be drastically dealt with, while Lord Byron held out that it was far better to let him alone and allow the rabbits and hares to look after themselves. This led to a somewhat heated argument, when Mr. Chaworth exclaimed: "Why, if it were not for Sir Charles Sedley and myself you would have no game at all at your place." Lord Byron retorted by offering to bet £100 that he could show more hares and rabbits than Mr. Chaworth. The latter gentleman promptly took up the wager, and, according to one of his historians, rather pointedly called for pen and ink to make a record of it, an action which might, but really ought not to, have nettled his lordship to some degree. Others of the party, however, intervened with the opinion that the bet had better not be booked, because the matter was one upon which it was impossible to come to any decision. Lord Byron, whose temper was fast getting the better of him, asked heatedly: "Where is Sir Charles's property? I know nothing of any land of his." Mr. Chaworth replied with equal warmth: "Why, Nuttall, to be sure; some of my people sold it to him, and if you are not satisfied you can easily find him and ask himself: he lives in Dean Street, and your lordship knows where to find me also."

After this they quieted down again, and, just like the Oneby-Gower party, resumed their seats, and continued in good-humoured conversation for another hour, when Mr. Chaworth left the room, followed by Lord Byron, who said he wished to speak to him, called a waiter, and bade him show them into an unoccupied room, which the man did, leaving on the table a tallow candle and no other light. The two gentlemen shut the door, and after some further words drew their swords and attacked one another.

Mr. Chaworth made a lunge, and, having pierced and entangled his sword in Lord Byron's waistcoat, thought he had severely wounded him, and, believing the affair to be over, paused in order to extricate his weapon, whereupon Lord Byron drew his hand back as far as he could and, with his shortened sword, stabbed Mr. Chaworth in the belly.

The clash of arms brought back those members of the club who had not left the house, and with them the landlord. They speedily disarmed and separated the combatants, when Mr. Chaworth was seen to be seriously hurt. A surgeon was sent for, who after due examination pronounced the wound to be a mortal one.

Lord Byron was arraigned on the charge of wilful murder, but the Peers found him guilty only of manslaughter, on which he claimed the benefit of a statute of the time of King Edward VI., by which he was discharged, and thus got away scot-free.

Shortly after this affair such a rencontre became impossible, as the constant wearing of the sword as a necessary part of a gentleman's dress went out of fashion.

How Richard Brinsley Sheridan fought twice with Captain Matthews.

It is the year 1772, and we find ourselves at Bath, a very fashionable place, where much gaiety is required to attract and retain the smart sword-wearing gentlemen and bepowdered ladies who congregate there in search of health or excitement. Music is one of the leading features, wherefore good musicians make the city their rendezvous. Among these is a certain Mr. Linley, who has been blessed with a family so handsome, so charming, and so skilled in their art that the well-known Dr. Burney dubbed them the "nest of nightingales," and one of them, Miss Elizabeth, so far excels the rest, both in talent and in beauty, that she is known as "the Maid of Bath," and it is only natural that she should be followed by a host of admirers.

About four years before the time of which we speak there arrived in Bath an Irish family of the name of Sheridan, the head of which, having retired from the theatrical profession, adopted that of a teacher of elocution. The arts practised by the two families were sufficiently similar to promote mutual sympathy, but not sufficiently identical to engender professional jealousy, so they shortly became extremely intimate. Miss Sheridan was the bosom friend of the Maid of Bath, and the elder brother, Charles, speedily enrolled himself among the number of her courtiers. But a Cæsar suddenly arose in the shape of a junior member of the Sheridan family, Richard Brinsley by name, a young fellow of twenty, who had just finished his education; a most attractive young gentleman. He was something of a poet, he was remarkably handsome, with a keen wit and a spice of romance about him; moreover, he rode well, danced to perfection, and understood the handling of the small sword to a remarkable degree, an accomplishment highly desirable in those days. He possessed a chivalrous soul, and was, in fact, a sort of youthful Don Quixote, only minus the age, the wrinkles, and the absurd extravagance. He was liked and admired by everyone, the only person in the whole of Bath with whom he could not get on being his own father, the old professor of speech-making, whose pedantic rules of the art of elocution his son could in no way put up with. Small wonder, then, that, like Cæsar, he came, he saw, and he conquered.

The crowd of Miss Linley's admirers gradually melted away, the faithful Charles being the last of them, and much tittle-tattle thereon arose among the scandalmongers of the city, who were promptly taken to task by the chivalrous Richard, who espoused the cause of the young lady from a feeling of friendship, which soon developed into one of a more romantic kind.

At this juncture a Mephisto appeared on the scene in the person of a Captain Matthews, a married man who had left his wife behind him in the country, and who turned out to be an unmitigated scoundrel. This fellow got himself introduced to old Linley under colour of being able to assist him largely with his influence in the matter of placing concert tickets and getting up musical performances, and although the real reason of his attentions was a vastly different one, neither the father nor the mother of the young lady was aware of it, or they must have been so greedy of gain as to ignore it altogether. Matthews carried on the siege for a long time, but without the success he had anticipated, and he at last so far transgressed the rules of decency as to threaten to carry the fair one off by force. The poor girl was so terrified that she decided to take refuge, at least for a time, in a convent in France, whither Richard Sheridan escorted her; but during the journey he declared his unalterable affection for her, and they were privately married by the parish priest of a little village near Calais.

Matthews, balked of his prey, was beside himself with rage and wounded vanity, and in revenge inserted letters and other matter in the Bath papers attacking the character of the lady as well as that of his successful rival. Charles Sheridan, the brother, took the matter up, contradicted the slanders, and was on the point of requiring satisfaction at the sword's point, when the cowardly Captain, hearing that hostilities were in the air, bolted from Bath and took refuge in London. But "out of the frying-pan into the fire": the refugee found himself face to face with a more implacable enemy, Richard Brinsley, who immediately sent his friend Mr. Ewart to him to demand reparation after the fashion of the day. He was referred by Matthews to a Captain Knight, whom he chose as his second. It was decided that the meeting should take place in

Hyde Park, and that the instruments used in it should be swords, Matthews having a strong objection to the pistol.

The momentous hour has arrived; the pair of combatants appear on the ground attended by their seconds, when Matthews, even on the field itself, makes use of every tricky excuse that he can imagine to postpone the duel. Sheridan tells him that he is trifling, and bids him come to business at once. Matthews, stung by the taunts of his enemy, at last draws his sword; they take up their positions, and at a word from one of the seconds they cross blades. Coward as Matthews is, he has some skill at fence. Several fierce thrusts are exchanged and are cleverly parried on both sides, when, in his eagerness, he overlunges himself, a mistake by which Sheridan profits. He parries strongly, seizes his enemy's sword by the forte with his left hand, wrenches it away from him, and strikes up his heels, thus giving him a heavy fall. He has the slanderer now at his mercy, and the latter, with Sheridan's point at his throat, begs that his life may be spared, and signs a complete confession and retractation of the calumnies which he had circulated. Sheridan, having secured the written confession, departs at once for Bath where he takes measures to make it as widely known as possible.

The real character of Matthews is now a matter of common talk. He is irretrievably disgraced, both as a man of honour and a man of courage. He retires to his estate in Wales, but his ill-fame has arrived before him, and he finds himself shunned by everyone. Infuriated by the reception he meets with in his own district, he repairs again to Bath in the hope of retrieving something of his lost honour by another encounter with Sheridan, whose friends are most averse to his descending to meet one so utterly disgraced as this fellow. The overchivalrous Irishman, however, waives this consideration and accepts the challenge. At this particular period it was sometimes the custom for gentlemen to void their differences, not with sword *or* pistol, but with both, and such is the arrangement between Sheridan and Matthews.

Attended on Sheridan's part by a Mr. Barnett, and on Matthews' by Captain Knight, they meet on Kingsdown, they take their ground, and exchange shots, but without effect. The empty pistols are thrown away ; the swords are drawn, and the pair approach one another. Several thrusts are given, some of which take effect, for both men are bleeding. Sheridan again attempts his favourite trick of disarming by seizure of the blade. Matthews, however, this time eludes it, and closes with him. They fall to the ground together, and in the fall both of the swords are broken. They struggle furiously while on the ground, and both are seriously injured. The seconds at last part them : Sheridan is conveyed to his father's house, where his wounds confine him to his bed for several weeks, while Matthews is taken away by his second, never to appear again.

CHAPTER XXIV

Three Famous Fencers.

In the eighteenth century there flourished a trio of fencers whose like the world has scarcely ever seen—the Chevalier de Saint Georges, the Chevalier d'Eon de Beaumont, and last, but not least, our Henry Angelo. These three, consummate as was their skill at arms, seem very seldom to have used that skill in real earnest, although we hear occasionally of a sound lesson being given by one of them with the foil to some person of presumptuous insolence. Millingen, indeed, in his "History of Duelling," hints at the numerous affairs of honour of both Saint Georges and of D'Eon, but he fails to furnish his readers with the description of a single instance. The fact was that they were swordsmen of such extraordinary calibre that no one cared to provoke them, while Henry Angelo, from his becoming a professor of the art of fence, was precluded from a hostile encounter with any but a member of his profession.

The Chevalier de Saint Georges.

Angelo throws some light on to this remarkable man. He tells us that "the Chevalier de Saint Georges was born at Guadaloupe. He was the son of M. de Boulogne, a rich planter in the colony. His mother was a negress, and was known as 'la belle Nanon.' She was considered to be the finest and most graceful woman that Africa had ever sent to the plantations. The Chevalier united in his own person the grace of his mother with the strength and firmness of his father. The youth's sprightliness and vigour were highly pleasing to M. de Boulogne, who frequently laughed and said he thought to have produced a man, but that, in fact, he had produced a sparrow. This sparrow, however, grew into an eagle. No man ever united so much suppleness with so much strength. He excelled in all the bodily exercises in which he engaged. An excellent swimmer and skater, he was frequently known to swim over the Seine with one arm, and to surpass all others by his agility on its surface in the winter. He was a skilful horseman and a remarkable shot; he rarely missed his aim when his pistol was once before the mark. His talents in music unfolded themselves rapidly, but the art in which he surpassed all his contemporaries and predecessors was fencing. No professor or amateur ever showed so much accuracy, such strength, such length of lunge, and such quickness. His attacks were a perpetual series of hits; his parade was so close that it was in vain to attempt to touch him; in short, he was all nerve.

"Saint Georges had not attained his twenty-first year when his father proposed him to go to Rouen to fence with M. Picard, a fencing-master at that place, with a promise that if he beat him he should have, on his return, a little horse and a pretty little cabriolet. This Picard had formerly been in the army, and harangued very foolishly against the necessity of science. Saint Georges, whom he called 'the mulatto of La Boëssière,' would, he publicly asserted, soon give way to him. But he was mistaken, for La Boëssière's pupil disposed of him very easily indeed.

'The various talents of Saint Georges were like a mine of gold: he might have amassed considerable wealth if he had united prudence to his other qualities. He was very liberal in money matters, and indulged freely in all the pleasures which then made Paris such a delightful residence; he mixed in every circle, and yet seemed to neglect nothing."

"To this memoir," adds Angelo, "I have only a few remarks to make as to what I personally knew of that extraordinary character, as also the particulars of my acquaintance with him.

"While I was in Paris, under the tuition of M. Mottet and M. Donardieu, I often went to fence with Saint Georges. My introduction arose from his being well known to my father, who occasionally corresponded with him for the purpose of directing his attention to my improvement.

"In the summer of the year 1787, on returning to my residence in St. Alban's Street, I was surprised by the appearance of lights and a crowd of people entering Mr. Rheda's Fencing Academy. On inquiry, I was informed that Chevalier Saint Georges had arrived in England, and was about to exhibit his great talents at that place. I immediately went and renewed my acquaintance with him, and, as it is customary for fencing-masters of celebrity to engage with each other at such meetings, I proposed myself, and was accepted as the first professor who engaged him in this country. It may not be unworthy of remark that from his being much taller, and, consequently, possessing a greater length of lunge, I found that I could not depend upon my attacks unless I closed with him. The consequence was, upon my adopting that measure, the hit I gave him was so 'palpable' that it threw open his waistcoat, which so enraged him that, in his fury, I received a blow from the pommel of his foil on my chin, the mark of which I still retain. It may be remarked of that celebrated man that, although he might be considered as a lion with a foil in his hand, the contest over he was docile as a lamb, for soon after the above engagement, when seated to rest himself, he said to me: 'Mon cher ami, donnez-moi votre main; nous tirons tous les jours ensemble.'"

Saint Georges and the Captain of Hussars.

Our great fencer happens to be staying at Dunkirk, where a man of such varied accomplishments is naturally much sought after. He finds himself one day among a party of ladies and gentlemen, when a young Captain of hussars makes his appearance. He has a most overweening sense of his own importance, especially in matters concerning the sword, and has the hardihood to boast that not a fencer in the whole of France can touch him at all. "That is interesting," says one of the ladies, "but did you ever happen to meet with the celebrated Saint Georges?" Quoth the Captain: "Saint Georges? Oh yes; I have fenced with him many a time. But he is no good; I can touch him just when I please." The ladies all look at one another. Saint Georges remarks quietly: "Dear me, how very odd! I should rather like to cross blades with you myself, and if a pair of foils were forthcoming a few thrusts might amuse the ladies." To this suggestion the hussar accords a supercilious assent. As luck will have it, the needful weapons are in the house, and they are at once produced. The Captain, seeing that he is opposed to a man much older than himself, is inclined to treat him with contempt, when the veteran fencer calmly turns to the ladies and asks them to name the particular buttons on the gentleman's coat which they would like him to touch. They select half a dozen or so.

The pair engage. The famous swordsman plays with his man for a few minutes for the benefit of his audience, and then proceeds to hit each of the named buttons in rapid succession, and finishes by sending the foil of his vainglorious enemy flying out of his hand, to the great delight of the ladies, and the discomfited Captain is so enraged that he wants to make the affair a serious one there and then. His victorious opponent corrects him with: "Young gentleman, such an encounter could have but one ending. Be advised;

reserve your forces for the service of your country. Go, and you may at last tell your friends with truth that you have crossed foils with me. My name is Saint Georges."

Physic for the Fencing-master.

Saint Georges is reputed to have administered corrective medicine somewhat similar to the above to a certain fencing-master who approached him in a discourteous manner, and finally challenged him to a trial of skill. This Saint Georges accepted for the next day, naming a time and place which would insure a fair number of chance spectators. At this the fencing-master was not a little disconcerted, but having given the challenge himself, he could not draw back.

On arriving at the ground he finds Saint Georges waiting for him. They take their places, cross blades, when away flies the fencing-master's weapon out of his hand! Thirsting for revenge, he picks it up again, when, behold! on a sign from Saint Georges, a huge black man advances, carrying in his arms a great bundle of foils. "What are you going to do with all these?" he asks. "To teach you civility," replies Saint Georges. "You will not leave this place until I have broken every one of them upon you." He is as good as his word, for in less than twenty minutes the disagreeable master has received a disagreeable lesson: he is standing surrounded by fragments of foil blades, and looking exceedingly sheepish, to the immense merriment of the bystanders.

Concerning the Fencing-mask.

During the three centuries at which we have glanced, anything in the shape of protection for the face in a fencing-bout was unheard of; wherefore the need of the enormous buttons "so big as a tennis-ball," recommended by fencing-masters in the rapier days, as also of the ultra-academic custom in the *salles d'armes* during the earlier part of the small-sword period, that a man, having made a successful parry, should withhold his riposte until his opponent had recovered from the lunge, in order to obviate the danger of injury to the face, of which the blow on the chin given by Saint Georges to young Angelo is an example.

The elder La Boëssière is credited with having been the first to advocate a covering of some kind for the face, but his invention did not become popular, partly by reason of professional vanity, the masters proudly considering such protection beneath their notice, and partly from the very inadequate nature of this protection. The earliest kind of mask was clearly of solid metal (not of the steel meshwork afterwards introduced), in which holes were cut for the eyes, which, although they were the parts which needed defence more than any other, were thus left entirely open to any thrust, chance or otherwise. An unfortunate event—we cannot call it an accident—at last brought this need clearly before the eyes of the masters by the loss of an eye on the part of one of them. The injury was, as will be seen, purposely inflicted by that unmitigated scoundrel, George Robert Fitzgerald, the man who had gained for himself the sobriquet of Fighting Fitzgerald, on account of the numerous duels in which he had been successfully engaged, until in the last of them it was discovered that he owed his supposed courage to a strong shirt of mail which he wore under his clothes. Henry Angelo, of whom more anon, gives an account of the "accident" in his Reminiscences, so he shall tell us the story himself:

"Fitzgerald had the reputation of not only being a good shot, but a capital fencer, though, in fact, he knew very little of the art, and was only desperate when opposed to the button of a foil, rushing on when there was no danger to apprehend. I can speak to this fact, as I have often been his antagonist, and know that if the point of a sword had been opposed to him

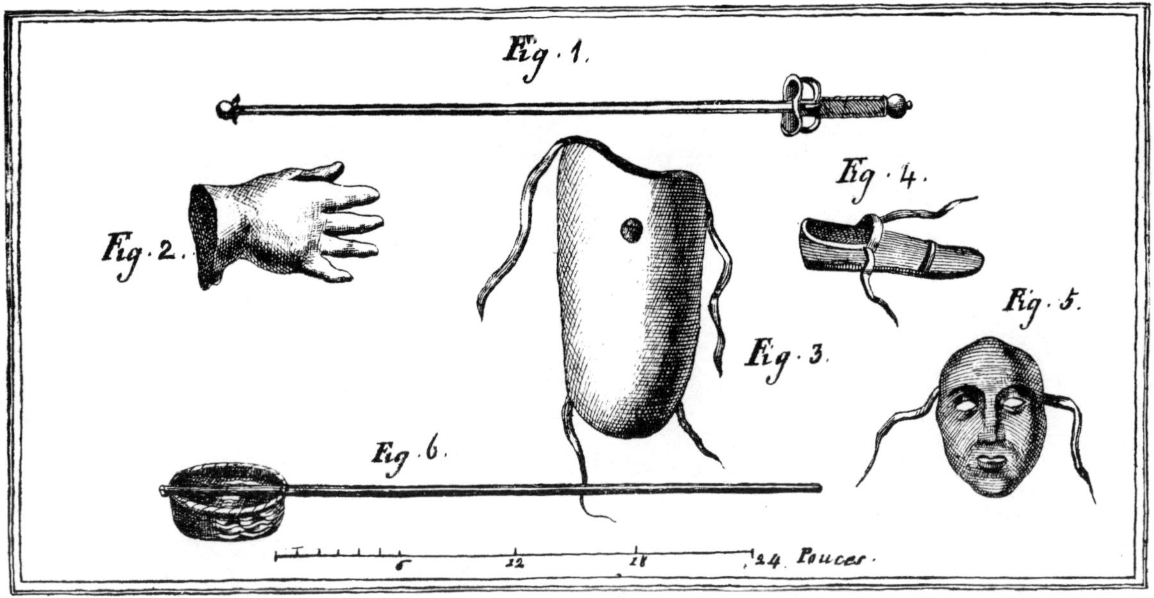

Fencing implements in use about 1760, *after Diderot and d'Alembert*: 1. *Foil*; 2. *Glove*; 3. *Plastron*; 4. *Sandal*: 5. *Mask*; 6. *Singlestick.*

it would have very much altered his ardour. At that time, M. Redas, a famous fencing-master, taught at the Opera-house previous to my teaching there, and had an assistant who was the *plastron de salle* (a mark for everyone to push at). Among the many he had to contend with, Fitzgerald preferred him to all the other fencers, making him subservient to his pretended skill. The fact was that the Frenchman (M. Charriot), who was the prévôt, now and then got some little douceur from him, and was too *politique* to hit his lucrative adversary too often. It was far different with all the others who fenced with Fitzgerald: not suffering themselves to be beat, they took care never to spare him.

"One day I was present when Charriot was not pleased with the number of hits he had quietly and voluntarily received; and Fitzgerald, having boasted that he had been beating him, so roused monsieur's pride that the next time, forgetting the presents his forbearance had procured him, he retaliated on his vaunting antagonist, determined no longer to be his tool. Charriot made the first attack, and so enraged Fitzgerald that he stretched out his arm and poked his eye out. With the loss of one eye and a ten-pound note from his enraged opponent for the accident (which was an intentional one), this catastrophe proved *tout pour le mieux*, for Charriot's salary was but small, his dependence being more on the occasional presents from the scholars. Baron Wensell, who was the famous oculist at that time, making immense sums of money here by his performance of the cataract operation, was present when the calamity happened, and on Charriot's recovery took him home to his house, where, no longer assistant fencing-master, through the Baron's instruction he became an oculist. The year following, the Baron, having made an ample fortune, returned to his own country; his *en seconde* in the course of four years did the same. This, therefore, proved a lucky *hit* for him."

The Chevalier d'Eon de Beaumont.

This strange personage—who was for many years of his life believed to be a woman, wore to the day of his death the dress of the fair sex, and was everywhere received as Mdlle. la Chevalière—was of noble descent. He was born at Tonnerre in Burgundy on October 5, 1728, and was christened Charles-Geneviève-Louis-Auguste-Timothée, masculine names, be it understood, and not feminine ones, as some of his biographers will have it. He was educated at the Collége Mazarin in Paris, on leaving which he became secretary to M. de Sauvigny, who held a high office in that city, and it was in the *salle d'armes* of the famous master Taillagori—where he made the acquaintance of the elder Angelo—that he conceived his passion for the foil. Accomplished swordsman though he became, he was not a person of great physical strength : he was five feet seven inches in height, and of distinctly slight build. As a child, he was so delicately formed that his mother used to amuse herself with dressing him up in his sister's clothes, and passing him off upon her friends as a little girl. This facility of apparently changing his sex adhered to him all through life, and he made use of it more than once when employed in certain matters of diplomacy. In 1763 he was sent to London as Minister Plenipotentiary to ratify the treaty between England and France, where, as the story goes, he had a quarrel with Count de Guerchy, the French Ambassador, whose face he slapped—a most unpardonable affront, especially when offered to the representative of his Sovereign. The Count died not long after, and his young successor was anxious to retrieve the family honour by an encounter with D'Eon, which could have but one ending, the Chevalier being about the best swordsman in Europe ; indeed, he had but one rival, the famous Saint Georges. The young gentleman's mother, fearing this, implored the intervention of the King, when an event occurred which greatly facilitated the granting of her request. During a fencing-bout D'Eon chanced to receive a thrust from a particularly stiff foil on the breast. This caused the growth of a small tumour, which had to be surgically treated—a fact which decided the mind of the French monarch as to the sex of D'Eon, who was commanded to "resume" the proper costume of "her" sex. "She" was permitted to retain all her decorations and honours, the cross of Saint Louis included, and a pension of something like £500 a year—a respectable sum in those days—was granted to her so long as she continued to wear petticoats. Young Guerchy was saved.

Mdlle. la Chevalière, as we must now call her, enjoyed her pension until the downfall of the French monarchy, when it was abolished entirely. She established herself permanently in this country, where she gained her livelihood by fencing in public at assaults of arms, and also by giving lessons in her art. Her income was augmented by a modest pension obtained for her from the British Government. The Prince of Wales, afterwards George IV., delighted in her society, and often crossed foils with her. At his instance she consented to encounter no less a person than the famous M. de Saint Georges at an assault of arms which took place at Carlton House on April 9, 1787. Notwithstanding the inconvenience of her female attire, she completely vanquished her formidable opponent, hitting him seven times without being touched at all herself. In this assault the celebrated English master Henry Angelo took a prominent part. D'Eon died in 1810 at the advanced age of eighty-three.

Angelo.

This famous family of fencers, of whom there were four generations, lived and taught their art in England for more than a hundred years, and the author of this volume had the honour of being instructed, when a boy, by the last of the house, who died in 1864. Of the history of the Angelos we unfortunately know nothing beyond what is contained in the Reminiscences of the second of the name, the celebrated Henry, for the widow of the last of them ordered in her will that all the family papers should be destroyed, and the executors were only too obedient to her wishes.

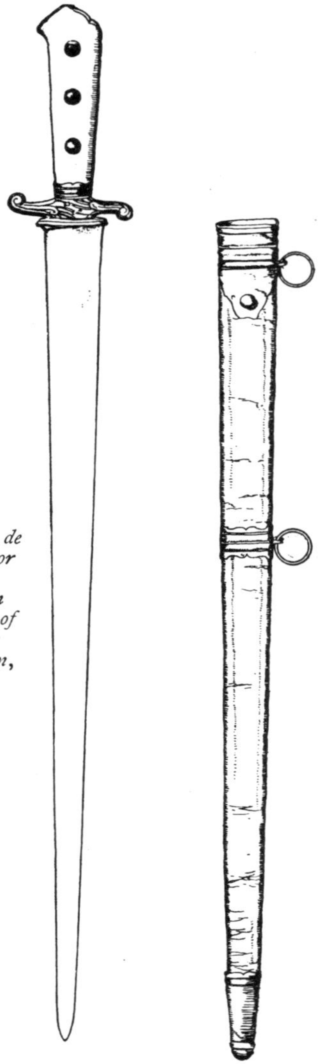

"Couteau de Chasse" or undress sword in possession of Captain A. Hutton, F.S.A.

Concerning the art of fencing, these four generations of eminent masters, although they were highly educated men, have left us nothing beyond the magnificent album of plates, engraved by the unhappy Rylands, with the explanatory text, published in 1763 by the founder of the house, in the composition of which he was greatly helped by his firm friend the Chevalier d'Eon, and an "Infantry Sword Exercise," first published by the military authorities in 1817. This latter was mainly the work of a sturdy English master of the broadsword, John Taylor by name, who did little more than transmit the lessons

Parry of Quarte and disarm by seizure, after Angelo.

as he had learned them, in a style differing not much from that in vogue in the days of Good Queen Bess.

The Angelos, even before they adopted fencing as a profession, were by no means quarrelsome people; they seem to have drawn their swords in earnest but once or twice, and then only under circumstances of very great provocation.

In the year 1753 there came to London one Domenico Angelo Malevolti Tremamondo, a native of Leghorn, where his father was a wealthy merchant. Young Domenico had been educated with lavish care in all the accomplishments, especially fencing and horsemanship, which were needful for the forming of a well-bred gentleman in those days, and, to complete his education, was sent forth by his father to travel and see the world. After visiting various parts of the Continent, he took up his abode in Paris. He seems to have had but one hostile encounter during his residence there, which his son describes as follows:

"When my father was at Paris he knew a French officer who always boasted of being a first-rate fencer. Motives of jealousy induced him to waylay my father one night, and he was cowardly enough to insult and then draw his sword upon him. My father happened to be only armed with a *couteau de chasse*, a short, small, edged sword usually worn in undress; but he acted on the defensive for some time, when at last he made a home thrust at the officer, who fell directly groaning, and at the time there was every reason to think that he was mortally wounded. The officer was taken home. The next day my father waited on him, when to his surprise, although it was thought that he was dangerously wounded, and that there was very little hope of his recovery, there was not that alteration in his countenance that might have been expected. My father instantly suspected that he must have had a cuirass (*cotte de maille*), and, throwing the bedclothes off, suddenly discovered the disgraceful stratagem to which he had resorted."

Peg Woffington and the Bouquet of Roses.

"A short period before his quitting France there was a public fencing match at a celebrated hotel in Paris, at which were present many of the most renowned professors and amateurs of that science, most of whom entered the lists. My father, who was honoured with the particular esteem of the Duke de Nivernois, was persuaded by that nobleman to try his skill. He had long before acquired the reputation of the first amateur swordsman, and was no less reputed for his scientific knowledge in the management of the horse.

"No sooner was his name announced than a celebrated English beauty, Miss Margaret Woffington, the renowned actress, then on a visit at this gay city, who, having met my father at a party, became suddenly captivated by his person and superior address, and, following him hither in presence of a crowd of spectators, she stepped forward and presented him with a small bouquet of roses. The company, as well ladies as gentlemen of rank, surprised at this, were no less struck by the gallant manner with which he received the gift. He placed it on his left breast, and, addressing the other knights of the sword, exclaimed, 'This will I protect against all opposers!' The match commenced, and he fenced with several of the first masters, not one of whom could disturb a single leaf of the bouquet."

Signor Domenico at last began to find that the life of a gentleman at large in Paris was something beyond his means, so he decided to try his fortune in England, whither his fame had preceded him, and where he was cordially received by many eminent people. Shortly afterwards he married an English lady, and settled down permanently in this country. He adopted at first the *manége* as his profession, and does not seem to have included in it the art of fencing until some time later, although in 1758, having been introduced

Parry of Tierce and disarm by seizure, after Angelo.

to the Princess Dowager of Wales, he was induced to undertake the tuition of the young Princes both in riding and swordsmanship.

His long, sentence-like string of Italian names he found not a little inconvenient among his new friends, most of whom were innocent of any knowledge of the Italian language, so he let drop the Malevolti-Tremamondo altogether, and Anglicized himself into simple Mr. Dominick Angelo.

Only a few months after his arrival he was taken under the patronage of the Earl of Pembroke, who ever afterwards treated him as a personal friend, and never as a dependent. The Earl possessed fine riding-houses both in London and at his seat in the country.

"My father," says his son Henry, "had endeavoured to introduce a new and superior method of riding in the English cavalry. This was a favourite object with him, even to a late period of life—one, indeed, which was recommended by some of the first military characters of the age to the attention of the Government, which, though admitting its utility, never could be persuaded to adopt it. This, I may be permitted to remark, is the more extraordinary, as my father had made several experiments by selecting certain men from two or more cavalry regiments, whom he instructed gratuitously, and whose superior skill in the management of the horse, consequently, was sufficiently manifest to procure them applause from every master of equitation in the kingdom.

"It was at the Earl's *manége* at Wilton that my father commenced his instructions for this purpose, and amongst the most active men selected from Elliot's regiment was old Philip Astley, who afterwards became so celebrated for his horsemanship at his own amphitheatre.

"My father's celebrity in the *manége* was scarcely less spread than the fame of his skill in the exercise of the sword, though he had hitherto only practised fencing as an amateur. On his return to London with his patron and friend, the Earl of Pembroke, he received a card inviting him to a public trial of skill with Dr. Keys, reputed the most expert fencer in Ireland. The challenge being accepted, the Thatched House Tavern was appointed for the scene of action, where my father attended at the time prescribed—two o'clock—though he had been riding the whole morning at Lord Pembroke's. His lordship, with his accustomed condescension, walked into the apartment arm-in-arm with his friend and protégé. My father was not prepared, however, for such an assemblage, many ladies of rank and fashion as well as noblemen and gentlemen being present, and he, expecting only to meet with gentlemen, was in his riding dress and in boots.

"My father, who had never seen his antagonist until this moment, was rather surprised at the doctor's appearance, he being a tall, athletic figure, wearing a huge wig, without his coat and waistcoat, his shirt-sleeves tucked up, exposing a pair of brawny arms sufficient to cope in the ring with Broughton or Slack; and thus equipped, with foil in hand, he was pacing the apartment.

"The spectators being all assembled, after the first salutation of the doctor, which was sufficiently frank and open, previous to the assault he took a bumper of cogniac, and offered another to my father, which he politely refused, not being accustomed to so ardent a provocative.

"The doctor, having thus spirited himself for the attack, began with that violence and determined method which soon discovered to those who were skilled in the science that, in the true sense of the term used by the French, he was no better than a *tirailleur, jeu de soldat*—anglicized, 'a poker.'

"My father, to indulge him in his mode of assault, for some time solely defended himself against his repeated attacks without receiving one hit, for, as the brandy operated, a *coup d'hasard* in the doctor's favour would only have encouraged him the more. Hence,

Parry of Prime and disarm by seizure, after Angelo.

allowing his opponent to exhaust himself, and my father having sufficiently manifested his superior skill in the science by thus acting on the defensive with all the elegance and grace of attitude for which he was renowned, after having planted a dozen palpable hits on the breast of his enraged antagonist, he made his bow to the ladies, and retired amidst the plaudits of the spectators.

"It was soon after this public display of his superior science that the elder Angelo, urged by his friends, first commenced teacher of the science of fencing. Indeed, the splendid offers which were made him were too tempting for a person in his state of dependence to refuse. His noble patron, though desirous of retaining his valuable services, yet with that generous spirit which marked all his actions, advised my father to accept the offers that were pressing upon him. This at once settled his future fortune, and his first scholar was the late Duke of Devonshire."

Henry Angelo, born in 1755, the second of the house, seems not to have been originally intended by his father for the profession he himself followed, although his success in it had been phenomenal (at the zenith of his career he was said to be making a good four thousand a year), but rather to be something of the fine gentleman. Accordingly he was sent to Eton, and in 1772, when he reached the age of seventeen, in order to study French, to Paris, where he was placed *en pension* with a M. Boileau, a stingy old rascal who half starved him until, "having imbibed the national notion that one Briton is worth half a dozen French," he seized monsieur by the collar, and gave him such a shaking that he put matters on a better footing for the rest of the quarter, at the end of which he was received into the family of a very different sort of person, M. Liviez, who had been at one time ballet-master at Drury Lane Theatre, and had married an English wife. This worthy man was as much addicted to self-indulgence as old Boileau was to the reverse, so that under his roof young Angelo fared sumptuously.

As regards his fencing, he must have already been well grounded in that art by his father, and, the elder Angelo having at last decided to bring up his son to the profession of arms, he was placed in the hands of M. Mottet, one of the first masters in Europe. "Much more attached," says the son, "to this exercise than to my books, I made a rapid progress in the science of attack and defence, to which circumstance I more than once owed my life, and in that period of boyish rashness acquired momentary fame.

"At this time every person having the least pretensions to gentility wore his sword. At Paris few youngsters who ventured out at night, or frequented any of the places of public entertainment, escaped one of those rencontres, wherein swords were point to point as readily as fist opposed to fist in London streets. I had the ill-luck to get into many a scrape; though, to balance the account in my favour, I had the good luck to get out of them again without the slightest damnification. Indeed, the only accident that befell my person, during my two years' residence in that gay city, happened as I was amusing myself in fencing, without a mask, with Lord Mazarene, when I swallowed some inches, button and all, of my noble opponent's foil.

"My first rencontre, which was with a French officer, happened at one of the fairs, of which two were annually held at Paris: that of the summer, Foire St. Ovid; that of the winter, Foire St. Germain. The playhouse there was entitled L'Ambigu Comique.

"One evening, whilst at this theatre, and standing up between the acts, a military officer near me, notorious for quarrelling, trod on my toe. Supposing it might be accidental, I took no other notice than by gently withdrawing my foot. He, however, contrived to tread on that tender part again. Perceiving now that he intended it as an insult, I beckoned him out, left the box, and he followed. We retired up a narrow street, arrived at a cul-de-sac, and, drawing, began the contest, which had lasted but a short space when two officers of police, attired in blue and red with silver lace, interposed. One seized my antagonist, the other conducted me home, where, M. Liviez making himself responsible for my appearance, I was permitted to remain, after engaging to appear at the police office on the following morning.

"Little evidence on my part was necessary; these officers, being of the *corps d'espion*, saw what had passed at the theatre, and, having followed us, took the said quarrelsome hero into custody. He was a desperate character, a public annoyance, indeed, and was punished for the assault."

On his return to England Henry Angelo was received as a master in his father's school, then established at the Opera-house in the Haymarket. This theatre was burned down in 1789, whereupon they set themselves up in those rooms in St. James's Street which they and their successors occupied for nearly a century. Old Dominick lived to a very advanced age; his son Henry married, and had certainly two sons, the elder of whom received a commission as Colonel in the army, and an appointment in connection with the supervision of that above-mentioned sword exercise which he was the means of introducing. The younger brother, William Angelo, whom we remember as a little old man, with his right hand so injured by an accident that he was obliged to have his foil strapped to his fencing-glove, taught regularly in the school. Henry Angelo died in the forties of the last century at the age of ninety, and his grandson, also named Henry, preserved the high credit of the house until his death in 1864.

There was now no scion left of the Angelo stock, but the conduct of the school of arms, under its old name, was undertaken by the famous William MacTurk, who had been for some years their senior assistant. He was in every way a gentleman of the old school,

17

now, alas! quite extinct. Courtly in manner and kindly in disposition, he was undoubtedly the finest all-round swordsman that this country has ever produced, and the present author owes to the superb teaching of that splendid master all that he knows of real value in the art of swordsmanship.

MacTurk died in 1888 at the mature age of seventy, and with him departed the glory of the illustrious old house. But the name of Angelo will survive in history.

BOOK IV

THE PRIZE-PLAYERS AND THE PRIZE-FIGHTERS

CHAPTER XXV

The Prizes and their Players.

THE prize-player must not be confounded with the prize-fighter. The two did not co-exist; the hundred years during which the prize-player flourished had ended before the hundred years (for they both lasted about the same time) of the prize-fighter commenced.

As we have before remarked, in the days of chivalry the art of fencing was confined to the lower orders; hence, the men who practised and taught what of art there was in it were of a very rough stamp indeed, and were ready to make use of any unseemly trick to get the better of an opponent, whether in play or in earnest; the exuberance of their spirits required curbing.

Where there is a demand there is sure soon to be a supply. Accordingly, in the reign of Henry VIII. we find the most respectable men of the profession organizing themselves into a corporate body, with distinct rules for the maintenance of fair play and decent behaviour, and as a punishment for the breach of these rules they agreed upon a system of fines and other penalties as under:

17—2

"It Is Agreed gennerally by & betweene every of vs the saide m^{rs} of the noble Science of Defence eche to the other, That if any one or twoe or more of vs doe breake any of the Orders and Constitutions whatsoever belonging to o^{r} Scyence, That then he or they of vs or any of vs so offending shall be fyned by the rest of vs the saide m^{rs} as in o^{r} discrecōns according to the breache shall fyne him or them, And he or they so being fyned not to sit in Judgem^{t} till the saide fyne & eūy ꝑte thereof be satisfied or payed, neither he or they shall receyve any dutyes wch belongh to a m^{r} till the same be payed as aforesaide."

Whether or no the "Maisters of the Noble Science of Defense" received an actual charter from King Henry is undecided, no such document having so far been discovered; but that he recognised them as an authoritative body is proved by a document containing a grant in 1540 to—

"Ric. Beste, Humph. Bassett, Rob. Polnorth, John Legge, Peter Beste, Philip Williams, Ric. Lord, John Vincent, Nic. de la Hage, masters of the "Science of Defence," and Will. Hunt, John Frye, Hen. Whytehed, Gilbert Beckett, Edw. Pynner, Thos Towner, Jeffrey Gryffyn, Thos Hudson, Thos Tymsey, Hen. Thyklyppes, & Johnap Ryce, provosts of the same science. Commission to enquire & search, in all parts of England, Wales, & Ireland, for persons being scholars of the said science of defence many of whom (regardless of their oaths made to their masters on first entering to learn the said science, upon the cross of a sword in remembrance of the Cross whereon Our Lord suffered) have for their own lucre of their 'unsociable covetous minds,' without sufficient license, resorted to all parts of England, keeping open schools, and taking great sums of money for their labours, & yet have insufficiently instructed their scholars, to the great slander of the masters and provosts of the science, and of the good and laudable orders and rules of the same, and to take any scholar so misusing himself before the nearest justice of the peace to be bound in sufficient sureties not to repeat his offences against his said oath and the said orders & rules, or in case of refusal to be committed to gaol. Westm. 20 July, 32 Hen. VIII."

In the Sloane MSS. at the British Museum there exists a most interesting book compiled in the reign of Queen Elizabeth, containing a record of this Association of Masters, with its rules, the oaths of fealty required from its various members, notes of prizes played by them, and many other details. For access to this book, and for much other valuable assistance, I am indebted to my friend Mr. G. T. Longley, of the MSS. Department.

The association consisted of, first, the "Scholler," an absolute beginner who was on his probation, and did not as yet rank as a member; next, the "Free Scholler," the junior grade; then the "Provost," or assistant master; and, lastly, the "Maister." From the "Maisters" was chosen the governing body, known as "The Four Ancient Maisters of the Noble Science of Defense."

To become a member of the association, the simple "Scholler" had to pass an examination, which usually took place in one of the schools kept by the "Maisters." This consisted of bouts at certain weapons, in which he had to encounter a given number of young men who had already passed that ordeal. It was known as "Playing his Prize"; it was, in fact, his matriculation, and when successful he was received as a "Free Scholler."

An order of the governing body touching costs, etc.

"Yf anny Prouost doth dwell within twentye myles of the Citye of London wheare all prizes oughte to be playd, then he oughte to beare his owne costs and Charges but if he Dwell more then Twentye myles distant from London Then the Prizor oughte to beare the one halfe of his Charges And so oughte everye maister in like manner at a maisters Prize // ALLSO EUERY maister oughte to be thear to play with the prizor, excepte onely his owne maister whome he playeth vnder / every provost and freescholler oughte to be thear to make rome as they shall be apoyncted by the maisters / And the youngest maister oughte to begine firste / and so in order / And at anny priz Whether it be maisters priz Provosts priz or freschollers priz who soever dothe play agaynste y[e] prizor, and doth strike his blowe and close withall so that the prizor cannot strike his blow after agayne, shall wynn no game for anny veneye [*bout*] so geven althoughe it shold breake the Prizors head.

"GOD SAUE THE QUEENE."

"The ruills and constitucons of the schole.

"OUR soveraigne Lady Elizabeth by the grace of god Quene of Englande ffranc and Irelande Defendor of the faithe and supreme hed (vnder God) of the church of Englande and Irelande &c of her moste ryall and abowndant grace hath licensed eṽy maister and Provost beinge Englishe men as well within this realme of Englande Irelande and Calleis and the precincts of the same to kepe and teache in their scholes all manner of estats gentilmen ore yomen of what estate so eṽ he or they be w[ch] ar willinge to learne the noble sciense of defence as playinge wth the two hande sworde the Pike, the bastarde sworde, the dagger, the Backe sworde, the sworde and Buckeler and the staffe, and all other manner of weapons apperteyninge to the same scienc / yf their be anny of them willinge to learne the same sciense To thentent that they and every of them beinge schollers of this present schole may knowe the ruills constitutions and ordenancies thearof I Willyam Mucklowe beinge one of the maisters of the same scienc proved and alowed accordinge to order have caused this present table to be written That they may soe heare and reade the same ruills constitucons and ordinanceis of this present schole in manēr & forme as hereafter folleth FIRSTE every scholler of what estate or degree soever he or they be shalbe at an agreement with the saide maister or his Deputye of and for soch weapon or weapons as the same scholler or schollers shall be willinge to learne And that donne the same scholler or schollers shal sweare by the crosse of his sworde or weapon, wch crosse signifieth and betokeneth the crosse which our Saviour Jesus Christe suffered his death vpon / and for the gevinge of his othe he muste pay xij^d vnto his maister and for his entrance iiijd And the same scholler shall paye for his learninge accordinge as his maister and he canne agree And for what soever that he dothe agre the sayde scholler shall pay in hande the one halfe / that is to say, yf he make his bargayne for xl^s then he muste pay in hande xx^s / yf he make his bargayne for xxx^s then he muste pay in hande xv^s and so as the maister and the scholler doth agree / to paye the one halfe in hande and the other when he is taken out of his quarters AND also the same scholler muste bringe his weapons / or ells to agree wth his maister or his maisters Deputye for them."

"The Order for playinge of a Schollers Prize.

"FIRST THAT EUERY Scholler at his first entrye to playe a priz shall geve his owne maister (wch he is sworne vnto) knowledge of his mynde what he doth intend to do as touchinge his priz / And then his maister to let the other anchiant maisters vnderstand his schollers pretence concerninge his sayde priz And vppon the agrement and conclusion of the sayd maisters, the sayd scholler shalbe content in anny schole or other place whearesoever the sayd anchiant maisters shall appoyncte, to play wth vj schollers at the leste at the longe sword and backe sword for a tryall or profe, to se whether he be hable to goe forwards in his priz, or not, And so if they fyend him hable and sufficient in that behalfe / That then as the sayd anchiant maisters shall agree and conclude to appoyncte and set his daye when he shall playe his priz, and when that daye is come / the sayde scholler shall at the longe sworde play with so manye schollers as will playe with him that Daye And the nexte daye w[ch] shall be appoyncted, to playe at his other weapon with so manye schollers as will play that daye according as the sayd anchient maisters will permit and suffer him / AND SO to stand and agree vnto all manner of orders constitutions and agreements which the sayd ffour anchiant maisters will that he should observe and keepe And farther to pay all orders and duetyes w[ch] belongith to soche a scholler / MORE OUER the sayde scholler after he hathe playd his schollers priz and is admitted a free scholler by the maisters / shall not at anny tyme within the space of seven years after his sayd admittance attempte or endevor to speake vnto anny maister or maisters concerninge anny other priz vntill the sayde seven yeares shall be fully expyred And then if he be mynded to play his Provost priz / to do as hearafter followeth.

"VIUAT REGINA."

The manuscript contains "A Note of all the Free Schollers," how they played their prizes, and with what arms. It would seem that the "scholler" (or beginner) was only compelled to engage at two weapons, which were very generally the two-hand sword and that typically English set, the sword and buckler. A few instances of these "Notes" may interest the reader :

"GREGORYE GREENE playde his schollers priz at Chensforde in Essex vnder Richard Donne at two weapons / the two hand sworde and backe sworde with viij at two hand sword and vij at backe sworde / he playd the xviij[th] of Aprill.

"JOHN GRENE playd his schollers priz at the Bull wthin Bishopps gate at ij weapons the longe sword and staffe Thear playd certeyn schollers wth him at both weapons He playde vnder Richard Smyth the second of Julye.

"EDWARD HARVYE playde his schollers priz at the Bull within Bishopps gate at ij weapons, the two hande sworde and the sword and buckeler Thear playde with him xiiij at the two hand sworde at xxviij at sworde and buckeler / with two free schollers called Rayson, and ffrauncies Caverly / the xxviij of January vnder Richard Smyth.

"WILLIAM MATHEW playde his schollers priz at the Bull within Bishopps gate at two kynd of weapons the two hand sword and the backe sworde. Theare playd wth him xij at the two hand sword and xvj at the backe sworde / and one fre scholler whose name was ffrancies Calverly / The vjth of maye and so was admitted free scholler vnder Willyam Thompson als Glover.

"ROGER HORNE playde his schollers priz at Oxforde at ij kinde of weapons that is to saye the two hand sword and the sword and buckeler Thear playde with him five at the two hand sword and viij at the sworde and buckeler with iiij free schollers That is to say John Blinkinsopps ffrauncies Caverly Edward Harvie and Willyam Mathewe / the 25 day of May and so was admitted vnder Willyam Mucklow maister.

"THOMAS NOBLE playde his schollers prize at the Bull within Bishoppsgate the ixth day of ffebruary at two weapons That is to say the longe sword and the sworde and buckeler.thear playd with him at longe sworde x / and two fre schollers / at the sword and buckeler xxij bysids the ij fre schollers whose names weare Willyam Mathew wch playd at both weapons and John Grene who playd at longe sword & no more And so the sayde Thomas Noble was admittet vnder Gregory Greene m^{r} / 1578.

"ROBERT BLISSE playd his schollers priz at the Bull in Bishopps gate th fiveth day of Juyn at two kynde of weapons That is to say the two hand sworde and the sworde and buckeler Thear playde with him three at the two hand sworde and 16 at the sworde and buckeler And three fre schollers at both weapons That is to saye John Harris Valentyn Longe and John Dawell and so the said Robert Blisse was admitted a fre scholler vnder Richard Smyth m^{r}—1581 /.

"GEORGE MUCKLOWE did agree wth the maisters and so was admitted a free scholler vnder Gregorye Greene m^{r} th vjth day of december 1591 /.

"JOHN BLINKENSOPPS playde his schollers priz vnder Willyam Glover at Burntwode in Essex at iij weapons the longe sworde, the backe sworde, and sword and buckeler and thear playde with him x at longe sworde xij at backe sworde and xviij at sworde and buckeler But he was not admitted, by cause of misdemenōr by him committed and for want of his games wch weare not in place / He was allowed a fre scholler the Tenth of Juyn at the Kings hed at Pye corner by Wm Joynor Ric : Donne Ric : Smythe and W : Mucklow."

"The Order of a Provost's Prize.

"IMPRIMIS THAT every free scholler which is mynded to proceede to anny other degree of the noble scyenc of Defence, to be a provoste, shall first desyer his owne maisters goodwill / And then his maister and he together shall goe to the four anchiant maisters and informe them of his Provosts priz and that he is willing to play it AND yf it chance that the free schollers maister whom he was sworne vnto be dceased, that then the sayde free scholler shall chose for his m^{r} one of ~~one~~ ~~of~~ [*sic*] the ancient maisters to play his Provosts priz vnder which he hath moste mynd vnto And shall be sworne to him as he was to his first maister in all poyncts / And accordinge as the four ancient maisters shall agree together and conclude of the matter so he to goe forward with his provosts priz, so that he be contented to abyde all manner of orders wch the ancient maysters will that he shold kepe, and to make them an obligacōn of the same and to sett to his hand and Seall as the maysters will that he shold do in all poyncts / In so doinge the four ancyent maisters to appoyncte his daye, and when he shall playe his Provosts priz / And he to playe at the two hand sword, the backe sword, and staffe with all manner of Provosts which do come into that place to play with him And allso the sayd free scholler shall at his owne proper Costs go and geve warning to all the Provosts which ar within three score myles of the place wheare he is appoynctd to play his Provosts prize That they may come to his priz wheare he doth play it, and so to play with him, and every Provost wch is within thre score myles that hath no warninge to come to his prizes the sayd free scholler shall pay to the ancient maisters fyve shillings of lawfull mony of England And yf theire be no Provost to play with him And for to geve them iiij weickes warning at the leaste before the Day become which the maisters have sett him And as many Provosts as do dwell farther then Twentye myles That then the free scholler shall paye the one halfe of thear Charges Thus doinge when the appoyncted day is come to proceede in his sayd priz And to make his Provosts Lcē [license], payinge to the four ancient maisters for seallinge thearof after the rate wch is set amongst them with all manner of other Duetyes belonginge to them And more over he to be bownd to the iiij ancient maisters not to keepe anny scholle within the space of seven myles of anny maister, without speciall leave of the sayd four ancient maisters And allso to be bound in his sayd obligacōn not to teach anny scholler this noble scyenc of defenc xcepte he doth sweare him vnto his owne maister, whom he was sworne himselfe And farther he be bownd to pay vnto his sayd maister (to whom he is sworne) for every scholler w[ch] he shall teache, x to pay xijd And so in lik wyes to the most anciet mayster of the four syd And to yeald vp his true accoumpt onc in every quarter of a yeare AND ALLSO yf he Dwell with in the space of thre skore myles wheare anny Provosts priz is or shall be playde havinge warning or knowledge thearof Then to come and play at the same priz without anny Lett vppon payne of payinge vj[s] viij[d] vnto the fower ancient maisters / except he be sicke in bodye or other wyes busied in the Queens affayers AND FINALLYE he to be bound in his obligacōn aforesayd vnto the four ancient maisters, to kepe and performe all that is above sayd Allso he shall not loke to play his maisters priz within vij yeares after his provosts priz n[r] to vsurp or grudge agaynst anny m[r] of y[e] same scienc Thus doing he is to have his Provosts Lcē sealled by the iiij ancient maisters And then to give him his provosts shipp & all things belonginge thear vnto.

"*Vingo manet nostri gloria sola soli.*"

Notes on the Provosts' Prizes.

The "Free Scholler," for his promotion, seems usually to have encountered a certain number (decided by the examiners) of provosts, and also of young men of his own rank, with three kinds of weapons.

It would appear that the playing of the prize was sometimes dispensed with, as we find instances of the candidate agreeing with the "Maisters."

The Provosts' Prizes were played in public, usually at some tavern or place of amusement, the most popular of which were the "Bull" in Bishopsgate, the "Bellsavage" at Ludgate, and the "Theatre" and the "Curteyn" in Holywell.

"John Goodwyne did agree with the maisters to playe his provosts priz wth in a schole at the longe sword, backe sword, sword and buckeler, and staffe / at the Tower Ryall, with two provosts Willyam Muckelow, and Richard Smythe and so was made a provost at . . . . . . he playd his schollers prize at safferne walden in Essex at two weapons the longe sword and the backe sword / with nyne at longe sword and twelve at backe sword / vnder William Glover.

"John Evanes als Gerkinmaker playd his provosts prize in Hartford vnder Willyam Glover als Thompson at thre weapons the longe sword, the backe sword and the sword and buckeler / with two provosts, Willyam mucklowe and Richard Smythe / He playd his schollers prize att Baldocke in Hartford shire at two weapons / vidz with seven at the longe sword, and six at sword and buckeler.

"Izake Kennard playd his provosts priz at the Bull within Bishopps gate the vijth of June at thre weapons, the longe sword, the sword and buckeler, and the staffe / Ther playd wth him two free schollers for want of Provosts / Willyam Wilks / and ffrancis Calverte / vnder Richarde Smyth in anno dñi / 1575 /

"Gregorie Grene playd his provosts priz the fivetenth daye of October at the Bull within Bishopps gate at thre weapons the longe sword, the backe sword, and the sword and buckeler Ther playde with him two provosts / Izake Kennard and Willyam Wilks Izake had a sore hand and so he playd but twyce at longe sword / And so the sayd Gregorie was made provoste vnder Willyam Muckelow.

"John Blinkinsopps playd his provosts priz the nyneth daye of June at the Bull within Bishoppsgate at thre weapons the longe sword, the backe sword, and the staffe There playd with him John Goodwyne a provost and ffrancis Calverte a fre scholler, which had a provosts licence for that tyme And so John

Blinkinsopps was made provoste vnder Willyam Thompson als Glover.

"Edward Harvie playd his provosts priz the five and twentith daye of August at the Theatour at thre weapons the two hand sword the backe sword and the sword and buckeler There playd with him one Provoste whose name is John Blinkinsopp / And one fre scholler called by name ffrauncies Calvert who had a Provosts lysence for that tyme And so the sayd Edward Harvye was made a provoste vnder Richard Smythe maister / 1578 /

"Thomas Pratt did agre with the maisters And was made Provost the seventh daye of Juyne vnder Gregorye Greene / maister / 1582 /

"Roberte Blisse playde his Provosts prize at the Theator in Holiwell the firste day of Julye at thre weapons / the longe sword the backe sworde and the sword and buckeler Their playde with him thre Provosts vidz Alexander Reyson, Thomas Prat and Valentyne Longe And so the sayd Robert Blisse was admitted Provoste vnder Richard Smyth / 1582 /

"Vallentyne Longe playde his provosts priz at the Courten in Holiwell the fiveth daye of August at thre weapons the longe sworde, the backe sword and the sworde and buckeler Theire playd with him two Provosts vidz Roberte Blisse and Androwe Bello; And John Dewell who had a Provosts licence for that tyme And so the sayd Valentyne Longe was admitted provost vnder Gregorye Grene / m^r^ / 1582 /

"John Dewell playd h[is] challenge at the Theator in Holiwell agaynste all Provosts and free schollers at thre weapons, the longe sword, the sword and buckeler and the sword and dagger Their playd with him Thomas Pratt, Roberte Blisse & Androw Bello Provosts Valentyne Longe John Harris Willyam Otte, and George Muckelowe free schollers And the sayde John Dewell was not admitted Provoste at that tyme for his disorder But he was alowed provoste by the goodwills of the maysters the Tenth day of Auguste vnder Willyam Joyner / 1582 /"

"The Provosts Othe.

"1. INP'MIS YOU shall sweare so helpe you God and halidome and by the christendome wch god gave you at the fount stone and by the Crosse of this sworde whiche dothe represent vnto you the crosse wch our saviour Jesus Christe did suffer his moste paynefull deathe and passion vppon for our redemption / That you shall vpholde mayntayne and kepe to you^r^ power all soch articles as shalbe declared vnto you by me beinge your maister in the presenc of theis my bretheren and maisters hear / wch you intend to procede vnto.

"2. ITEM you shall be true to the Catholike churche to augment and farther the true faythe of God to your power as all true Christians ought to do.

"3. ITEM you shalbe true subiecte tour soveraigne Ladye Quene Elizabethe and to her successors kings of this realme of Englande and not to knowe of anny treason but that you vtter it w^th^in four and twentie howers at the farthest, & soner yf you canne and to serve her and hers agaynst all nations to the vttermoste of your power.

"4. ITEM you shalbe true provoste from this daye vnto the last daye of your life to love and serve the trueth and hate falshode, never to rebell or go agaynste anny m^r^ or provost of this scienc, allways to be ruelled by me your m^r^ of this scienc, as all provosts ought to be ruelled by their owne maister and the rest of the maisters his bretheren, as other Provosts have donne heartofore, accordinge to the ancient orders of our scienc.

"5. ITEM YOU shall sweare not to teache anny suspecte person as a murtherer, a thefe, a common drunkarde or soch as be common quarellers but to avoyde your hands of them, and to kepe no companye with them so nigh as you canne.

"6. ITEM you shall not teache anny person whatsoever he or they be without you do sweare him with soche alike othe as your maister and other maisters my bretheren shall assigne you and no other othe but the verye same.

"7. ITEM you shall not challenge anny m^{r} or compare with anny m^{r} as to disprayese his doings / and especially you shall not compare with me your maister / vnder whome you do now procede / and of whome you have had your Cunninge / nether in Challendge or with approbrius words as touchinge our scienc in anny wyes.

"8. ITEM that at anny priz or game which you shalbe at ether to stick or to stande by you shall saye the trueth of that wch you shall see when you be asked or called to speake, and not ells yf there be anny maister in place, or anny ꝑvost beinge your elder and ancient / And when you shalbe so asked or demaunded you shall geve true Judgement of that which you have seene so nighe as you canne, settinge all affections aparte and rightely to Judge without fraud or guyle even as you woulde be Judged of God / helpinge them to that wch they have wone so nighe as you canne or maye by your good will.

"9. ITEM you shalbe alwayes mercifull and whearas it maye happen you to have the vpper hande of your enimye That is to saye vnder your feete or without weapon or some other advantage you shall not kill him, yf he be the Queenes true subiecte, savinge your selfe without danger of deathe or bodeley hurte accordinge to your first othe wch you Receved entringe to learne the scienc.

"10. ITEM you shall not make anny vsher without the licenc of your maister, but for neade you may have a deputie / wch shall not geve anny other othe but this That is to saye / yf you be absent he may take in soch as wilbe schollers sayinge to them thus / YOU shall sweare so help you God and holydome and by the crosse of this sworde that you shalbe content to receave soch an othe as my m^{r} or his ꝑvost shall geve vnto you at your next metinge together / And so to take him scholler and geve him his first lesson.

"11. ITEM you shall not entice or trayne anny other maisters scholler to teache or cause him to be taughte without the goodwill of his first maister Excepte the sayd scholler have well and truelye contented and payde his fore saide maister his full duetye And furthermore you shall kepe or cause to be kepte our orders ruills and constitutions in all prizes as we have partely / declared vnto you / and shall more at large hearafter as you shall farther procede in the scienc of defence.

"12. ITEM you shall sweare to kepe this Provosts othe in all poyncts nowe geven and declared vnto you by me beinge your maister in the precense of theis my bretheren / and maisters of this scienc so helpe you God and your holydome."

"A Prouosts Letter.

"BE IT KNOWNE vnto all manner of officers vnder the Dominions of our soveraigne Ladye Elizabethe by the grace of God of England ffranc and Ireland Quene Defendor of the faith &c // as Justices of peace maiors sheriffs Bailiffs Cunstables Hedborowes and other her ma^{ts} lovinge subiects Certifieng you by this lc̄ē That it pleaseth our saide moste dreade soveraigne Lady the quenes ma^{tie} wth her moste honorable privie Counsel to admitt wth. authoritie and by especiall commission vnder her highnes greate Seale to geve licenc to vs maisters of Defenc playinge wth all manner of weapons vsuall to admit and allowe all soch maisters and Provosts to instruct and teach and have experienc and counninge sufficient by profe and triall and before vs the saide maisters of the same scienc or the moste of vs openly wth warninge geven to all schollers by bills set vp within the citie of London fourtene dayes and then playinge their prizes wth so manye schollers as will playe that daye / and after that prize so Discharged to challendge for his Provosts prize by bills set vp xxj dayes, all Provosts And so to abide the triall of so many Provosts as will also play that daye Thus doinge openly within the citie of London before vs the ancient maisters of the saide scienc with all other Duetyes wch to a Provoste do belonge THEN we, Richarde White Thomas Weaver, Willyam Hearne, Willyam Glover als Thompson, Willyam Joyner, Henrye Naylor, Richard Donne and Edmond Darcye being all maisters of the same scienc dwellinge wthin the citie of London Do admitt Willyam Mucklowe as a Provost vnder Thomas Weaver Maister of our saide scienc the xiijth day of Juyne in the yeare of our Lorde God 1568 in the xth yeare of the raigne of our soveraigne Ladie the Quenes Matie for as much as the saide Willyam Mucklowe did play his Provosts priz within the Citie of London the day and yeare abovewritten And before vs the maisters of the said scienc We thearfore do by theis p̃nts admitt the saide Willm̄ Mucklow to instructe and teach wthin the Quenes ma^{tis} Dominions as an hable and well tried man with diverse weapons as, the Longesworde, the backsworde the rapier and dagger and the staffe AND thearfor we beinge Maisters admitted by the Queenes moste excellent Matie and her honorable Counsell as aforesaide, do praye and desyer all her highnes officers and true subiects to ayde the saide Willyam Mucklow agaynst all strayngers and soch as take vppon them to teach without authoritie wilfully forswearinge them selves / wch have a longe tyme deceaved her Ma^{ts} lovinge subiects Whearfore we the saide Maisters Thomas Weaver, Willyam Hearne, Willm̄ Glover Willm̄ Joyner, Henry Naylor, Richard Donne and Edmond Darcye desyer all her highnes officers as they love God and our soveraigne Ladye the queenes Matie to suffer none to teach or kepe anny schole of Defence whatsoever he or they be excepte he or they have authoritie to shew in like case as this Provost hath Thus doinge you shall shewe your selfes true and faythfull subiects and officers vnto our moste dreade soveraigne Lady the Quenes Matie Thankes be geven to God for maynteyninge of the truethe IN WITNES whearof &c."

"The Order for Playinge of a Maisters Prize.

"WHEN ANNY PROUOST is mynded to take the degree of a m^{r} That is, to play a maisters priz, he shall first declare his mynd vnto his m^{r}, vnder whom he playd his Provosts priz, yf he be livinge / and yf he be ded then shall he chuse for his maister one of the four ancient maisters, to play his priz vnder, whom he liketh best And shall be sworne vnto him, as he was to his first maister And then shall he desyer his maisters favor for the playinge of his sayd maisters priz and so to crave the good Wills of all the ancient maisters of the noble scienc of Defenc And accordinge as the ancient maisters do agree in that cause, he to procede in his sayd priz SO THAT he will be content to agree vnto them, and to all their orders and ruills accordinge as they have amongste them And never survince or invent by anny kynd of meanes to put anny maister of that noble scienc to anny displeasure or hinderanc, but shall be contented to fulfill all their constitucōns orders and ruills to the vttermost of his power, And shall byend himselfe in an obligacōn to the iiij ancient m^{rs} for performanc therof AND so doinge the sayd maisters shall appoynct him his day, wheare he shall play his maisters priz / at theis weapons followinge vidz the two hand sword, the Basterd sword, the pike, the backe sword, and the rapier and Dagger And then the sayd provost, to gev warninge to so many maisters as dwell within xl myles of the place appoyncted for his priz, eight weikes at the lest, before the day cometh to play his priz AND WHEN he hath playd his maisters priz he then to mak his maisters Lc̄ē and pay for th sealling of it to thancient maisters, wth all manner duetys to them belonging And so to byend him selfe in an obligacon to the sayd ancient maisters to fulfill all that is abovesayd and to set his hand and seall thearvnto Those done the four ancient maisters to gev him his maisters othe with all things that apperteyneth to the same."

"Notes of Maister's Prizes.

"Richarde White played his maisters priz at the graye ffriers wth in Nuegate at thre kinde of weapons, that is to say, the longe sworde, the Bastarde sword and the Backsworde with thre maisters, vidz Willyam Hunte, Peter Beste, and Willyam Browne, And he plaid his Provosts priz at Leaden Hall with two Provosts, that is to saye Edward Brytten and John Barsett at thre kinde of weapons vidz the longe sworde, the backesword, and the staffe. He plaide his Schollers priz at Leaden Hall with xxiij schollers at the backesword and at Hampton Courte wth xiiij at the longe sworde.

"Robert Edmonds played his maisters priz at the Whitehall before kinge Philipp and Quene Marie at thre kind of weapons that is to saye, the longe sworde, the backesworde and the staffe thear played agaynste him two maisters vidz Richard White and Thomas Weaver.

"Thomas Weaver was made maister by Kinge Edward the sixthe at Grenwitche.

"Izake Kennard came into the place to play his maisters priz at the Bull wth in Bishopps gate the one and twentith daye of Apprill at four kynde of weapons That is to saye the two hand sword the backe sworde the sword and buckeler and the rapier and dagger / ther playde with him thre maisters vidz Gregorie Grene Willyam Mucklowe and Willyam Joyner / The sayd Izake playde with the thre maisters at the longe sworde / and was stroken downe at the backe sworde by Willyam Muckelowe and so was dismiste for that tyme / The said Isake came the Mondaye after and playd the reste of his weapons, that is to saye the sword and buckeler and the rapier and dagger /. ther playde with him the thre maisters aforesayd vidz Gregorye Grene William Muckelowe and Willyam Joyner the 28 daye of Aprill and so the sayde Izake was, by entreatye made mayster vnder Rycharde Smyth mayster the Tenthe daye of Maye / 1598.

"John Blinkinsop playd his maisters prize the firste daye of June at the Artillerye garden at four kynde of weapons That is to saye the two hand sword the backe sword, the sword and buckeler and the staff Ther playd with him six maisters vidz Richard Peters / Anthonye ffenruther / Gregorie Grene Richard Smyth Richard Donne & Henrye Naylor An so the said Blinkinsop was admitted maister vnder Willyam Thompson maister / 1579 /.

"Franceis Calluert did agre wth the m^rs^ & so was mad m^r^ vnder Willyam Joyner maister / 1581 /

"Willyam Mathewes playd his maisters prize at Canterburye ye fiveth day of June at four kynde of weapons That is to saye the longe sworde the back sworde the sworde and buckeler and the rapier and dagger, ther playd wth him 8 maisters vidz ffranceis Calverte, John Blinkinsop John Goodwin Izake Kennard Gregorye Grene, John Evans Richard Smith and Henrye Naylor . And so was admitted m^r^ vnder Richard Peter / 1583 /

"Mr Paull Warren was aloweth a M^{r}. the 17. of october 1587 vnder Mr Rychyarde Pitter M^{r}.

"Mr Carlton was alowed a m^{r} the xxiijth of octobere vnder George Nayllore m^{r} 1587 ordenary grome off her majestes chamber.

"James Cranydge playd his Masters prize the 21 of Nowember 1587 at the bellsavage wth ovt Lvdgate at iiij sondry kinde of weapons that is to say the Long sword the Backsword the sword & Dagger and the Rapier and Dagger ther playd wth him 9 masters that is to saye Avndreve bellowe at ij weapons the Longe sword & the Backsword & no more & the other viij m^{rs} At all the weapons that is to say John Dawell Wallentine Longe Richard ffiecher Robard Blisse Wm Mathewes John Goodwyne Gregory Grēne Henry Naylor in the presents of ther Bretheren that is Wm Joynor John Evans pawlle Weran and Richard Carlton & so the sayd James Cranydge was allowed a m^{r} vnder Richard Carllton m^{r} of the Noble syence of Deffence, &c.

"John Mathewes playd his masters prise the 31 daye of Janvarie 1588 at the bell savege wth out lvdgate at iiii sondry kinde of weapons that is to saye the longe-sworde the backesworde the sworde and dagger and the Rapier and dagger there played wth him vii that is to saye James Cranydge John Dawell Wallentine Longe Richarde flether Robart blisse John Goodwyne and Gregorye Grine and in the presents of the reste of the masteres that is William Joyner his master masther Rycharde Petter William Mathewes Powlle Weran a Rycharde Carlton and so the sayde John Mathewes was allowed a master vnder Williame Joyner master of the noble syenes of deffence 1588."

"The maisters othe.

"1. FFIRST you shall sweare (so helpe you god and

halidome and by all the Christendome which God gave you at the fount stone and by the Crosse of this sworde which doth represent vnto you the Crosse w[ch] our saviour Jesus Christe suffered his most paynefull deathe vppon, That you shall vpholde maynteyne and kepe to your power all soch articles as shalbe heare declared vnto you and receved in the presenc of me your maister and theise the reste of the maisters my bretheren beinge psent hear with me at this tyme.

"2. ITEM you shalbe true to the Catholicke churche to augment and further the true faythe of Christe to your power as all true xpīans [*i.e.*, *Christians*] oughte to do of righte.

"3. ITEM you shalbe true subiecte to our soveraigne Ladye quene Elizabethe and to her successors Kings of this relme of England And not to know of anny ꝑson or persons committinge anny treason although it weare your owne father but that you vtter it within xxiiij howers or soner yf you canne / or yf it lye in your power / And alwayes to be ready to Spende bothe your lyfe and your goodes In the Sarvis of the quens majestye wher she shall Command yowe at all tymes agaynst her Enymyes /

"4. ITEM you shalbe true maister from this daye forward to the laste daye of your life, loving trueth, hatinge falcehod and not grudginge or disdeyninge anny maister of this scienc when you or anny of vs you shall not breake the ancient orders Excepte it be donne by the Consent of thre of the maisters for the better orderinge of our scienc And you alwayes to be rueled by your bretheren beinge maisters of this scienc, and especially yf anny maister be in place w[ch] is your ancient or elder.

"5. ITEM you shall not teache anny suspecte person, as a murtherer a thefe a common Drunkearde nor soch as you knowe to be common quarellers / nor to kepe company with them But to avoyde all soch so nighe as you canne A maisterlesse man you shall not mayn-teyne or succour within your schole yf you may knowe of him.

"6. ITEM yf it chance that you come to anny manner of priz or game or anny kynde of play at weapons touchinge our scienc, you shall without respecte favor or hatred of either partye, saye speake and geve true Judgement of that which you shall se theare Even as you would be Judged your selfe wth out respecte of either partye Declaringe the trueth and right so nigh as you can or maye.

"7. ITEM you shall take in no scholler to thentente to teache him or cause him to be taughte anny manner of weapon or weapons apperteyninge to the scienc except you geve him his right oth which belongeth to a scholler And to take for his learninge as other maisters do vse to take, not to take lesse the other maisters do, to spyte or to hinder any other maister of this scienc but to do as you woulde be donne to.

"8. ITEM you oughte not to challenge anny maister within this realme of Englande beinge an Englishe man / And especialy you shall not challenge your maister of whome you had your counninge and vnder whome you do procede and ar made maister AND farther vppon your maisters othe you shall well and truelye contente and paye yor maister for all soche manner of debts duetyes and demaunds which be dew betwyxte your maister and you And him to love and honor as your maister and your Ancient.

"9. ITEM you shalbe mercifull, And whearas you happen to have the vpper hande of your enimye That is to saie w^th^out weapon or vnder your feete or his backe towards you then you shall not kill him savinge your selfe harmlesse without daunger of death Excepte it be in the service of the prince: And also yf you heare of anny varyance betwyxt mr & mr / or mr and ꝓvost, or ꝓvost and provst or free scholler and free scholler you shall do the beste y[t] you can to make them frends And alwayes to kepe the peace yf you can.

"10. ITEM you shall ayde and strengthen to your power (yf you see them wrongede) and helpe all maisters and Provosts of this scienc, all widdowes and fatherles childeren / And yf you knowe anny maister of scienc that is fallen into sicknes being in povertye you shall put the maisters in rememberance at all prizes and games and other assemblies that they may se him to have duetye and to hav him in rememberanc the soner for your good worde / Even as other shall do for you yf the cause weare a like.

"11. ITEM you shall not sett forthe anny prize nor to kepe but one skolle in London within twelve moneths and a daye after the playinge of your maisters prize, nor teache or cause to be taughte anny other maisters scholler excepte you have the goodwill of his firste maister, without the saide scholler hath payde his first maister all his duetye for his learninge.

"12. ITEM you shall at no tyme set forwarde anny manner of provst or free schollers priz but that you firste calle the maisters together requieringe thear goodwills in that behalfe And with the consents of them havinge their goodwills to geve lawfull warn[i]ng as you shalbe instructed by the assents / wheare it shalbe playde, and what daye is appoyncted.

"13. ITEM you shall not for lucar sake set forwards anny priz of a m[r] provost or free scholler w[th]out a lawfull cause of him or them had and taken by you and at the leste ij maisters more besydes you[r] selfe, for vnto that you ar sworne And at anny prizes set forwarde by you and the consents of the maisters, you to see that everye maister and provost have his duetye w[ch] he oughte to have in the place for the prizes beinge accordinge to our ancient orders and ruills.

"14. Item you shall not promisse any person learninge, but that you do teach him or cause him to be taughte as a maister oughte of righte to do That is to saye, a scholler like a scholler a Provost like a Provost and a maister like a maister to the vttermoste of your power Entringe in his degrees without hidinge from them that which belongethe to them of righte Recevinge their othe and kepinge it truelye, soch ought to be taughte the effecte of our scienc, savinge the same which shall kepe the scienc out of Slander.

"15. Item you shall not cause anny othe to be geven in your name by anny person vnder the degre of a Provoste except it be your vsher wch is your deputie for that tyme so longe as his covenāt doth laste wth you / And he that you do appoynt in that rome ought to be knowne a sufficient hable and honest parson as well by the other maisters as by your selfe for that he is a Provost licensed during his covenant with you being placed in y^{t} rome.

"16. Item you shall not alowe or able anny Provosts licenc w^{th}out the consent of two maisters at the leste besydes your selfe And you shall not compact with anny person vnder couller or deceipte to kepe schole for you or in your name so that he or they shall have the proffit thearof and you beare the name by which meanes other maisters and Provosts wch stoode in place for it have their livings taken from them but you shall farther do your dilligenc and goodwill to the apprehendinge and puttinge downe of all soch as do take vppon them to teach without sufficient licenses or lawful authoritie to the great sclander and hinderance of our scienc."

"A Maisters Letter.

"Be it knowne vnto all men by this present writinge whearesoever it shall come to be read hearde or vnderstanded and especially to all manner of officers vnder the dominions of our soveraigne Ladye Elizabethe by the grace of God Quene of England ffranc and Irelande defendor of the faith and in earth (next vnder Christe) of the churche of England and also of Irelande the supreame hed / as Justices Maiors Sheriffs, Bayliffs Counstables Hedboroughs and to there Deputies, certifienge you by theis our letters. That it pleaseth our saide soveraigne Ladye the Quenes ma^tie^ with her moste honorable counsell to admitt with authoritie and by especiall Commission vnder her highnes broade Seall to geve licence vnto all vs beinge maisters of Defence playinge with all manner of weapons vsuall And also to admitt all soch to instructe and teach from henseforth, and to admitt all maisters and Provosts to teache havinge couninge sufficient and beinge experte, and tryed before the maisters of the saide scienc openly within the Cittye of London, geving all schollers warninge xiiij dayes And then to playe his prize with so many schollers as will come that daye And also he to challendge all Provosts gevinge them xxj dayes warning and thear to abyde the triall of so many Provosts as will playe that daye for his maisters priz And then playinge his priz with so many maisters as will playe Gevinge them a monethes warninge And thus doinge openly in London before all the maisters / with all dueties that belonge to a maister Then we the saide maisters R. W: T W: G. F. and, A R: beinge the four ancient maisters of the saide scienc of Defence within the Citye of London do admit E.B. maister of the saide scienc the ffive and twentithe daye of Maye in anno &c in so much as the saide E, did playe his priz with vs the saide maisters And we do also admit the saide E to teache and instructe in anny place within the Queenes dominions as an hable well tryed and sufficient man with divers weapons as the longe sworde &c And thearfore we the saide masters admitted by the Quenes ma^tie^ and her moste honorable Counsell, desyer all her hignes true subiects to ayde the said E. B: agaynst all strangers and soch as teach without authoritie, and soch forsworne men agaynste God and the Quenes ma^{tie} wch of longe tyme have deceaved her highnes true subiects whearfore we the saide R W. T W. G F and A R. beinge four ancient maisters of this scienc wthin the citie of London desier all her ma^{ties} true subiects and officers as they love god and our saide soveraigne Ladye / to suffer none to kepe anny schole of Defenc whatsoever he be excepte he have authoritie to shew in like case as this m^{r} E B hath In so doinge you shall shew your selves true & faith full officers & subiects vnto your power / thankes be geven to God for the maynteyninge of the trueth whearof we be maisters of defenc In witness whearof &c."

"*Hear followeth an Indenture of covenants made betwen the four anciant maisters of the noble scienc of Defenc within the Citye of London.*

"This Indenture made the last daye of October In the Therd yeare of the raigne of our soveraigne Lorde Kinge Edward the sixte by the grace of God &c Be twene Willyam Hunt on th one partye, R.G. on the second partie and W B. on the therd partie beinge ancient maisters of the noble scienc of Defence With in the citie of London Witneseth that the sayde parties have Covenanted condiscended and agreed together in manner and forme followinge That is to saye every of the same pties covenanteth and grantith to and with the other parties that neither of the saide parties shall from henceforth set forth anny of theire schollers prizes without the consent and agrement of all the sayd parties And allso that none of their schollers shall play his provosts priz within vij years after his schollers priz Allso the saide parties do likewyese covenaunte and graunt everye of them with the other that none of them shall permitt or suffer anny of their saide schollers after he hath playd his Provosts priz, to playe their maisters priz within five yeares after their

Provosts priz MOREOUER the same parties ar consented and agreed together That everye of them shall kepe one Boxe whearin they shall put for every scholler that he hath (or from hence forth shall have) ij[d] towards the mayntenance of necessaries belonginge to the saide science And every of them shall kepe a Juste and a true boke of the monye in the sayde boxes severally And every of the same parties shall bringe att two sundry tymes in the yeare, all the monye in theire sevall boxes gathered, To soch a place as the same maister * * * *" [ends *sic*]

This Association of Masters of Defence arrived at its zenith in the time of Queen Elizabeth, although so far we have been unable to discover the granting of a distinct charter even in her reign. In the following reign, that of James I., we find a trace, but that only, of the existence of the body. King James was not a person likely to regard with much favour an association of fighting men. Randle Holme, a most voluminous writer, a contemporary of Joseph Swetnam, gives a list of the weapons with which fencers fight their prizes, and the number of them was a goodly one :

Single sword, or back sword.
Sword and dagger.
ffiles, or *single rapier.*
Rapier, or ffile, and *punniard.*
Sword and *gauntlett*—that is, a left-hand arm gauntlett.
Sword and *buckler*, or targett.
ffauchion.
Two-handed sword.
Quarter-staff.
Halberts.
fflaile, or threshall.

CHAPTER XXVI

The "Gladiating" Prize-fighter.

WE are now in the days of the "Merry Monarch." During the troublesome times of the Civil War and the Puritanical ones of the Commonwealth that truly respectable body "The Association of Maisters of the Noble Science of Defense," together with its well regulated "Prizes," had died out, and its place was taken by a set of men, brave certainly, and skilful without doubt, who fought for prizes—not such as those of Elizabeth's time, which were played for promotion and good fame, but for a mere pecuniary stake, and, in addition, whatever coins might be thrown on to the stage to them by the public.

At this time the two-hand sword, the axe, and the long rapier had gone out of fashion, the latter having been displaced by the small sword, a weapon rejected by the prize-fighting community as being too deadly for their purposes. They retained the staff and the back-sword, used either "single" or accompanied by the great gauntlet or by a basket-hilted dagger; this was also the weapon of the soldier. As Captain Godfrey puts it, "The Small Sword is the Call of Honour, the Back-Sword the Call of Duty." The cudgel, too, must not be lost sight of; it was employed on the fighting stage, and it was used, and is so still, as a means for studying the art of the broad-sword.

The method of back-sword play was handed down by a succession of professors, who learned it partly by rote, but mostly by practical experience (for of books there were very few indeed), and down to the end of the eighteenth century there were practically no changes in it.

In Charles II.'s time these prize-fights were a matter of interest even to such respectable gentlemen as Mr. Samuel Pepys, who on June 1, 1663, witnessed a fierce combat of this kind.

Ancient leathern cudgel hilt in possession of Captain A. Hutton, F.S.A.

"I," says he, "with Sir J. Minnes to the Strand Maypole, and there light out of his coach, and walked to the New Theatre, which, since the King's players are gone to the Royal one, is this day begun to be employed for the fencers to play prizes at. And here I come and saw the first prize I ever saw in my life: and it was between one Matthews, who did beat at all points, and one Westwicke, who was soundly cut both in the head and legs, that he was all over blood; and other deadly blows did they give and take in very good earnest. They fought at eight weapons, three boutes at each weapon. This being upon a private quarrel, they did it in good earnest, and I felt one of their swords, and found it to be very little, if at all, blunter on the edge than the common swords are. Strange to see what a deal of money is flung to them both upon the stage between every boute."

"*May 27th*, 1667. Abroad, and stopped at Beargarden stairs, there to see a prize fought. But the house so full there was no getting in there, so forced to go through an alehouse into the pit where the bears are baited; and upon a stool did see them fight, a butcher and a waterman. The former had the better all along, till by and by the latter dropped his

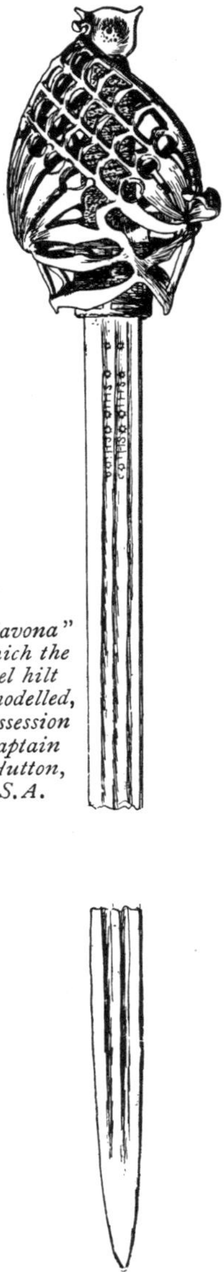

"*Schiavona*" *on which the cudgel hilt was modelled, in possession of Captain A. Hutton, F.S.A.*

sword out of his hand, and the butcher, whether not seeing his sword dropped I know not, but did give him a cut over the wrist, so that he was disabled to fight any longer. But Lord! to see in a minute the whole stage was full of watermen to revenge the foul play, and the butchers to defend their fellow, though most blamed him; and there they all fell to it, knocking down and cutting many on each side. It was pleasant to see, but that I stood in the pit, and feared that in the tumult I might get some hurt. At last the battle broke up, so I away."

"*Sept.* 1*st*, 1667. To the Beargarden, where now the yard is full of people, and those most of them seamen, striving by force to get in. I got into the common pit; and there, with my cloak about my face, I stood and saw the prize fought, till one of them, a shoemaker, was so cut in both his wrists that he could not fight any longer, and then they broke off. The sport very good, and various humours to be seen among the rabble that is there."

"*April* 12*th*, 1669. By water to the Beargarden, and there happened to sit by Sir Fretcheville Hollis, who is still full of his vainglorious and profane talk. Here we saw a prize fought between a soldier and a country fellow, one Warrell, who promised the least in his looks, and performed the most of valour in his boldness and evenness of mind, and smiles in all he did, that ever I saw; and we were all both deceived and infinitely taken with him. He did soundly beat the soldier, and cut him over the head. Thence back to White Hall, mightily pleased all of us with this sight, and particularly this fellow, as a most extraordinary man for his temper and evenness in fighting."

Donald MacBane.

In the days of good Queen Anne, the heyday of sword prize-fighting, there lived a sturdy Highland soldier, named Donald MacBane, who by dint of application and of hard experience made himself a first-class swordsman. Unlike the majority of his class, he was something of a scholar, for he left behind him a work, "The Expert Swordman's Companion," which contains a number of wise lessons for both the small and back sword; but perhaps the most interesting part of it is the account he gives of his life when serving in Flanders under the great Duke of Marlborough. There is a rough quaintness in the style of his narrative that adds flavour to the curious anecdotes of fights in which he was engaged. The autobiography is as a whole eminently unsuited to the drawing-room table, but certain parts of it we are able to reproduce. MacBane recites a story against himself with as much relish as one in which he had the best of it, so he may well tell us his tale in his own words:

In the year 1690 "General M'Kay and his army marched off, and left Collonel *Hills'* Regiment in the Fort (Fort William), and him Governour of the same. I remained there, and served in one Collonel Forbes' Company; at that time I had very little skill how to manage my Pay, so there was an Old Soldier ordered to take care of me, and to manage my Pay as he pleased; he gave me nothing but what he thought fit, when I asked him for Money he would for ordinary give me a Blow, I resented it several times, but I came off Second best; I complained to my Officer, but found it in vain, for at that time, if any Difference fell

19

out betwixt two Soldiers, they were obliged to Decide it with their Swords. I was afraid to venture on my Governour, he being a Bold old Soldier, being a sort of a gentleman was allowed to wear a Sword; I had nothing but a Wooden Handled *Bayonet*, and did not know how I should be upsides with him, by Chance I got some Money from my Friend, so I went directly to a *Sergeant* who taught Gentlemen the Art of the *small Sword*, I desired the Favour of him to Teach me that Art of the Sword; he answered he could not, because my Pay would not satisfy him, I desired but Fourteen Days Teaching, and gave him a Crown in Hand, which he Imbraced: I was taught privately so that none might know of it, then I took some Spirits to me, and would live no longer as I had done but would Fight the Old Fellow: I got a Sword of one of my Neighbours, and went privately with it under my Coat unto the *Canteen*, where the Old Gentleman was; I Demanded the remainder of my Pay, his answer was, you saucie Rogue, if you ask any Money of me, I'll beat you Back and Side, when I think fit I'll give you Money. I replyed, Sir that will not do, either give me Money, or give me Gentlemens Satisfaction immediately: says he, Sirra, with you it's not worth my while, I urged him so that he and I went to the Back of the Garrison in the Dusk of the Evening, lest any Person should see us, we drew on each other, I had a *Small Sword*, he had a *Broad;* after two Turns he beat my Sword out of my Hand, I took my Heels, he runing after me overtook me, and gave me a blow with the flate side of the Sword, obliging me to submit to him; he carried away my Sword and Pauned it in the *Canteen* for Two Gallons of Ale, my Neighbour seeing his Sword go for Ale was very displeased with me, but there was no help for what was past.

"Next Morning I went to my old Master, and gave him some more Money, and asked what Guard I should keep with a *small* Sword against a *Broad;* he shew'd me to keep a low Guard, and slip from his Blow, and

Push above his Sword when it goes to the Ground, and make a half Thrust to his Sword Arm, and to save my small Sword from his. Next Day being Pay Day, he took up my Money as he had done formerly, I went and Demanded my Pay from him, he answered I got Meat and Drink, and what Occasion have you for Money; I told him I would have it whether he would or not, whereupon he gave me a Blow with his Sword and Scabard, which I took very ill, and went to see for a Sword, but could get none; I was at last obliged to take one of my Commerads' Sword, whether he would or not, and put it under my Coat; I came where the Old Gentleman was, he being in Company, I called him to the Door, desired the remainder of my Money without any further Delay, otherways walk to the Place we formerly were at, which he immediately did: In our way he was always saying, I should not come off so well as I did before, for he would Cut a Leg or Arm off me: I was resolute and no way afraid, we came to the Place where we Fought before, he put off his Coat, I would not, thinking it would save his Sword from cutting me, we looked about to see if any Person were in view, then we drew, and after two or three Turns, he making a great stroak at my Leg, I slipt him, and Thrust him through the Body before he could Recover himself; finding he was Wounded he struck furiously, and giving way he fell forward, I seeing that pusht him in the Leg, least he should run after me as before. I then commanded him to give me his Sword, which he did, I put the Sword into the Scabard, and went into the Garrison to the Drawer that Sold the Drink, and gave the Gentleman's Sword to him, desiring him to give me my Sword, and keep that Sword until he saw the owner of it, the Swords I had taken, I laid them down where I got them; by this time he was Carried into the Garrison by some *Cow-drivers*, a *Surgeon* was call'd to dress his Wounds: His Officer came and asked how he came by that Misfortune, he refused to tell, being a high spirited

19—2

Man: I then became Master of my own Pay, and his likeways time about, for it was half a Year before he fully recovered of his Wounds: I then began to think something of myself, and purchased a Sword, this was my first Adventure with the Sword, in the Year 1692.

"After this I Lived Peaceably for some Time, and continued learning at the Fencing School Publickly for Two Months, I had several bouts with the Scholars, I came off still Master."

1697: "I came home to my Parents at *Inverness*, my Father being Dead, I stayed with my Mother sometime, she being in no Extraordinary Circumstance to Maintain an idle Man, desired me to go Work for my Bread, or go to my old Trade again. I desired her to provide me some Money, and I would go seek my Fortune, my Mother gave me Twenty Shillings and a Suit of new Cloaths, and her Blessing. I took leave of all Friends and came off for *Perth*, where I listed in the Earl of *Angus's* Regiment. I served there as a *Pikeman* for sometime; one Day being on Guard, I happened to be absent from my Duty, the Corporal being angry upon my appearing, he obliged me to stand Four Hours Centrie, and beat me for my Absence; at which my *Highland* Blood warmed, I resolved to be Revenged on him when the Guard was relieved next morning, I told the Corporal he had affronted me on the Guard, for which I would have satisfaction, which he was very willing to give; he desired me to go to the *South-Inch* (which is very near to the Town of *Perth*) and he would follow me quickly, when he came he asked if I was for Death or Life, I told him I was for anything that happened, we drew on each other, after some turns he received a Thrust on the Breast-bone, he falling backward cryed you Rogue run, for I am Killed, I said I wished it were otherways, I took him by the Hand desiring him to rise, but he could not, he threw away his Sword, then

I returned mine, I said to him, are you Dead really? he answered, I am in very deed, he opened his Breast and shewed me the Blood, he again desired me to run away, for if I was catch'd I would be hanged; I desired him to give me what Money he had, in a very trembling manner he put his Hand in his Pocket, and gave me Three Shillings to carry me off, saying it was all he had, he took me by the Hand and said he forgave me, crying make your Escape; when I was about Two Miles from *Perth*, in the Road that goes to *Stirling*, I met with my Officer who asked me where I was going, I told him my Misfortune, and that I was afraid of six quarters of *St. Johnstoun* Ribbons, so I resolved to make my escape, he was very sorry for it, and gave me half a Crown to carry me to *Glasgow;* he wrote to one Captain *Cockburn*, who was Recruiting for the Royal Regiment of *Scots* then Lying in *Ireland*, he likeways said he would suffer none to pursue after me, I was not much afraid of any Man catching me, I was at that time as swift as a *Highland* Horse, I came for *Stirling*, and there met me two Soldiers and a Drum, they asked me where I was going, and what I was? I answered, it was none of their Business, they told me I must give Account and better Language, one of them drew his *Shable*, and said I was his Prisoner; immediately I jumpt over a Ditch and drew my *Sword*, then they attacked me, I thrust one through the Shoulder, the Drum threw his Stick at my Face and fled, the other one I thrust through the Hand, he fearing further Danger beged Pardon, so they made the best of their way to the Garrison, I fearing a Party to be sent after me, went to the *Tor-wood*, where I staid that Night, the next Morning I came for Glasgow, and found the Captain I was Recommended to, who immediately gave me a Line to his *Sergeant* then lying at *Saltcoats* with Recruits; he shiped me, and next Morning we set Sail for *Ireland*, then was I pretty safe.

"At that time I went to a *French* Master to Learn

to Push, I tarried with him a Moneth; my Fellow Scholar and I fell out, he said I was not able to do with the *Sword* what he could do with the *Foil*, we went to *Oxmentoun-Green* and drew on each other, I Wounded him in three places, then we went and took a Pot, and was good Friends. We remained in Limerick about Eighteen Months, I continued still at the School and had several Turns with my Fellow Scholars, and continued still formest Scholar in my Master's School. There was seven other Schools in the City, with whom my Master's Scholars had several Conflicts, at last one of the Masters and I fell out about a Sister of his whom I intended to Marry, all the Tocher I got was a Duel with her Brother: After which I set up for a Master my self, and keept a School while our Regiment lay there.

"Now follows an Account of my Transactions in Holland during my aboad there, our Regiment went to the *Bush* at *Brabin*, there I met with the Sergeant I had killed at *Perth*. I asked him if ever he was a *Corporal* in *Perth?* He said he was: I said was not you once killed at Perth as you said yourself? He said almost but not altogether, by a Roguish Fellow called Daniel Bane, and I believe you are the Man; I took him by the Hand, so we went and took a Bottle.

"I set up a School for Teaching the Art of the *Sword*, and had very good Business. But there being a great many Schools in the Town which caused great envy amongst us, they took all Methods and ways to do me a Mischief, which obliged me to be constantly on my Guard, and to Fight Twenty-four Times before they would be perswaded that I was Master of my Business.

"I continued keeping my School, a short Time after I came to know that there was Four good Swordsmen in the Town that kept Gaming, the Wheel of Fortune, and Ledgerdemain, by which they got vast Money; I resolved to have a share of that Gain, at least to have a fair Tryall for it. I Fought all the Four, one by one, the last of them was Left-handed, he and I went to the Rampart, where we searched one another for Fire Arms, finding none, we drew and had two or three clean Turns, at last he put up his Hand and took a Pistol from the Cock of his Hat, he cocked it against his shoulder and presented it to me, upon which I asked Quarters, but he refused, and Fired at me and run for it, one of the Balls went through my Cravat, I thinking I was shot did not Run as I was wont to do, but Run as I could after him crying for the Guard, the Guard being half a Mile distant I was not heard; at last I overtook him over against the Guard, and gave him a Thrust in the Buttocks; then I fled to the Flesh-market, nobody could take me out there it being a privileged Place; I tarried there till Night then went home to my quarters, and called for his Commerads that same Night, who agreed to give me a share of their Gain; with this and my School, I Lived very well for that Winter.

"In 1707 we took the Field, and Camped at *Pungdeperie,* during this Camp I had good Business by Gameing and other things; there was a wicked Fellow who belonged to the Dutch Blew Guards, he was a French Gascoon, he bullied all the Swordsmen belonging to them, he and I fell out about a Lady, he Challenged me immediately to Answer him, so we went out to the back of an old Trench where he showed me Five Graves which he had filled, and told me I should be the Sixth (we had a great many Spectators both Dutch and English) if I would not yield him the Lady, for shame I could not but Fight him, he drew his Sword and with it drew a Line, saying, that should be my Grave; I told him it was too short for me, likewise I did not love to ly wet at Night, but said it would fit him better; we fell to it, he advanced upon me so that I was obliged to give Way a little, I bound his Sword and made a half

Thrust at his Breast, he Timed me, and wounded me in the Mouth; we took another turn, I took a little better care, and gave him a Thrust in the Body, which made him very angry; he came upon me very boldly, some of the Spectators cryed Stand your Ground, I wished them in my Place, then I gave him a Thrust in the Belly, he then darted his Sword at me, I Parried it, he went and lay down on his Coat and spake none, I took up my Scabard and made the best of my Way to the Regiment, hearing no more about him, but that his Commerads were glad he was off the Stage, for he was very troublesome.

"In 1711 we took the Field and March'd to the Plains of *Dowie*, and stayed there a few Days until our Army Conveened; then we march'd to *Leward* between *Dowie* and *Bashaine*, we continued there for several Weeks, there I followed my old Trade, as well in the *Holland's* Quarters as in *Marleborough's* Quarters; there was Two *Hollanders* that was Angry that I should have a share in their Quarters, so they swore I should have it no more; they came to the Gameing Tent I had there, and cut it down, and abused my servant; they sent me a challenge to meet them next Morning, but being under Arms to be Reviewed by the General I could not attend, this offended them because I gave them not a Meeting; both of them came when I was in Bed, and said, if I would not arise and give them Satisfaction, they would stab me where I lay; I desired them to go to a Tent in the Rear and take a Glass of Wine, and I would be with them in a Minute, I sent for a Commerade one *Joseph Borrough* an *Englishman*, who came; then we went to the Tent where they were, and asked them what they Designed? they told us they would Fight in the Front of our Army, and that they had provided a Waggon to carry us off when Killed; the Landlord of the Tent as we were going out searched us for Fire Arms, he found Two Pistols upon one of them, and one upon the other, but none upon us, so we walked to the Place appointed in Front of the Army, they stript, and we likeways; then they took a Dram and Drunk to each other, I asked if they would give us a Dram, but refused, upon which my Commerade drew and Engaged his Man I likewise Engaged my Man we were not long untill we ended the Controversie, one lay on the Spot, the other was carried in the Waggon that was provided for us, we went to our Camp and kept quiet a day or two.

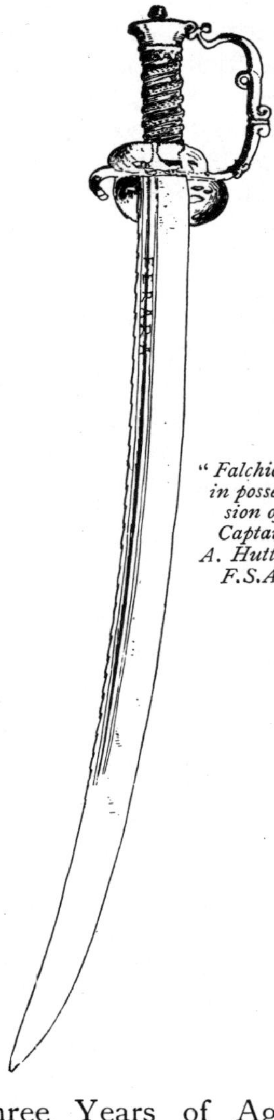

"*Falchion*" *in possession of Captain A. Hutton, F.S.A.*

"In 1712, while I stayed in *Dunkirk* I kept a School and had good bread, at length I took the Ague, and my Collonel sent me to *England*, and Recommended me to *Chance Colledge*. Some Time after I Recovered, I went and Married a Wife, I kept an Ale-House and a School, and Lived very well in *London*, I Fought Thirty-Seven Prizes at the *Bear-Garden*.

"In 1726 I Fought a Clean Young Man at Edinburgh, I gave him Seven Wounds and broke his Arm with the *Fauchon*, this I did at the request of several *Noblemen* and *Gentlemen*. But now being Sixty-three Years of Age, resolves never to Fight any more, but to Repent of my former Wickedness."

MacBane must have been a more than ordinarily tough fellow. He served all through the Duke of Marlborough's campaigns in the Low Countries, where he took part in sixteen battles and fifty-two sieges, besides skirmishes innumerable. He was twenty-seven times wounded, without counting an occasion when he was blown up by the bursting of his own hand-grenade. He retired from the service at the age of forty-nine, bearing within him, by way of a reminiscence, two musket-balls in his thigh and a plate of silver in his skull. Hampered with these he commenced his career at the Bear Garden (where, as he tells us himself, he fought thirty-seven prizes) at the age of fifty, a time of life at which most of the fighting men thought it wise to retire into private life. His last exploit, when, at the age of sixty-three, he beat the "clean young man" at Edinburgh, has been celebrated in verse :

"Whether in Private or in Publick Field,
He Victor was and made his Foes to yield.
Grown Old at length, and spent with Warlike Toil,
He did return unto his native Soil.
Resolved no more to Fight, when lo he's told,
An *Irish* raw Bravado stout and bold
Imperiously all *Scotish* did Defy,
He laid his former Resolution by,
And from great Distance came in haste to see
Who was the Man, and what a Spark was he.
He took the *Challenge* up, and modestly
He set a day, their Valour for to try.
When met, our *Hero* mov'd with generous Rage
Beat at first Time *O'Bryan* of the Stage ;
His luck was good he fell, for had he stood,
He there had lost his life and *Irish* Blood.
Foolhardy he Appear'd on Stage again,
And all his Bragadocia Threats were vain ;
For Valiant *Bane* like *Lyon* void of Fear,
With furious Blows did this the Youngster tear.
Seven Bloody Wounds he gave, but none he got,
And this the *Tague* was Vanquished by the Scot."

* * * * *

Combat with Falchions, after James Miller.

"The Atlas of the Sword."

Such was the title conferred by Captain John Godfrey upon James Figg, the famous prize-fighter; but before we introduce the latter we ought to say something about Godfrey himself.

This gentleman was one of the number of enthusiastic amateurs of the art of fence, such as George Silver, "J. G.," "A. C.," the author of "Pallas Armata," Sir William Hope of Balcomie, and others, who have handed down to us in print the methods in use in their time. The "Treatise upon the Useful Science of Defence," written by Captain Godfrey in 1747 at the instance of many of his friends, contains not only sound ideas on the practice of both small and back sword, for the latter of which he shows strong predilection, but also interesting accounts of several leading prize-fighters and teachers of his day, and in the preface to his book he introduces the name of his favourite master.

"I think," says he, "I have had some knowledge of the Theory and Practice of the SWORD: The following Reasons may be some Excuse for my Conceit. If I am mistaken, no Man living has been more abominably abused by Flattery; for I have for many Years been fed with that Notion from the Town, and have been told that I could execute what I knew, and give better Reasons for what I did in the SWORD, than most Men, by Men of Rank so far above me, that it is scarce to be supposed they would ever debase themselves by idly flattering one so insignificant. I believe it will be farther acknowledged, that I have a considerable Time supported this opinion of myself, by proving it upon all who were willing to dispute it with me. I have purchased my Knowledge in the BACK-SWORD with many a broken Head, and Bruise in every Part of me. I chose to go mostly to FIG, and exercise with him; partly, as I knew him to be the ablest Master, and partly, as he was of a rugged Temper, and would spare no Man, high or low, who took up a Stick against him. I bore his rough Treatment with determined Patience, and followed him so long, that FIG at last, finding he could not have the beating of me at so cheap a Rate as usual, did not shew such Fondness for my Company. This is well known by Gentlemen of distinguished Rank, who used to be pleased in setting us together.

"I have tryed with all the eminent Masters since FIG's Time, and I believe, made them sensible of what I could do; and it has been so publickly proved, that I cannot think any one will deny the Fact.

"I have followed chiefly the Practice of the BACKSWORD, because Conceit cannot be so readily cured with the File in the Small, as with the Stick in that: For the *Argumentum bastinandi* is very strong and convincing; and though a Man may dispute a full Hit of a File, yet if he is knocked down with a Stick, he will hardly get up again and say, it *just brushed him*. This has been my Reason for preferring the BACKSWORD."

James Figg was born at Thame, in Oxfordshire. He was neither a man of family, like Rob Roy MacGregor, nor an honest soldier of his Sovereign, like Donald MacBane. A prize-fighter pure and simple, he was undoubtedly the head of his profession, both as a "gladiator" and as a teacher of his art. Godfrey says of him:

"FIG was the Atlas of the Sword, and may he remain the gladiating Statue! In him, Strength, Resolution, and unparalleled Judgement conspired to make a matchless Master. There was a Majesty shone in his Countenance, and blazed in all his Actions, beyond all I ever saw. His right Leg bold and firm, and his left which could hardly ever be disturbed, gave him the surprising Advantage already proved, and struck his Adversary with Despair and Panic. He had that peculiar way of stepping in, in a *Parry*; he knew his Arm and it's just time of moving, put a firm Faith in that, and never let his Adversary escape his

Parry. He was just as much a greater MASTER, than any other I ever saw, as he was a greater Judge of *Time* and *Measure.*"

The "battles" Figg fought upon the stage numbered nearly three hundred. This seems enormous compared to the modest thirty-eight which MacBane confesses to; but it must be remembered that the former commenced and pursued his battles at the Bear Garden at the time of life when the Highland soldier was fighting his in Flanders against the enemies of his King and country, and that MacBane appeared on the gladiatorial stage at an age when the mighty Figg was thinking of retiring into private life.

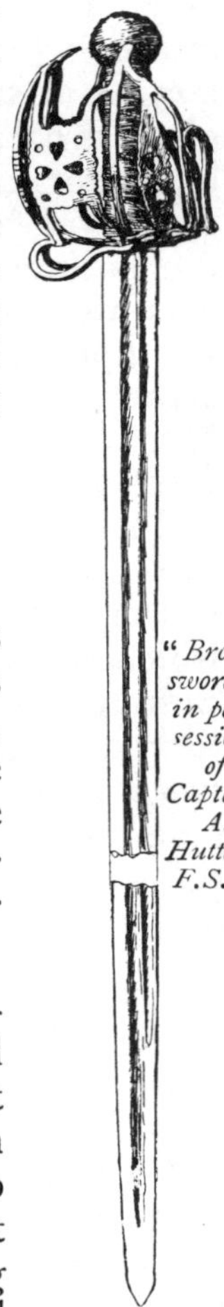

"*Broad-sword*" *in possession of Captain A. Hutton, F.S.A.*

Perkins the Gladiator.

Like other great men, James Figg was not without his rivals, one of whom was an elderly Irishman, Perkins by name, whose success at his trade was mostly due to the peculiar engaging guard which he adopted, that one which we moderns recognise under the name of "sixte." Godfrey speaks of him as follows:

"The Man certainly was a true Swords-Man, but his Age made him so stiff and slow in his Action, that he could not execute all that his Judgment put him upon; yet, by Dint of that, he made up for his Inactivity. He always at first setting out, pitched to this Posture, lying low to the *Inside* so wide as to hide all the *Outside*, with his Wrist so ready raised, that nobody knew what to do with him. I have seen FIG, in Battles with him, stand in a kind of Confusion, not knowing which way to move, the old Man would also move so warily upon the Catch, that he would disappoint him of most of his Designs."

The old Bear Garden so often frequented by Samuel Pepys was at Hockley-in-the-Hole; but a new place of pleasure bearing the same name came into being at Mary-le-bone. Both of these resorts were famous in the early part of the eighteenth century for gladiatorial shows. Figg, however, who had prospered in his craft, erected in the Oxford Road an amphitheatre of his own, which at once attracted the élite of the patrons of the fighting stage. Here occasionally even women entered the arena sword in hand. There was none of the romance about them that there was about our fair friend "Long Meg of Westminster." Meg played her pranks for the fun of the thing; but these viragos fought on the public stage for filthy lucre, and for nothing else. We are informed that "August, 1725, produced a conflict for the entertainment of the visitors of Mr. Figg's amphitheatre, Oxford Road, which is characteristic of savage ferocity indeed. Sutton the champion of Kent and a courageous female heroine of that County fought Stokes and *his much admired* consort of London; £40 was to be given to the male or female who gave most cuts with the sword, and £20 for most blows at quarterstaff, besides the collection in the box."

Sutton the Pipe-maker and James Figg.

"SUTTON," says Godfrey, "had a nimble Body and very agile Joints under a heavy Head. He was a resolute, pushing, awkward Swords-Man; but by his busy intruding Arm, and scrambling Legs, there were few Judgements but were disordered and disconcerted. FIG managed him the best of any, by his charming Distinction of *Time* and *Measure*, in which he far excelled all, and sufficiently proved these to be the Sword's true Foundation."

Sutton was Figg's greatest rival of all, and for a

time the honours were divided between them, they having fought two big "battles" with varied success. In order to decide the victory, they agreed upon a third contest, to be fought first with swords and afterwards, should it be possible, with the quarterstaff. A poetical description of this combat has been left to us, as it is said, by the author of the pastoral in Addison's *Spectator* beginning "My time, O ye Muses, was happily spent." The poem gives so graphic a description of the details of the "battle" that it is worth while to preserve it:

"Long was the great Figg by the prize-fighting swains
Sole monarch acknowledged of Mary-bone plains;
To the towns far and near did his valour extend,
And swam down the river from Thame to Gravesend.
There liv'd Mr. Sutton, pipe-maker by trade,
Who, hearing that Figg was thought such a stout blade,
Resolved to put in for a share of his fame,
And so sent to challenge the Champion of Thame.
With alternate advantage two trials had past,
When they fought out the rubbers on Wednesday last.
To see such a contest the house was so full,
There hardly was room left to thrust in your scull.
With a prelude of cudgels we first were saluted,
And two or three shoulders most handsomely fluted;
Till, wearied at last with inferior disasters,
All the Company cry'd, 'Come the Masters, the Masters.'
Whereupon the bold Sutton first mounted the Stage,
Made his honours as usual, and yearned to engage;
Then Figg with a visage so fierce and sedate
Came, and entered the list with his fresh-shaven pate,
Their arms were encircled by armigers two,
With a red ribbon Sutton's, and Figg's with a blue;
Thus adorned the two heroes 'twixt shoulder and elbow
Shook hands, and went to 't; and the word it was *bilboe*.
Sure such a concern in the eyes of spectators
Was never yet seen in our Amphitheatres!
Our Commons and Peers from their several places
To half an inch distance all pointed their faces;
While the rays of old Phœbus that shot through the sky-light
Seemed to make on the stage a new kind of twilight;

And the Gods without doubt, if one could but have seen
them,
Were peeping there through to do justice between them.
Figg struck the first stroke, and with such a vast fury,
That he broke his huge weapon in twain I assure ye.
And if his brave rival this blow had not warded,
His head from his shoulders had quite been discarded.
Figg armed him again, and they took t' other tilt,
And then Sutton's blade run away from its hilt;
The weapons were frighted, but as for the men
In truth they ne'er minded, but at it again.
Such a force in their blows you'd have thought it a wonder
Every stroke they receiv'd did not cleave them asunder.
Yet so great was their courage, so equal their skill,
That they both seemed as safe as a thief in a mill;
While in doubtful attention dame Victory stood,
And which side to take could not tell for her blood,
But remain'd like the Ass 'twixt the two bottles of hay
Without ever moving an inch either way;
Till Jove to the Gods signified his intention
In a speech that he made them too tedious to mention.
But the upshot of it was, that at that very bout
From a wound in Figg's side the hot blood spouted out;
Her ladyship then seemed to think the case plain,
But Figg stepping forth, with a sullen disdain,
Shew'd the gash, and appeal'd to the company round
If his own broken sword had not given him the wound.
That bruises and wounds a man's spirit should touch,
With danger so little, with honour so much!
Well, they both took a dram, and returned to the battle,
And with a fresh fury they made the swords rattle;
While Sutton's right arm was observed to bleed
By a touch from his rival, so Jove had decreed;
Just enough for to shew that his blood was not *icor*,
But made up, like Figg's, of the common red liquor.
Again they both rush'd with as equal a fire on,
That the company cried, 'Hold, enough of cold iron,
To the quarterstaff now, lads;' so first having dram'd it,
They took to their wood, and i' faith never shamm'd it.
The first bout they had was so fair and so handsome,
That to make a fair bargain it was worth a King's ransom;
And Sutton such bangs to his neighbour imparted,
Would have made any fibres but Figg's to have smarted.
Then after that bout they went on to another;
But the matter must end in some fashion or other,

Combat with sword and dagger, after James Miller.

So Jove told the Gods he had made a decree,
That Figg should hit Sutton a stroke on the knee;
Though Sutton, disabled as soon as it hit him,
Would still have fought on, but Jove would not permit him.
'Twas his fate, not his fault, that constrained him to yield,
And thus the great Figg became lord of the field."

Captain James Miller.

James Miller commenced life as a soldier, and also as a fighter on the stage. He rose to the rank of Captain in the army, and did good service in 1745 in Scotland under the Duke of Cumberland. He was evidently a man of education, as he brought out a very handsome album of gladiatorial figures, from which Mr. Angelo must have derived the idea of his magnificent work published some thirty-five years later. Godfrey says of Miller: "Mr. Millar was the palpable Gentleman through the Prizefighter. He was a most beautiful Picture on the Stage, taking in all his Attitudes, and vastly engaging in his Demeanour. There was such an easy Action in him, unconcerned Behaviour, and agreeable Smile in the midst of Fighting, that one could not help being prejudiced in his Favour."

The *Spectator* gives an interesting account of a "battle" between Miller and one Timothy Buck, whom Godfrey describes as "a most solid Master," in which our friend seems to have fared rather badly.

In the number of the *Spectator* of July 21, 1712, Steele tells us that "Being a person of insatiable curiosity, I could not forbear going last Wednesday to a place of no small renown for the gallantry of the lower order of Britons, namely to the Bear-garden at Hockley-in-the-Hole; where, as a whitish brown paper, put into my hands in the street, informed me, there was to be a trial of skill between two masters of the noble science of defence, at two of the clock precisely. I was not a little charmed with the solemnity of the challenge, which ran thus:

"'I James Miller, sergeant, lately come from the frontiers of Portugal, master of the noble science of defence, hearing, in most places where I have been, of the great fame of Timothy Buck of London, master of the said science, do invite him to meet me, and exercise at the several weapons following, viz. :

Backsword	Single falchion
Sword & dagger	Case of falchions
Sword & buckler	Quarterstaff.'

"If the generous ardour in James Miller to dispute the reputation of Timothy Buck, had something resembling the old heroes of romance, Timothy Buck returned answer in the same paper, with the like spirit, adding a little indignation at having been challenged, and seeming to condescend to fight James Miller, not in regard to Miller himself, but in that, as the fame went out, he had fought Parkes of Coventry. The acceptance of the combat was in these words:

"'I Timothy Buck of Clare-market, master of the noble science of defence, hearing he did fight Mr. Parkes of Coventry, will not fail, God willing, to meet this fair inviter at the time and place appointed, desiring a clear stage, and no favour.

'*Vivat Regina.*'"

The battle "was carried out with great order. James Miller came on first, preceded by two disabled drummers, to show, I suppose, that the prospect of maimed bodies did not in the least deter him. There ascended with the daring Miller a gentleman, whose name I could not learn, with a dogged air, as unsatisfied that he was not principal. Miller had a blue riband tied round the sword arm.

"Miller is a man of six foot eight inches height, of a kind but bold aspect, well fashioned, and ready of his limbs, and such a readiness as spoke his ease in them was obtained from a habit of motion in military exercises.

A prize-fight, after James Miller.

"The expectation of the spectators was now almost at its height; and the crowd pressing in, several active persons thought they were placed rather according to their fortune than their merit, and took it into their heads to prefer themselves from the open area, or pit, to the galleries. This dispute between desert and property brought many to the ground, and raised others in proportion to the highest seats by turns, for the space of ten minutes, till Timothy Buck came on, and the whole assembly, giving up their disputes, turned their eyes upon the champions. Then it was that every man's affection turned to one or the other irresistibly. A judicious gentleman near me said, 'I could, methinks, be Miller's second, but I had rather have Buck for mine.' Miller had an audacious look that took the eye; Buck a perfect composure, that engaged the judgement. Buck came on in a plain coat, and kept all his air till the instant of engaging; at which time he undressed to his shirt, his arm adorned with a bandage of red riband. No one can describe the sudden concern in the whole assembly; the most tumultuous crowd in nature was as still and as much engaged, as if all their lives depended on the first blow. The combatants met in the middle of the stage, and shaking hands, as removing all malice, they retired with much grace to the extremities of it; from which they immediately faced about, and approached each other, Miller with a heart full of resolution; Buck with a watchful untroubled countenance; Buck regarding principally his own defence, Miller chiefly thoughtful of annoying his opponent. It is not easy to describe the many escapes and imperceptible defences between two men of quick eyes and ready limbs; but Miller's heat laid him open to the rebuke of the calm Buck, by a large cut on the forehead. Much effusion of blood covered his eyes in a moment, and the huzzas of the crowd undoubtedly quickened the anguish. The assembly was divided into parties upon their different ways of fighting; while a poor nymph in one of the galleries apparently suffered for Miller, and burst into a flood of tears. As soon as his wound was wrapped up, he came on again with a little rage, which still disabled him further. But what brave man can be wounded into more patience and caution? The next was a warm eager onset, which ended in a decisive stroke on the left leg of Miller. The wound was exposed to the view of all who could delight in it, and sewed up on the stage."

William Gill.

This hero was the foremost pupil of the renowned Mr. Figg, his assistant in his school, and his faithful companion in his fights. Godfrey thus describes him:

"WILLIAM GILL was a swordsman formed by FIG's own Hand, and by his Example turned out a complete Piece of Work. I never beheld any Body better for the Leg than GILL. His Excellence lay in doing it from the *Inside*; and I hardly ever knew him attempt it from the *Outside*. From the narrow way he had of going down (which was mostly without receiving) he oftener hit the Leg than any one; and from the drawing Stroke, caused by that sweeping Turn of the Wrist, and his proper way of holding his Sword, his Cuts were remarkably more severe and deep. I never was an Eye-Witness to such a Cut in the Leg, as he gave one BUTLER, an *Irishman*, a bold resolute Man, but an aukward Swords-Man. His Leg was laid quite open, his Calf falling down to his Ancle. It was soon stitched up, but from the Ignorance of a Surgeon adapted to his mean Circumstances, it mortified: Mr. *Cheselden* was applied to for Amputation, but too late for his true Judgement to interfere in. He immediately perceived the Mortification to forbid his skill; and refused to be concerned in what he knew to be beyond his Power. But another noted one was applied to who, through less judgement, or Value for his Character, cut of his Leg above the Knee, but the Mortification had got the Start of his Instruments, and BUTLER soon expired."

The taste for these gladiatorial shows was already on the wane. The pugilist had for some time been gradually displacing the swordsman in the public esteem, and the accident to the unfortunate Butler put the finishing stroke to it.

CHAPTER XXVII

The Broadsword.

"Rob Roy."

THE popular idea of this famous swordsman is that he was nothing better than a robber and a cattle-lifter. Doubtless he did transact a little business of that kind on occasion, but it must be remembered that at the time in which he lived (he was a contemporary of that Donald MacBane who has just amused us with his account of his exploits) cattle-lifting was of common occurrence in the northern parts of Scotland, so that in that matter Rob was no worse than his neighbours; indeed, he seems to have been quite as much an adept at recovering such property when stolen, as at helping himself thereto on his own account. Early in the last century, Dr. K. MacLeay published a very interesting account of Rob's life, and there is still more to be gleaned about him from various chapbooks:

"Though possessed of qualities that would have fitted him for a military life, the occupations assigned to Rob Roy were of a more homely description. It was customary at that time for gentlemen of property, as well as their tenantry, to deal in the trade of grazing and selling of cattle, and to this employment did Rob Roy also dedicate himself. He took a track of land in Balquhidder for that purpose, and for some years pursued a prosperous course. But his cattle were often stolen, in common with those of his neighbours, by hordes of banditti who infested the country, so that to protect himself from these marauders he was constrained to maintain a party of men, and to this cause may be attributed the warlike habits which he afterwards acquired.

"In the latter days of his father, Rob Roy assisted him in all his concerns, especially in that of collecting his fees for protection, and after the old man's demise he pursued a similar course of life, and received such blackmail from many proprietors of his vicinity, an engagement which he fulfilled with more determination and effect than had before been experienced; and it was in a pursuit after some thieves that he gave the first proofs of his activity and courage. A considerable party of Macras from the western coast of Ross had committed an outrage on the property of Finlarig and carried off fifteen head of cattle. An express informed Rob Roy of the circumstance, and being the first call of the kind he had received, he lost no time in collecting his followers to the number of twelve, and they set off to overtake the men of Ross and their spoil. They travelled two days and a night before they obtained any other information as to their track than at times seeing the impression of the cattle's feet on the ground. On the second night, being somewhat fatigued, they lay down on the heather to rest till morning, when one of them discovered a fire at some distance. This he communicated to his companions, and they went on to reconnoitre, when they found it was a band of tinkers who had pitched a tent close by, and were carousing. Their mirth, however, was turned into terror when they beheld Rob Roy and his party, as they little expected such an intrusion in so secluded a place, but they soon recognised MacGregor.

"The tinkers informed him that they had seen the Macras, who were at no great distance, and two of the fraternity agreed to conduct his party to the spot, for which they set out after having partaken of such hospitality as the wallets of the gang could afford. The freebooters had halted, for the security of their spoil, in a narrow part of the glen, confined by semicircular rocks, where the MacGregors overtook them just as they were setting out. Rob Roy charged them to stop at their peril, but, as they disregarded the order, he instantly rushed upon them, and before they had time to rally six of their number were wounded and lay prostrate on the ground. Eleven who remained made a stout resistance, and it was not until two were killed and five more wounded that they gave up the contest. Four of Rob Roy's lads were sorely wounded, and one killed, and he himself received a cut on the left arm from the captain of the banditti. The booty being thus recovered, was driven back and restored to the rightful owner. Rob Roy received great praise for this exploit, and those who had not formerly afforded him their countenance were now anxious to contribute a donation of blackmail."

Rob Roy and the Soldiers of King James.

During the reign of that miserable bigot, James II., both civil and religious discord reached their climax, and most odious deeds of oppression and cruelty were constantly enacted under the cloak of piety. At some such scenes Rob Roy had occasionally been present as a spectator, regretting that, strong man though he was, he was not powerful enough to crush down the perpetrators.

It happened on a time that he had been to Carlisle to receive some money that was due to him, and returning home by way of Moffat, he comes upon an officer and a party of soldiers, who are engaged in hanging on a tree four peasants, whom they describe as fanatics, Covenanters, and Nonconformists ; the daughter of one of these unfortunates they have bound to the same tree. Their cruel work being completed, they proceed to unloose the girl, tie her hands and feet, and drag her towards the verge of a precipice, from which, regardless of her cries for mercy, they are about to throw her into the river. It is now Rob's turn; he steps forward and demands why they are treating a helpless woman so barbarously. The officer replies in an arrogant fashion: "Be off, you rascal, or we will serve you the same for your insolence in interfering with His Majesty's commands." This infuriates Rob: he springs upon the soldiers, who are by this time close to the edge, and hurls eight of them into the stream, where they are carried away and drowned in the rapid current; he next whips out his skene dhu, and cuts the cords by which the girl is bound. The officer and the rest of his men are for the moment paralyzed with astonishment, when Rob draws his claymore, attacks him, and promptly stretches him dead on the ground. The soldiers now attempt to surround Rob and avenge their commander; but the herculean Highlander lays about him so vigorously that he soon despatches three more of them to keep the good gentleman company. The remainder take to their heels, and never stop till they arrive at the garrison of Moffat, where they report that, while they were about their holy work, no less a person than Satan himself sprang from the earth, armed with a sword which no mortal arm could resist; that he slew their officer and eleven of their comrades, and that it was all that the remainder could do to save as much as their lives.

Rob Roy to the Rescue.

One autumn evening MacGregor was travelling alone through a lonely part of the passes of Glenetive; he sat him down to rest, and, struck with the beauty of the scene, fell a-musing; but he was awakened from his daydream by the sound of distant voices and the shrieks of a female. The sun was setting, and darkness coming on; but he determined to follow the voices, since he doubted not that the cries were those of some helpless woman who needed his aid. At last he came to an open space in the midst of the woods.

He had scarcely arrived there, when two men emerged from the trees. Rob couched in the long grass till they approached, when he heard the younger of them say: "But what will her father think of our ungrateful conduct?" "Oh," said the other, "I care little for what he thinks now that I have got possession of his daughter!" "Surely," rejoined the other, "you do not mean to use her ill; she is too lovable." "Hold your tongue!" said the elder. "You have assisted me, it is true, but you shall not dictate to me." Quoth the younger: "I have a right, Sir James, to insist on honourable behaviour, and I shall maintain that right." "Well, well," replied Sir James, "this is no time for quarrelling. Let us get our prize away from this wilderness. The old laird has by this time given up search for us in despair, so we can leave in safety." "Not quite so safely as you think," said Rob to himself as he prepared to follow them. He traced them to a ruined castle of the feudal times, and here they disappeared altogether. The gateway was so completely blocked with fallen masonry that entrance was impossible. He searched about among the thick bushes which surrounded the place, and at last discovered a vaulted passage which seemed to lead into the interior. He proceeded cautiously along it, with his dirk drawn in his hand, till he reached an enlarged space, from which he could clearly hear the voices of men in angry dispute. The place was very dark, but he saw at last a faint ray of light, which proceeded from a closed door. This he gently pushed open, when he beheld by the light of a wood-fire which was blazing on the ruined hearth the form of a woman lying on a litter of dried grass. On seeing him, the terrified lady thought her last moments were come; but Rob speedily reassured her, saying, "Madam, your cries reached my ears, and I am come to help you. But who are you, and what has brought you to this horrible place? For my own part, I am Rob Roy MacGregor, and I mean to rescue you; but tell me briefly your name."

She replied : " I am the daughter of the Chief of —— " (" My most truculent enemy," thought Rob to himself). " I have been decoyed and forcibly carried off by one of my father's guests, Sir James ——, a wicked, cruel Englishman." "Well," says Rob, "trust to me, and remain here till I return. I am going to find your Englishman." The sounds of altercation recommence. He leaves the lady, gets his claymore ready for action, and softly approaches the door from which the noise emanates. "You are treating me nicely, Percy, threatening to leave me in the lurch," says one voice. " No, Sir James," replies the other. " I went to that castle as your friend. You have betrayed me into a villainous breach of hospitality and most inhuman behaviour to the daughter of our host. I'll have no hand in such a business." Hearing this, Rob Roy steps boldly into the chamber, where the two disputants with three other men are pacing up and down. All are armed ; but so astonished are they at the fierce appearance of their unexpected visitor that they shrink back into a corner, taking him to be some evil spirit that haunts the place. But they are shortly to discover that he is made of much more tangible material. " What men are you," he demands, " who brawl here at such an hour ? This is no place for human quarrellers." Sir James at length in a measure recovers himself, and says faintly : " Sir, we have indeed no money with us. We are travellers who have lost our way ; we have done harm to no one." " Harm to no one !" retorts Rob. " What, then, of the Chief of ——? Hark you, Sir James (you see, I know you) : I am not a brigand, and it is not your money I come for, but yourself. You and your gang will go back with me to the castle, in order that the chief may give you that Highland benison which your abrupt departure prevented."

The party, seeing Rob to be so far alone, pluck up their courage. Two of the men attack him vigorously, but with two sweeps of his broadsword he lays the pair of them dead on the floor, and turns his attention to Sir James, who, being a better swordsman than his followers, gives Rob some little trouble, but with no better result than to draw upon himself some severe cuts from the terrible claymore, the last of which places him *hors de combat.* Percy, who has wisely taken no part in the fighting, now implores Rob to spare Sir James's life, which he consents to do, saying that the blood of such a cowardly wretch would only stain his sword, and that he shall be reserved for a more humiliating punishment.

Sir James, meanwhile, is in a very bad way indeed. Rob Roy leaves him to the care of Percy and the remaining attendant that they may bind up his wounds, goes straight to the young lady, who has been terribly alarmed at the clash of steel, tells her that she has no longer any cause for fear, that Sir James has been well paid for his villainy, that he is incapable of further mischief, and that she shall be escorted back to her friends without delay. He shortly procures a boat, in the bows of which they place Sir James and his servant, while Percy, the young lady, and Rob, who takes charge of the tiller, make themselves as comfortable as they can in the stern.

During the voyage the lady describes her adventure to Rob. Sir James and Percy were young Englishmen of good family, who, having an introduction to the chief, were invited to stay at his castle. They both—but with feelings of a totally different nature—fell in love with the daughter of the house, and Sir James, without confiding his intentions to his companion, conceived a plan for carrying her off by force. One evening she was persuaded to go with them in a boat which Sir James had ready, manned by ruffians in his pay. When they were a considerable distance from the shore, he declared his passion for her, and his intention to carry her off to his own country. Percy perceived that the only thing he could do was to remain with the party, to keep quiet, and to trust to chance for an opportunity of rescuing the girl. Knowing nothing whatever of the country, they wandered about for some days till they came by chance to the ruined castle, where they took refuge, and where Rob Roy luckily found them.

As the voyage proceeds, Sir James, who is now thoroughly frightened, repeatedly implores his companions to put him ashore ; but this Rob Roy peremptorily refuses, giving him the sole consolation that he will intercede for his life. To the joy of everyone else, they at last arrive at their destination. To the old chief Rob Roy exclaims : " I restore you your daughter —— at the peril of my life, for I well know on whose ground I stand. It shall never be said that MacGregor is incapable of a generous action, even to a man who has so often grievously injured him." The chief, much moved, seized his hand, saying : " Brave MacGregor, you have done me a service which I can never fully repay ; henceforth reckon me your stanchest friend." Then, glancing at the boat, he saw Sir James and Percy, towards whom he rushed with his sword drawn. Rob, however, stayed him with, " Hold your hand ! your anger is justifiable, but I have promised that the life of this man shall be safe, and I must have it so. Percy, though, has been true, and has preserved the honour of your daughter. Know him as your friend. As for Sir James, spare his life, but otherwise do with him what you will."

MacNeill of Barra.

Rob Roy was a man of herculean strength ; he had even been known to seize a deer by the horns and hold it fast, and he was possessed of arms of such abnormal length that, when standing upright, he could touch his garters with the ends of his fingers, which gave him an unexpected advantage at broadsword play, as MacNeill of Barra found to his cost.

The Laird of Barra, MacNeill by name, had long

prided himself on his skill as a swordsman, and, having heard of MacGregor's fame in that respect, made up his mind that by some means or other he would contrive to have a turn with him. One day, with this in his mind, he betakes himself to Buchanan as the most likely place for his man to be found in, and, being arrived there, is informed that Rob has gone to the market at Killearn, whither he proceeds at once. Meeting several gentlemen on horseback who have just finished transacting their business, he asks them if Rob Roy MacGregor is at the market. "He is here with us," says one of the gentlemen. "What do you want with him?" "I have never seen him, and I wish to do so," is the answer. Rob now comes forward, saying: "I am the man you ask for. What is your pleasure with me?" The other replies: "I am MacNeill of Barra. I have never seen you before, but have heard great talk of your skill, and I have come to find out which is the better swordsman, you or I." The temerity of Barra excites the hilarity of most of the party, when Rob replies: "Laird of Barra, I am far from questioning your skill at arms, but I would have you to know that I am not a prize-fighter nor a seeker of quarrels, and I never fight without a just cause." "Then," says Barra, "I will give you a just cause. You are afraid to fight me; you are a coward, and your boasted valour is all moonshine." This is too much for Rob, who replies: "These gentlemen can attest that I have not provoked this battle; but, Laird of Barra, since you have come so far in quest of a quarrel, you shall not go home unsatisfied. Dismount from your horse." Whereupon down they both get and fall to work, when Rob deals MacNeill such a fearful cut on the sword-arm that he nearly lops it off, and the victim is so injured that he is unable to move from the village of Killearn for three months afterwards.

Colonel Jonah Barrington.

In "Personal Sketches of his own Times," Sir Jonah Barrington gives, as follows, an interesting account of a duel fought in "the ancient mode" between his grandfather, Colonel Barrington, and a Mr. Gilbert, on horseback, armed with a broadsword, a pair of pistols, and a huge dagger:

"The ancient mode of duelling in Ireland was generally on horseback. The combatants galloped past each other, at a distance marked out by posts which prevented a nearer approach; they were at liberty to fire at any time from the commencement to the end of their course, but it must be at a hand-gallop; their pistols were charged alike with a certain number of bullets, slugs, or whatever was most convenient, as agreed.

"There had been, from time immemorial, a spot marked out on level ground near the Doone of Clapook, Queen's County, on the estate of my granduncle, Sir John Byrne, which I have often visited as classic ground. It was beautifully situated, near Stradbally; and here, according to tradition and legendary tales, the old captains and chieftains used to meet and decide their differences. Often did I walk it over, measuring its dimensions step by step. The bounds of it are still palpable, above sixty or seventy steps long, and about forty wide; large stones remain on the spot, where, I suppose, the posts originally stood to divide the combatants, which were about eight or nine yards asunder, being the nearest point from which they were to fire. The time of firing was voluntary, so as it occurred during their course, and, as before stated, at a hand-gallop. If the quarrel was not terminated in one course, the combatants proceeded to a second; and if it was decided to go on after their pistols had been discharged, they then either finished with short broadswords on horseback or with small-swords on foot; but the tradition ran that when they fought with small-swords they always adjourned to the rock of Donamese, the ancient fortress of the O'Moors and the Princes of Offely. This is the most beautiful inland ruin that I have seen in Ireland. There, in the centre of the old fort, on a flat, green sod, are still visible the deep indentures of the feet both of principals, who have fought with small-swords, and their seconds. Every modern visitor naturally stepping into the same marks, the indentures are consequently kept up, and it is probable that they will be deeper a hundred years hence than they were a twelvemonth ago.

"My grandfather, Colonel Jonah Barrington, of Cullenaghmore, had a great passion for hearing and telling stories of old events, particularly respecting duels and battles fought in his own neighbourhood or by his relatives, and his face bore to the day of his death ample proof that he had not been idle among the combatants of his own era. The battle I remember best—because I heard it oftenest and through a variety of channels—was one of my grandfather's, about the year 1759. He and a Mr. Gilbert had an irreconcilable grudge (I forget the cause, but I believe it was a very silly one). It increased every day, and the relatives of both parties found it must inevitably end in a combat, which, if it were postponed until the sons of each grew up, might be enlarged, perhaps, from an individual into a regular family engagement. It was therefore thought better that the business should be ended at once, and it was decided that they should fight on horseback on the green of Maryborough, that the ground should be one hundred yards of race, and eight of distance; the weapons of each, two holster pistols, a broad-bladed but not very long sword (I have often seen my grandfather's) with basket handle, and a skeen, or long, broad-bladed dagger, the pistols to be charged with one ball and swan-drops.

"The entire country for miles round attended to see

the combat, which had been six months settled and publicly announced, and the county trumpeter who attended the judges at the assizes was on the ground. My grandfather's second was a Mr. Lewis Moore, of Cremorgan, whom I well recollect to have seen. He long survived my grandfather. Gilbert's was one of his own name and family, a Captain of cavalry.

"All due preliminaries being arranged, the country collected and placed as at a horse-race, and the ground kept free by the gamekeepers and huntsmen mounted, the combatants started and galloped toward each other. Both fired before they reached the nearest spot, and missed. The second course was more fortunate. My grandfather received many of Gilbert's shot full in his face; the swan-drops penetrated no deeper than his temple and cheek-bones; the large bullet luckily passed him. The wounds not being dangerous, only enraged old Jonah Barrington; and the other, being equally willing to continue the conflict, a fierce battle hand-to-hand ensued; but I should think they did not close totally, or they could not have escaped with life.

"My grandfather got three cuts, which he used to exhibit with great glee: one on the thick of the right arm, a second on his bridle-arm, and the third on the outside of the left hand. His hat, which he kept to the day of his death, was also sliced in several places; but both had iron skull-caps under their hats, which probably saved their brains from remaining upon the green of Maryborough.

"Gilbert had received two pokes from my grandfather on his thigh and his side, but neither disabling. I fancy he had the best of the battle, being as strong as, and less irritable than, my grandfather, who, I suspect, grew towards the last a little ticklish on the subject; for he rushed headlong at Gilbert, closed, and, instead of striking at his person, thrust his broadsword into the horse's body as often as he could, until the beast dropped with his rider underneath him. My grandfather then leaped from his horse, threw away his sword, and putting his skeen, or broad dagger, to the throat of Gilbert, told him to ask his life or die, as he must do either one or the other in half a minute. Gilbert said he would ask his life only upon the terms that, without apology or conversation, they should shake hands heartily and be future friends and companions, and not leave the youths of two old families to revenge their quarrel by carving each other. These terms being quite agreeable to my grandfather, as they breathed good sense, intrepidity, and good heart, he acquiesced, and from that time they were the most intimately-attached and joyous friends and companions of the county wherein they resided."

BOOK V

THE NINETEENTH CENTURY

CHAPTER XXVIII

The Duelling Sword.

In all civilized countries the walking-sword had vanished from the side of the gentleman, but it was not forgotten. A form of it still survived in the *épée de combat*, the favourite duelling weapon of the French. Stripped of the knuckle-bow and *pas d'âne*, its hilt retained only the shell, which in the early half of the century closely resembled both in size and in shape that of the discarded small-sword; it retained its triangular blade, and the method of using it was very little altered. Of its use M. Vigeant, the famous literary master of our art, has recorded many interesting examples.

Jean-Louis.

Born about the year 1784, Jean-Louis, like his predecessor, Saint Georges, was a man of colour, which fact, in addition to a weakly and almost deformed frame, hampered him greatly in his early days; but he conquered these defects by his assiduity in the school of arms, and at the age of twenty we find him among the leading swordsmen in France. He had already fought many duels, but, being of a merciful disposition, his consummate skill enabled him to spare the lives of his antagonists as well as to save his own.

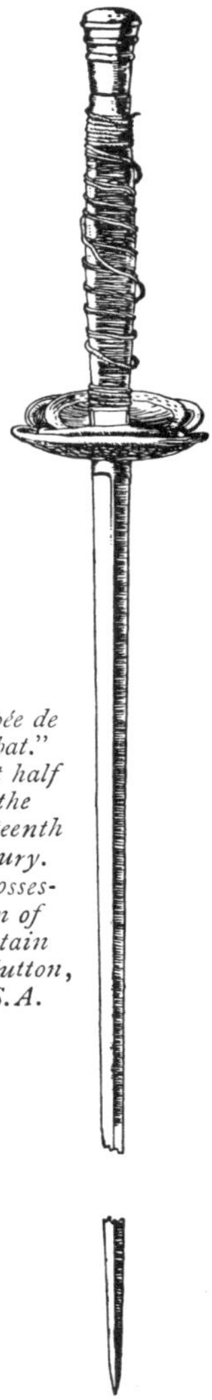

"*Épée de combat.*" *First half of the nineteenth century. In possession of Captain A. Hutton, F.S.A.*

In those days any meeting of skilled fencers could hardly be called so if Jean-Louis had no part in it. Upon a time, having just achieved a fresh success in one of these assemblies, and being surrounded by a crowd of felicitating friends, a voice struck his ear. It said in a contemptuous tone: "This is all very fine; but the fencing-floor and the *terrain* are two different things, and clever as this fellow may be with the foil, he might cut a different figure if the buttons were off." Jean-Louis glanced round, and immediately recognised the speaker, a well-known boaster, but whose merit as a performer was rather small. Seeing who it was, Jean merely shrugged his shoulders, and murmured: "Oh, it is only that fellow; I should be a fool to put myself out about anything he says."

Not long afterwards another *assaut d'armes* took place, where, on entering the room, the first person Jean-Louis saw sitting in the front-seats was the self-same individual, who immediately commenced making disparaging remarks. Our hero found himself opposed to several strong fencers, but not one of them could touch him at all, and, the affair over, he retired to the dressing-room. He was on the point of leaving the hall, when his ear caught a conversation between two of the audience. "You are very difficult to please," said one of them. "Jean-Louis has not been touched at all." "Nonsense!" replied the swaggerer. "These fine foil-players would play a very different game if their points were sharp." Jean marched up to him, clapped him on the shoulder, and said: "Sir, this is the second time that I have heard that remark of yours. Do you intend your words to apply to me?" The other replied haughtily: "And to whom else should they apply?" "Am I to understand, then, that you are attempting to force a duel upon me?" asked Louis. To which the other replied in a most insolent tone: "The sword is not intended for the hand of a nigger; keep you to your foil play." Jean-Louis looked at the man for a moment, and then said: "I am not particularly anxious to cross weapons with you; but since you are so keen on the matter, you shall have your wish, only on one condition." "Oh, there's a condition already, is there?" said the other sneeringly. "Make your mind easy," said Jean; "it is rather to your advantage. Knowing my own power as well as I do, I cannot, for conscience' sake, fight on equal terms with a tenth-rate performer like you. This is how it shall be: I will use a buttoned foil, and you shall have your sharp sword." At this the bystanders rushed forward, exclaiming: "Louis, you must be mad! We will not permit an encounter so utterly unfair to take place!" The master put them back with a motion of his hand, saying: "I am sane enough to give this gentleman to-morrow morning the castigation which he has so justly earned. I am certain of myself, and I know exactly what he is good for. Leave it to me to make a complete example of him."

The next morning the affair came off, Louis being armed with a foil and the other with a duelling sword. The latter attacked furiously. Jean-Louis broke ground slightly in order to allow the energy of his enemy to expend itself, parrying meanwhile his fierce thrusts, when, seizing his opportunity, after having executed a particularly vigorous parry, he dealt him by way of a riposte a terrific slash across the face with his supple blade. The wretched fellow rolled over and over, his beauty completely spoiled. Many months passed ere the mark of Jean-Louis was obliterated, and the offender took good care never to give him a chance of repeating it.

A Day of Duelling.

During the wars of Napoleon, at the time when his fortunes were on the wane, two regiments were brigaded together in Spain, the one being entirely French, and the other composed mainly of Italians. Between these two corps there was a considerable amount of racial ill-feeling. They were constantly quarrelling, and their animosities culminated at last in a serious riot, in which a number of men on both sides were injured; nor was the tumult quelled without the intervention of a body of infantry with fixed bayonets, and a number of men were arrested.

The General in command now summons a council of superior officers, who decide to terminate the trouble in a very drastic fashion. An order is given that the fencing-masters and their assistants of the incriminated regiments shall take the matter in hand, and that they shall fight in the presence of the whole army until one side or the other is unable to continue the combat. Jean-Louis is the chief fencing-master of the French regiment, and Giacomo Ferrari that of the Italian. Louis will have his work cut out for him, for his enemy is one of the finest blades in Italy, has been a swordsman from childhood, and, before receiving his military appointment, was the head of a famous school of arms in Florence.

The day has arrived. The troops are paraded and formed into a hollow square. A roll of the drum, and the two chief combatants make their appearance, each accompanied by fourteen masters and prévôts of his regiment. The two leaders at once prepare for action. They strip to the waist, and each receives his sword from the hands of his second. The command is given, "En garde, allez." The Italian assumes the offensive, and attacks furiously; but every thrust is quietly put aside by the cool-headed Frenchman, who is patiently waiting for his opportunity. Ferrari now moderates his ardour somewhat, hoping to draw his adversary on; but Jean still adheres to his defensive tactics. The Italian loses patience, gives vent to one of those shrieks with which fencers of his nation so often try to frighten their opponents, and rushes on Louis, who parries closely, rapidly extends his arm, and touches his man in the shoulder. The latter, slightly wounded, cries out, "It is nothing! Come on again!" They recommence, when with a vigorous lunge Jean-Louis drives his point deep into the chest of Ferrari, who turns pale, his sword drops from his hand, his knees give way, and he falls to the ground with a heavy thud. His last duel is over.

Jean-Louis calmly wipes his sword and takes a moment's rest, when a second adversary springs upon him; there is a click of steel, a sharp cry, and Louis alone stands upright. The Italian has gone to join his chief. A third meets the same fate, while ten others who afterwards oppose the terrible creole are seriously hurt, and only two remain. The General, thinking that enough has been done, stays the proceedings; Jean-Louis offers his hand to the two surviving prévôts, and the feud of the regiments is at an end.

M. le Comte de Bondy.

In the early years of the nineteenth century, the Count de Bondy was a very prominent man. He occupied a high official position: he was Prefect of the Seine. Of this, however, he thought but little; his chief pride was in his personal perfections, and they were something to be proud of. He was a superb specimen of manhood, six feet in height, of enormous and, moreover, well-cultivated physical powers, and, with forty years of a judiciously-spent life behind him, possessing the activity of a panther. But his greatest pride of all was in his magnificent swordsmanship. He had learned and loved the exercise of the foil from his very childhood ; he had encountered and beaten all the leading amateurs and many highly-respectable professors as well. On one particular occasion his skill had been called in question by a stalwart soldier of the guard, who insisted on a public trial of it, the result being that the Count gave him fifteen clean hits, and received only one himself ; it was a disaster to the soldier, as his ignominious defeat, in a measure, affected his professional career. The Count had one failing, the result of his many successes : he had come to believe himself absolutely invincible. There was one master in France who had never fenced with the Count; this man was the famous Lafangère, a native of Lyons, where he kept a school of arms which so completely monopolized his attention that his absences from home were few and far between. But he went to Paris one day in order to take part in an assault of arms which was being organized by one of his professional friends, and at this meeting he scored a remarkable success. Lafangère was a very little man, barely five feet high, so that the magnificent Prefect, who was present on the occasion, looked down upon him in more ways than one, and was so little sparing of his disparaging remarks that it was suggested to him that if they were to cross foils together he might not have it all his own way. These pretty speeches came to the ear of Lafangère, who very soon decided to prolong his stay in Paris in order to cause M. de Bondy to change his tone, and he further made up his mind that the encounter should be a public one. The Count was equally eager for the fray ; the preliminaries were arranged, a "jury" formed, with no less a person than the celebrated Jean-Louis as its president, and a large hall in a mansion on the Quai d'Orsay was placed at their disposal.

All is now ready for the assault. The judges take their seats on the front-benches, and so important is the event considered that the great room is crowded with masters, prévôts, and all the leading amateurs of the city. As the clock strikes, Lafangère makes his appearance at his end of the hall simply but correctly dressed in the costume of the fencing-room; he is greeted with deserved applause. Immediately afterwards his opponent comes forward. He is at once the cause of such astonishment among the spectators that one of them ejaculates: "Why, he looks as if he was going to a fancy-dress ball!" In point of fact, the gentleman, instead of the usual fencing-jacket, has arrayed himself in a doublet of white satin, quilted, bordered with fine lace, and finished off with a collar of the same rather too ladylike material. Lafangère notes this; he regards it as something of an affront to himself, and decides in his mind to make it the means of bringing consummate ridicule on its wearer.

The voice of the president is heard, "Gentlemen, are you ready?" They incline their heads in assent. "Then play." The combatants approach each other cautiously, they cross foils, and remain motionless, each watching and feeling the blade of his antagonist. The little man is imperturbably cool, which exasperates the Count, who at last loses his patience and leads off with a vigorous attack. Lafangère parries, plants a smart riposte on the breast of his opponent, and withdraws his foil, to the button of which adheres a piece of the beautiful lace. They cross blades again, and again a small piece of lace flutters in the air. The assault lasts about twenty minutes, at the end of which time every scrap of the costly ornament has entirely disappeared, and the superb white satin jacket is reduced to a mere mass of rags and tatters. The poor Count was so chagrined at this signal defeat that he went home and kept his bed for nearly a fortnight. Verily, "pride goes before a fall."

The "Stabber."

The late Mr. George Chapman, who was for about forty years secretary to the London Fencing Club, used to recount to us the following story, and, as we understood, he was an eye-witness of the singular accident which occurred. He told his narrative with the view of warning young fencers against being so foolish as to encounter a kind of opponent known in fencing circles as a "stabber." Those who cultivate the "noble science of defence" know this dangerous animal very well indeed, and give it a remarkably wide berth; but among our readers there may be one here and there who is not a votary of our honoured art, so to him we must present this creature. It joins the school of arms of some professor, or, if it has sufficient influence, gets itself elected as a member of some fencing club; when there, it provides itself with all the impedimenta needful to the fencing man, and it proceeds to take a dozen, or possibly two dozen, lessons from one of the professors (how we do feel for that poor professor!). It now finds itself, after a fashion, able to lunge and recover, and it possesses a very archaic and terribly rough idea about how a thrust is to be parried. Its object is now achieved; it requires no more lessons; it is able to, as it euphoniously puts it, "get a sweat," which it proceeds to do; it does not wait to be invited to fence, but inflicts itself at once on the most prominent swordsman who has the bad luck to be present. Once engaged, its tactics are simple: it draws its sword-hand as far back as it possibly can, it puts its head down, rushes like an angry billy-goat upon its opponent, and stabs at him with its foil as hard as it possibly can, utterly regardless of where it may strike him or what the result may be. Such a result is shown in the story told us by Mr. Chapman.

A Resuscitation.

About the year 1840 a certain Mr. R—— was a constant frequenter of the few schools of arms then existing in London. Off the fencing-floor he was a popular man, but once on it he was shunned by everyone as being a determined and thoroughly dangerous "stabber," and it was very seldom indeed that he found any person sufficiently careless of his existence to cross foils with him. One day, however, M. Pons, a French professor of note, who had taken up his residence in England, happened to visit the *salle d'armes* where Mr. R—— was, and no sooner had he donned his fencing costume than our stabber, as is the habit of stabbers, selected him as a victim, and invited him to fence. Someof the habitués, not overwell pleased at his forwardness in thrusting himself upon so distinguished a stranger, cautioned M. Pons about the dangerous qualities of the gentleman; but the Frenchman, prompted partly by his natural courtesy and partly by his confidence in his own skill, consented to play a bout with him. They commenced, and Mr. R—— soon found out that he could do nothing against so able an opponent; he therefore lost his head, rushed at Pons, and, drawing his hand back in his usual fashion, delivered a furious stab. Pons parried this naturally with some force; a small piece of the end of the foil broke off; the jagged end of the blade struck him full on the chest, and pierced his body through and through. M. Pons, turning round to a young professor, a great friend of his, exclaimed, "Mon ami, je suis tué!" and sank back insensible. The bystanders rushed to his support, placed him in a chair, and sent at once for a doctor. Mr. R——, horrified at what he had done, and well knowing that he was entirely to blame, fell on the floor in a dead faint. The doctor, a young practitioner, arrived, and proceeded at once to look after the prostrate gentleman, when the young professor called out to him:

"Not that fellow; here is your man." They withdrew the broken foil from the body of M. Pons, when the doctor exclaimed: "Oh, this is a bad case! We must take him home at once, and you had better send for So-and-so," mentioning the names of two of the most distinguished surgeons of the day. Pons, quite insensible, was conveyed to his lodgings and placed on his bed. The two surgeons arrived, examined him carefully, and pronounced the case to be hopeless. But the younger of the three, who had been called in first, turned to them, saying: "Surely there is a little chance for him." The two great men replied: "He has only about three hours to live; we can do nothing for him, and we give up the case. If you like to undertake it, by all means do so, but the responsibility must be yours." With that they left the house.

The remaining doctor turned to the young professor, who was almost distracted with grief, and asked him: "Is this man a friend of yours?" "Yes," he replied, "the greatest friend I have in the world." "Then there is one chance for him; it is but a chance. Tell me, will you run a risk to save him?" Said the professor: "I'll risk life itself for him." "Good," said the doctor, writing a prescription. "Get this at once, and make him swallow it if you possibly can. You see, I have not signed it; I dare not. You must take the matter in hand yourself; and, mind, there is no time to lose." The young man went out at once, procured the medicine, and contrived to get it down his friend's throat. Very soon M. Pons moved, turned on his side, and vomited forth an enormous quantity of blood. This went on for several minutes, when Pons, relieved by the violent emetic which had been administered to him, fell back on to his pillow and went off into a deep sleep, in which he remained many hours. He was a man of robust constitution and regular habits, and a month after the accident he was walking about as if nothing had happened to him.

The Sharpened Foils.

We are in the year 1860 and at the town of Luneville. It is a garrison town, and it possesses, among its many places of entertainment, a certain café which is largely patronized by the military element, and that for a remarkably good reason. The proprietor has a daughter who presides at the desk. She is a very charming girl, only just eighteen, with a wealth (isn't that how the poets put it ?) of luxuriant dark hair, and the sweetest brown eyes that imagination can dream of. Every soul in the garrison is madly in love with her, and the establishment does brisk business in consequence. There are quartered in the town, among other corps, the 2nd Regiment of Lancers and the 12th Regiment of Dragoons, both of which bestow most lavish patronage on the worthy host. The most prominent among the Lancers is Corporal Pierre, a fine, tall, handsome young fellow, about four-and-twenty, with a good deal of the gentleman about him, a pleasant voice, and decidedly nice manners. No wonder that the pretty little girl looks upon him favourably.

But she has another admirer, a gentleman in the 12th, Corporal Giraud by name, who is quite the opposite to the handsome Lancer. He is a good deal over thirty ; his face is nothing particular to look at ; he is losing his hair ; he has a disagreeable, harsh, sarcastic tongue ; and, as far as his person is concerned, he is a good deal inclined to embonpoint ; in point of fact, he is, as a certain brilliant poet—who, thank heaven, is still with us—pithily put it some few years ago, " everything that girls detest." It is the old story of the two dogs and one bone. Giraud is annoyed at the favour shown to his rival, and makes no effort to conceal his ill-temper. One evening, while he, Pierre, and some of their comrades are sitting at the table, he calls out roughly to the young lady, " Here, you girl ! fill our glasses again, and look sharp about it !" His coarse behaviour costs him very dear, for Pierre springs to his feet, seizes him by the ear, and demands hotly: "Pray, who are you speaking to, Master Giraud?" The two enemies are white with rage, and ready to throttle one another on the spot, but the bystanders intervene and separate them. Under such circumstances a duel is inevitable. The weapons selected for the encounter are foils with their points sharpened, and, as the two men rank among the best fencers in their respective regiments, excitement and speculation naturally run rather high.

The pair meet according to the usual form; the command is given to commence, and the first bout, which lasts some three or four minutes, is well played by both combatants, but without result. After a few minutes' rest they engage again, when Pierre, seeing the hand of his enemy to be slightly in pronation, makes a feint underneath it, so drawing it downwards, on which, far quicker than I can speak it, he disengages over, and plants his point full on Giraud's chest. The wounded man is carried away insensible, and everyone thinks that he is killed outright. He, however, has only fainted, and he survives just long enough to thoroughly repent him of his rudeness to the pretty girl.

The Red Gloves.

The Baron de Vaux, in his interesting book "Les Duels Célèbres," gives an entertaining account of an affair which took place in the year 1868 between the Vicomte de Lau and a M. des Perrières. During a discussion about the proceedings in a duel which had taken place some little time previously, these two gentlemen had a misunderstanding, which they decided to arrange in the customary manner. Perrières, although scarcely two-and-twenty, was a formidable antagonist, who, young as he was, had already "been out" some half-dozen times. But in this case he had his work cut out for him, for the Vicomte was a very tough customer, thoroughly well trained in the handling of arms, and of tried courage. He had the further advantage of being one of the most redoubtable left-handed players that it was possible to conceive; so the affair promised to be an interesting one. The Marquis of Hertford placed his park at the disposal of the party, and ordered his people to show them every needful attention. The seconds of De Lau were Prince Joachim Murat and the Comte de Biencourt, while the head of the family, the Marquis de Lau, accompanied the party; so his interests were well looked after by gentlemen of both position and experience.

"*Epée de combat.*" *End of the nineteenth century.*

Perrières, on the other hand, was assisted by two young sparks who were attached to a leading newspaper, who showed themselves not so *au fait* of affairs of honour as the seconds of his opponent. One of them, Fervacques by name, who liked a lord as much as most people do, was so overwhelmed at the prodigious honour of being able to rub shoulders with a Prince that he almost forgot to trouble himself about his principal; while the other, Nazet, being a bit of a dandy, could think of nothing but his patent-leather boots and a marvellous pair of red gloves, which no consideration in the world would induce him to take off and put in his pocket. They were rather nice boys, these two; but as seconds in a duel they were such uncommonly queer specimens that Perrières remarked, "If the issue of this affair is not really very serious, we shall be thoroughly well laughed at."

They chose for the scene of operations a nice shady walk, and were soon ready for the fray. The fight was a fierce one. The first encounter lasted fully five minutes, the Vicomte attacking his man so vigorously that he was compelled to break ground more than once, but he regained it again in making his ripostes. They rested awhile to take breath, and engaged a second time without any result, the fencing on both sides being magnificent.

At the third reprise the Vicomte thought it time to bring the matter to an end, and began to gather himself together for a decisive lunge. He tried to attract his enemy's attention by constant changes of engagement, while at the same time he was quietly drawing up his right foot (remember he was a *gaucher*) in order to increase his reach; but just before his manœuvre was completed, Perrières, whom all this did not escape, anticipated the attack in the very nick of time, effected a rapid disengagement, ran his man clean through the biceps muscle, and so brought the encounter to a finish.

On the way home, Nazet, delighted at the issue, and chatting gaily with Des Perrières, asked him, "How was it that, when you were fighting, you kept constantly glancing in my direction?" "My dear fellow," was the reply, "it was all owing to those dreadful red gloves of yours. The next time you come out with me, for Heaven's sake put them in your pocket; they catch one's eye terribly!"

CHAPTER XXIX

The Sabre.

AFTER having exchanged stately courtesies with the armour-clad knights of the fifteenth century, after having been to the field with the Soëilles and the Claudios of the sixteenth, after having revelled with D'Artagnan and his musketeers of the seventeenth, after having rollicked with Ravanne and Dubois in the eighteenth, with their great battle-axes and their two-hand swords, with their rapiers and poniards, with their tricky little "colichemardes," and all the romance pertaining to the men who fought and the splendid weapons they fought with, how difficult it is to settle down into that prosaic nineteenth century which we have only just left behind us! True, we have seen something of the foil play of that trio of famous friends, Angelo, D'Eon, and Saint Georges; we have witnessed the exploits of Jean-Louis, and the almost resurrection of that excellent master, M. Pons. All these were nineteenth-century men. But what have we in England left us now, either to tackle or to talk about, but the sword of the British officer, that official appendage of his, in the use of which he takes, as a rule, so very little interest. We must go to the Continent, where skill with the sabre is still needful, to see what this weapon can do.

The Bully of Bordeaux.

There existed in the first half of the nineteenth century an individual—a nobleman, if you please. He would have positively graced the era of the Vitaux and the Lafrettes, but in the days which he was destined to embellish with his presence he was distinctly an unmitigated nuisance.

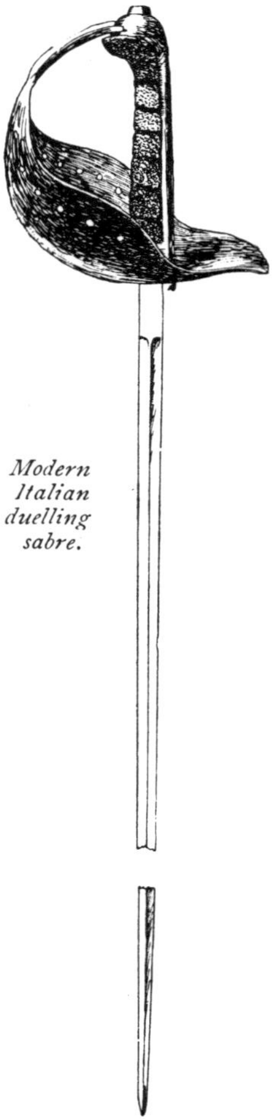

Modern Italian duelling sabre.

The Count de Larillière was a very nice fellow in some respects. He was a tall, handsome man; his manners were most elegant, and he had a way of saying the most outrageous things in so courteous a fashion, and with a voice so musical and sweet, that it charmed everybody, except, perhaps, the person to whom his remarks were addressed. At the same time he was a crack shot with a pistol, a remarkably fine fencer, and he prided himself especially on his skill with the sabre; but he had an unfortunate weakness, which eventually proved to be the undoing of him. He was afflicted with a sort of mental disease, in the shape of an insatiable thirst for blood—anybody's, it did not matter whose—and he had a sad habit of provoking the first gentleman he met in the street—a perfect stranger to him—in such a manner that a duel was bound to ensue, of then slaying the gentleman (of course, in every way strictly according to the rules of honour), and afterwards recording the event in what to the modern British sportsman would be his game-book.

Upon a time he betook himself to the city of Bordeaux in quest of an adventure. He went out for a stroll one evening with a friend of his who knew him well, and as they sauntered along they happened to meet a respectable merchant, who was taking the air with his young wife. The Count stopped the pair, took off his hat in the most polite fashion to the gentleman, and addressed him with, "My dear sir, I hope you will pardon me, but I have made a bet with my friend here that I will kiss your wife (I presume the lady is your wife) now, at this very instant. I should be sorry if my action should in any way inconvenience you, but, you see, I have got to win my wager." High words passed between them, during which the Count, who had planned out the entire scene previously, slapped the merchant's face. A duel with pistols ensued, in which the Count deliberately shot the poor gentleman dead, and inserted the event in his book.

Larillière had now become an absolute terror to the neighbourhood, just as did that swaggering Irishman at Edinburgh, whom that fine old sexagenarian, Donald MacBane, accounted for so gloriously. The Irishman was dismissed with seven sword-cuts and a broken arm, but this bloodthirsty Count was still more drastically dealt with.

A young officer, a native of Bordeaux, happening to be quartered in the neighbourhood, made up his mind that he would rid the good town of this pest. He was a vigorous young fellow, well trained in the use of all sorts of arms, and felt fully equal to the task he had imposed upon himself. He obtained leave of absence from his commanding officer, and betook himself to Bordeaux, where he speedily received information as to the usual haunts of the terrible Count. A masked ball was going on, and M. de Larillière was seated at a table sipping a glass of punch, when there approached a tall, athletic-looking personage, disguised in a black domino, and with his face concealed by a velvet mask. He marched straight up to the table, and, as the bully was in the act of raising the glass to his lips, with a sweep of his arm sent it flying across the room, calling out at the same time in a loud voice, "Waiter, a glass of barley-water for this gentleman!" The Count, foaming with rage, exclaimed, "You wretched fool! do you know who I am?" "I know you quite well," replied the domino. "The tables are turned; you have me to deal with this time. Here, waiter, quick with that barley-water." The servant produced an entire bottle full of the innocent beverage. "Now," said the mask, placing a small pistol to the head of the Count, "if you do not at once drink up the whole of that stuff, I will blow out your brains on the spot; if you do drink it, you shall have the distinguished honour of fighting me to-morrow morning with whatever weapons you may be pleased to fancy. Either way, the good city of Bordeaux will shortly be well rid of you." The infuriated Count blurted out, "It shall be sabres, then!" "Sabres, with all my heart," replied the domino, with that unpleasant little pistol still in its place; "but drink, pretty creature, drink;" and the bloodthirsty bully gulped down the liquid with about the same relish that Ancient Pistol experienced when he devoured the Welshman's famous leek. In the meantime a number of the townsfolk had collected and were watching the proceedings. The unknown glanced haughtily round to note what effect his little scene had produced; then, turning to the Count, he said: "I have given you enough for this evening; you shall have the remainder to-morrow; you will keep till then. And, mark me, I intend to kill you on the very spot where that unhappy merchant fell by your hand."

Arrived on the ground the next morning, Larillière finds himself face to face with a tall, active-looking young gentleman of about five-and-twenty, attended only by two private soldiers from the neighbouring garrison, and from the cool, resolute manner of this adversary he sees at once that he will have his work cut out for him. They are placed opposite to each other, the sabres are handed to them, the director of the duel pronounces the fateful words, "Allez, messieurs!" and they engage hotly. Larillière thinks this young officer the most troublesome customer he has ever yet had to deal with, for touch him he cannot, although he has recourse to every trick of fence that he can call to mind. At last his patience deserts him, and he calls out to his enemy: "Well, sir, you take a long time over your work; pray inform me at what particular hour of the day you propose to end the matter?" "At this very moment," replies the officer, as, with a vigorous lunge, he passes his weapon clean through the bully's heart.

That night the good folks of Bordeaux slept peacefully.

Self-slain.

As the event which we are about to narrate occurred within the last quarter of century, we think it right to suppress the actual names of the parties concerned, and will limit ourselves to relating what took place as clearly as the data from which we derive our anecdote will permit.

There was a young officer in the Italian army whom we will call Lieutenant Foscaro. This young gentleman, who, by the way, was a good-looking fellow, of agreeable manners and deservedly popular, being out for a stroll one day, chanced to meet a distant cousin of his, a Signor X——, who was accompanied by his young wife. The cousins fraternized, and Foscaro was, of course, introduced to the lady. It was in his garrison town, and he was in uniform. Foreign officers appear in uniform much more often than ours do. Some little time after, being on leave, he met them again, and took off his hat to them, but they failed to return the compliment. Foscaro said to himself: "Oh, they evidently do not recognise me in mufti," and he thought no more about it. But the same thing occurred several times, and at last it dawned upon him that they were cutting him on purpose. Coming across Signor X—— one day, he said to him: "You and your wife have cut me several times; please tell me what I have done that you should treat me thus." The other replied, with a haughty wave of his hand, "I do not choose to know you," and, what was worse, he struck him. After such an affront a duel naturally had to be fought, and that not only of "first blood," either.

The affair came off in a fencing-room in Rome, and the weapons employed were those feather-weight sabres to which Italian duellists usually have recourse. Foscaro was at an evident disadvantage, his right arm having been so seriously injured in an accident that it was useless, and he was compelled to fight with his left hand, a thing to which he was entirely unaccustomed; so he placed himself on guard, and every time that his opponent offered an attack he presented his point towards him. Fortunately for the Lieutenant, his man proved to be an excessively bad swordsman. He did not even handle his sabre properly, for, instead of placing his thumb along the back of the grip in order to direct the edge, he clenched it in his fist, which caused the sword to turn in his hand whenever he attempted to deliver a cut; consequently, although Foscaro received several severe blows on his arm and shoulder, they produced no worse effect than a series of disagreeable bruises. The fight was a fierce one, especially on the part of the cousin, and the pair were obliged to stop several times to rest and take breath. At last Foscaro received a furious blow on the shoulder near the neck, which, had it been correctly delivered, must have put an end to the encounter. The director cried, "Halt!" the doctors and seconds examined the part, and exclaimed: "Good heavens! there it not a drop of blood!" The sword had turned again.

One of the seconds, glancing round at the other principal, remarked to him: "Then, what about you?" As these words were uttered, Signor X—— turned ghastly pale, staggered, and fell to the ground. In his savage rush he had spitted himself on Foscaro's point.

The Withered Hand.

How history repeats itself! The story we are about to relate, the events of which happened during the last decade, is very similar in all respects to the foregoing one of Rob Roy and MacNeill of Barra. In both cases the men who had the worst of it brought their trouble on themselves by their folly in forcing a combat with sharps upon men with whom they had no quarrel whatever, and that for no better purpose than to find out which was the best swordsman of the two, a thing which might have been achieved much more peaceably. Moreover, curiously enough, both were punished in precisely the same manner. MacNeill, it will be remembered, received a cut on his sword arm which kept him in bed for three months. What happened to the nineteenth-century gentleman we shall see. The names of the parties concerned do not yet belong to history, so we think it right to suppress them, as we did those in the preceding anecdote.

A Mr. C——, a personal friend of the author, happened to be staying at a watering-place in Switzerland which is a great rendezvous for the better classes of the Italians. Among the other guests at the hotel there was a certain gentleman from North Italy, whom we will christen Count Alessandro. The Count had a peculiarity: his right hand was withered, and seemed almost useless, so much so that it more than once attracted the Englishman's attention. The Count, perceiving this, glanced mournfully at his disfigurement, and, turning to Mr. C——, said: "I see you are looking at my hand; it is as well that others should know how it came to be like this, so that they may avoid committing such an act of folly as I have done. Before this happened I was passionately fond of foil and sabre play. I met with constant success in the fencing-schools, and I fought several sabre duels with a result satisfactory to myself. I fancied myself almost invincible, when, as bad luck would have it, I heard of an Austrian gentleman whose prowess was described as equal, if not superior, to my own. Nothing would satisfy me but that I must cross blades with him, and had I been content with a friendly bout with blunts in a *salle d'armes*, my object of a trial of skill might have been accomplished without any unpleasant result; but a mere fencing match was not enough for me, and I made up my mind that our encounter should be with sharps.

"I met the Austrian, and contrived so to fix a quarrel on him that he was obliged to challenge me, sabres, of course, being the chosen weapons. We fought several bouts, which lasted a considerable time, when at last he gave me a cut on the inside of the wrist which disabled me completely. The surgeons who were present bound me up, and with much difficulty saved my arm from amputation. The wound at last healed, but the severed nerves and sinews never re-united; my hand withered up, and my skill of fence is gone for ever."

"L'Affaire Asselin."

M. Asselin does not seem to have been exactly a gentleman, but he certainly possessed all the facilities for developing himself into a good fellow of the very first water. He was a big, strong young man of some seven-and-twenty years of age, and sufficiently well-featured; he possessed plenty of money; he had nothing to do, and plenty of time to do it in. Part of this time, being fond of rural sports, he devoted to the duties of Lieutenant de la Louveterie (Master of the Wolf-hounds), a position, we take it, in some way analogous to that of M.F.H. in this country. But he neglected his opportunities, and he got himself looked upon as something of a bully, something of a gross liver, and something of a thoroughly good-for-nothing fellow to boot. He seems to have had rather a bad record, for during the trial which followed after the duel we are about to touch on, the President reminded him that he had been twice convicted of *délits de chasse* (which we should English as "poaching"), once for a row which resulted in fisticuffs (only fancy a British M.F.H. being even accused of such a thing!), and last, but not least, that, after having fought a duel with a certain journalist, he had gone about swaggering and openly expressing regret that he had not killed the man—a very unusual thing to do after an affair of honour.

M. de Saint Victor, a retired officer and a gentleman by birth, was a married man with a young daughter about twelve years of age. He was a very peaceable man, and deservedly popular. He was anything but well off, and to augment his means he had accepted the post of agent on the estate of the Marquis de MacMahon. M. Asselin got into difficulties with the Marquis, to whom he wrote a letter couched in such insolent terms that the nobleman, considering it undignified to reply himself, deputed his agent to do so for him. Asselin nourished a grudge against Saint Victor, who was agent also to the Comtesse de Talleyrand, with whom, in his capacity of Master of Hounds, he had taken a liberty. He had thought fit one day to assemble his men and to hunt wild-boar on the lady's property without having previously informed her or her people of his purpose, the result being that he was turned off the manor by the gamekeepers.

In consequence of this he wrote an uncivil letter to the agent, who replied in terms, courteous certainly, but not quite calculated to soothe an angry man. The correspondence waxed warm, and at last Asselin wrote to Saint Victor a letter so brutally insulting that he was obliged to send him a challenge. It was intended that the duel should be an affair of "first blood," but from what came out at the trial, whatever Saint

Victor's ideas may have been, those of Asselin were undoubtedly to kill him.

The weapons used were infantry officers' swords, and the combat was very soon over, for in the very first reprise Saint Victor received a thrust in the abdomen, from which he died in about four hours.

CHAPTER XXX

Cudgelling—Backswording—Singlestick.

EVEN so late as the middle of the nineteenth century there was a faint survival of the sword prizefighting of the early eighteenth in the form of "cudgel play" and "backswording," which still held their own in the West of England. Cudgel play was a distinct descendant of that short sword and dagger fight of Silver's time which James Miller's "gladiators" still recognised. Those heroes fought some of their "battles" on the stage with a Scotch broadsword in the right hand, and in the left a shorter weapon, some fourteen inches in length, furnished with a basket hilt similar to that of their sword, and this they employed to assist in parrying. The cudgel-players copied these in a less dangerous form, the steel blades being replaced by an ash stick about a yard in length and as thick as a country fellow's middle finger, the hilts (known by the name of "pots") being usually of wickerwork. Hence the term of "taking up the cudgels" (mark the plural) in the cause of some innocent or defenceless person.

The upper classes in those times had no particular need to cultivate this rather rough style of fighting; they confined themselves to the small sword, skill in the use of which was very needful to them, as we have already shown. But the fashions changed; gentlemen ceased to wear their swords, and consequently ceased to trouble themselves about what to do with them.

Our sturdy, honest country folk, on the other hand, were in no way affected by the shifting fancies of the fine gentlemen in London, and they continued to play at their wakes and other jolly meetings their bouts of cudgelling and backsword. Now, what was back-swording? It was simply the use of one stick—the big one—instead of two; and to prevent any unfair use of the left hand, that hand was tied in various fashions, according to the usage in the different districts. In Gloucestershire it was evidently fastened to the thigh, the arm being at full length; in Wiltshire it appears to have been fastened to the belt in such a way that the man could raise his elbow to protect his eyes, but nothing higher; while Donald Walker, in his "Defensive Exercises" (1840), tells us "the left hand grasps a handkerchief which is tied loosely round the left thigh, and the elbow is elevated and thrown forward." The men, when engaged, stood up within striking distance, the legs being straight, or nearly so; there was no lungeing, but at times a considerable amount of movement of the feet, as in the fencing of the rapier period. From the fact of the employment of only one stick, that weapon, and the game itself also, gradually came to be recognised as "single-stick." The object of these encounters was to break the opponent's head—that is to say, so to strike it as to draw a stream of blood an inch in length; and no hit on any other part of the person was recognised at all.

"Dover's Meetings."

In the first half of the seventeenth century there lived in Gloucestershire a genial, kindly gentleman, and a right good sportsman, too, by name Master Robert Dover, who took upon himself the task of organizing in an orderly and decorous fashion the rough country sports of which his humbler neighbours were so fond, among which sports were pre-eminent cudgelling, backswording, and wrestling, the latter of which does not concern us just now. He chose for his scene of action a piece of elevated waste ground

Backswording, after Donald Walker.

not far from the village of Weston Subedge, which is even now known as Dover's Hill. Like the keen sportsman that he was, he aimed at attracting not only the country players of his own district, but the best "gamesters" which the whole of England could produce, so he gave as prizes at his annual "meetings," which he arranged to take place every Whit Monday, not merely a new hat with a yellow ribbon round it—of which hat we shall have something further to say—but a good fat purse of golden guineas. No wonder, then, that the crack cudgellers of all broad England came to Dover's Hill to have a try for it.

It was a famous meeting. All the gentry round about came to see it, and some of the young sparks of them even took part in the play, not, of course, for the sake of the guineas, but for the mere fun of the thing. Verily, Dover's Meeting was a goodly show in those days. True, it received a check in the psalm-singing, kill-joy time of the Commonwealth; but when the Merry Monarch came to his own again, its fun and frolic revived anew as much as did the less innocent merrymakings of the Court of that festive King. And thus these honest country sports went on even into the reign of our present gracious Sovereign, whom God preserve!

These affairs, however, were not altogether unattended by serious results. Men sometimes lost their tempers and belaboured one another most unmercifully. There occurred on Dover's Hill somewhere in the forties a combat—a match it must have been—between two *gentlemen*—Mr. Ebenezer Prestage, of Campden, a famous "gamester," and Mr. Spyres, of Mickleton, equally renowned for his science with the stick. They played, or fought, if you will have it so, for a good hour or more, till both champions were utterly exhausted. The battle was a "drawn" one, for the coveted inch of blood was not achieved. The played-out combatants were taken away by their respective friends. Mr. Prestage had his ribs and shoulders handsomely roasted, but poor Mr. Spyres was so badly knocked about that he was incapacitated for any sort of work whatever, and shortly afterwards gave up the ghost. Strange to say, nothing more was heard of the occurrence.

"Dover's Meetings" live now in history alone, but it was not the mishap to Mr. Spyres that killed them. No; they were killed by the railway. The railway brought upon the scene all the roughest and most disorderly scum of the manufacturing towns for many miles around. These people encamped on the ground to the number of over thirty thousand during the whole of Whitsun Week. The gentry, of course, held aloof from them. The scenes of drunkenness, riot, and debauchery were such as to cause a scandal to the whole district, and an Act of Parliament had to be invoked to sanction the enclosing of the ground, which put an end to the historic "Dover's Meetings" once and for ever.

Purton Fair.

Purton, a village in Wiltshire, seems to have been a somewhat important centre of the art of stick play. William Hone, in his "Everyday Book," which appeared before these sports had ceased to be, gives in the form of two or three letters written to the editor, but unfortunately signed only with initials, some idea of their nature, and from Hone's pages we take our inspiration. It must be remembered that the events described took place in the early twenties.

The fair was held twice a year, on May 1 and September 3, on a pleasant little green called the Close. Here the young fellows were wont to assemble every evening to amuse themselves with a few pleasant sports, the most favoured of which was "backswording" or "singlestick." Some of them were such adepts in the noble art that they were regarded as beings of transcendent genius by their less skilful companions. One especially, the most experienced of them all, was revered by them as their "umpire," to whom all disputes were referred, and whose decision was, of course, accepted as final.

The fair lasted three days, on the second of which "several champions enter the field to contest the right to several prizes, which are laid out in the following order:

"1st. A new smock.

"2nd. A new hat with a blue cockade.

"3rd. An inferior hat with a white cockade.

"4th. A still inferior hat without a cockade.

"A stage is erected on the green, and at five o'clock the sport commences. A very celebrated personage, whom they call their 'umpshire,' stands high above the rest to award the prizes. The candidates are generally selected from the best players at singlestick, and on this occasion they use their utmost skill and ingenuity, and are highly applauded by the surrounding spectators. I must not forget to remark that on this grand and to them interesting day the inhabitants of Purton do not combat against each other. No; they are better acquainted with the laws of chivalry. Purton produces four candidates, and a small village adjoining, called Stretton, sends forth four more. These candidates are representatives of the villages to which they respectively belong, and they who lose have to pay all the expenses of the day; but it is to the credit of the sons of Purton that for seven successive years their candidates have been returned the victors. The contest generally lasts two hours, and after that the ceremony of chairing the representatives takes place, which is thus performed: Four chairs made with the boughs of trees are in waiting, and the conquerors are placed therein and carried through the village with every possible demonstration of joy."

A noted champion of Purton was Blackford the butcher, one of the most noted backsword players of his day. He did not confine his efforts to the stage at Purton Fair, but carried off prizes in London, Bath,

Bristol, and Gloucester. On one particular occasion he succeeded in breaking fourteen heads in succession, but in the fifteenth bout he pretty nearly found his match in the person of one Isaac Bushel, a blacksmith, who could bite a nail asunder, eat a shoulder of mutton with appendages, or fight friend or foe for love or money. It was a saying that Bushel could take enough to kill a dozen men.

About the year 1826 Purton Fair was "entirely done away with, as the principal farmers of the place *done* like it, and so don't suffer it."

Stoulton Wake.

In the good old times every small village in the West Country had its annual festivity, in which this famous backswording was the favourite game. Likely enough, the event was not such an important one as Dover's Meeting, or even Purton Fair; but in the matter of genial kindness and liberality the good folks of Stoulton in Worcestershire were in the forefront. They did not keep their prize all to themselves, but they admitted strangers from far and near to contend for it. And what about the prize? These brave Stoulton lads played their backsword fights right lustily; they hammered one another terribly sometimes, chiefly for the mere credit of the thing. Like the Greek athletes of old, who wrestled and boxed at the Isthmian games for a wreath of laurel, or for an even more perishable one of fresh parsley, so did our Stoulton friends play—not for a fat purse of golden guineas, as at Dover's Hill, but for nothing more valuable than a new hat with a yellow ribbon round it; they fought for glory, and not for pelf, and many a sturdy cudgeller came to the cross-roads to have a try for the far-famed Stoulton hat.

It is very difficult—it is more than very difficult—to obtain any reliable information about what went on at games of this kind. Apparently no records of them were ever kept, and we have to rely solely on mere legendary gossip of very, very old village folk, who have almost disappeared. We should have failed hopelessly in the matter had it not been for the valuable assistance kindly given to us by the Rev. Hamilton Kingsford, the Vicar of Stoulton, who during a residence of thirty-three years has amassed an immense fund of interesting details gathered from the lips of his aged parishioners.

The Wake was held on Ascension Day (so that it did not clash with Dover's Meeting) on an open space at Stoulton cross-roads, where at that time there was a comfortable inn. The Stoultonites had a recognised head, whose functions were something like those of the "umpshire" of Purton. He was known as "the bully o' the wake": not that he was in any way a village tyrant, but a big, burly, noisy, cow-mouthed fellow "as knaowed everything," and by common consent assumed the dictatorship. A famous "bully" was one Perry, who by his loud shouting, heard far away, called people to the sports. One of his duties was to "cry the belt" for the "wrustling," and "the 'at" for the "backswording" contests, and thus to gather the spectators to the trysting-place. This was the formula he used:

"Oh iss! oh iss! oh iss! this is to gi'e notiss that a 'at ull be plahyed fur at Stoulton Wake, a go'd lace 'at; three men ov a side, the best two out o' three, and no booty plahyin', no booty works; blood to run a hinch; no plahy, no 'at."

The term "booty playing" meant playing unfairly for one's own "boot" or advantage, whatever the game might be, and so acting contrary to the rules, which varied in different localities, as by kicking, cutting at the face (instead of the head), hitting below the belt, getting the left arm loose, or allowing an opponent to win by a previous arrangement with some other person. "Booty" play, in fact, was "foul" play.

The arrangements at Stoulton are of a more primitive kind than those at Purton. No platform is erected, but a ring is formed on the open space by the inn, where the backswording and wrestling take place. Here the services of the "bully" are again required to perform the operation known as "beating the ring." In response to his previous shouting a goodly crowd has collected, and to clear the ground Friend Perry takes off his leathern belt and swings the buckle end of it about him in all directions, giving it smartly to anybody who will not budge, by which means he quickly forms a space for the combatants to play their bouts in. The ring having been "beaten," one of the competitors throws his hat into it; another accepts the challenge by doing the same, and they join issue. They strip to their shirts and set to work; they cut and slash each other desperately and beat one another "amos' to dyuth"; their shirts (to say nothing of the skins underneath them) are torn to tatters; but nothing of it counts until at last one gets a "broken head," a cut sharp enough to cause the "blood to run a hinch," according to the previous announcement. That fight is over, and the next pair make their appearance. If the man on the side of the previous victor is successful, the contest is decided; but if so far the sides are "level-handed," there must be the third bout to end the matter as to who shall carry off the hat.

How delightful it is to be brought into contact, not only with deeds that have been done, but also with the personalities, the actual men who did them, and here it is that Mr. Kingsford has helped us so effectually! Among his humble friends at Stoulton there is an old, old man, George Merriman by name, who recounted to our friend many curious events which occurred at Stoulton Wake in its later years. One of the last affairs of backswording took place somewhere in the late forties, and was one of the most desperate. A keeper of Lord Coventry's named James Graves and a man called Pratt, as old George put it, "turned on at the jaub. Pratt wuz wot I ca's a riglar bu'-dog, and niver didn't knaow when a wuz 'urted." They "fote" for a long time without effect, when two of Graves's brothers, who were looking on, called out to him: "'Ef 'ee cosn't bre-ak 'is yud, cut 'im out of the ree-ung'" [ring]. This interference annoyed Pratt, who cried out: "'Ef thur's another Graves,' a said, 'let 'im come on!' An' thur was two moer, but a udn't come." They went at it again without doing much, when Graves at last remarked to his opponent: "'Us be two nahibours, an' 't yeant wuth while fur we to maul each other about.' And they gen in, an' left off level-handed." But they had already mauled each other about pretty considerably, and had cut each other's shirts all to pieces.

Another famous local hero was one David Staight.

"Oye!" said old George, "I remembers Dahvid Staight as wull as I remembers you. 'E wuz a despret, gre-at, big, strung, bwony mon, an' a deadly mon to plahy at backsword. A dooesn't see sich a mon about 'ere nowadahys; but 'e wuz poor—a means i' flesh. 'E worked fur Mr. Whitaker—done 'es 'osses. An' thur wuz another, Gearge Hosbun, as lived agen Pirton's Church. 'E wuz a despret mon fur back-swordin' an' fightin' an' summat. I remembers as 'e an' Dahvid Staight plahyed at backsword, an' 'e wuz despret lissom, an' 'e jumped hout o' 'es wahy, 'e wuz sah quick. An' 't stirred Dahvid's mettle, I suppose, an' 'e sahys, 'Ef 'ee dooes thot agen,' 'e sahys, 'a'll cut thy guts hout.' An' the nex' time folks said as 'e cut the buttons off 'es breeches i' front."

One George Nutting, who had a hare-lip (a "harshar"), was a prominent backsword man. He had on a time a tremendous set-to with a stranger, a professional fighting man, who frequented all the meetings, fairs, and wakes for miles around, where there was anything to be picked up. Only a few days previously he had attended Dover's Meeting, and had met with some success there. Old George Merriman did not very much approve of this stranger. "'E niver," said he, "wuzn't at no plaace fur lung. 'E wuz a drunken, scampin' 'ound as hever nid be. 'E'd goo scampin' about hall hover Henglan' pritty nigh, but a'd be suer to be 'ere o' 'Oly Thu'sday. 'E rommled about 'mos' hall hover the world." On this particular occasion Mr. Nutting gave the "rommler" such frightful punishment as to put a stop to his "scampin'" altogether, for he died a few days after it; his dissipated habits had made him a bad subject for a mauling of that sort.

The farmers at Stoulton were more favourable to these sports than were those at Purton, for they not only managed and arranged the "playing," giving money prizes, but the younger and more adventurous among them actually took part in the games on the spot as well as elsewhere.

Singlestick at Angelo's.

It was in the late fifties. In the West Country Dover's Meeting had come to an end in the year of the Great Exhibition, backswording and cudgelling had gradually smouldered out, and were no longer heard of; but in London, in a more refined form, singlestick still held its own: it was recognised as the medium for studying and practising the use of the officer's sword. At Angelo's famous rooms in St. James's Street the best gentlemen in England were wont to assemble to receive their lessons, and to prove among themselves which of them had best assimilated the lore taught them by their great master. In their bouts they preserved something of the hardiness of the backswordmen of the older time (true, they did not play for the "blood to run a hinch": for Henry Angelo imposed upon them the wearing of a stout helmet), for when they played singlestick it never occurred to them to use any clothing of more defensive nature than their shirts or their jerseys; good honest knocks on ribs and shoulders and on arms and on legs did they both give and receive, and that most good-naturedly. We only remember one instance of bad loss of temper; we will not mention the names of the people concerned: our reason is obvious. Angelo, as may be remembered, taught fencing at a large number of great schools, and he was very hospitable to his young pupils; no person was better received in St. James's Street than any one of those boys who liked to go there. One youngster, a lad of sixteen or thereabouts, was a particularly keen customer. If a certain gentleman, whose name is not always to be quoted, had condescended to come up from below and grace Angelo's rooms with his august presence, that boy would not have been happy without a tussle with him. One afternoon our boy found himself engaged with a shortish, stout, strong gentleman who had achieved for himself the reputation of a crack player, not so much from the "finesse" of his play, but for his merciless hard hitting, and for this same reason it was not everybody who cared to take him on. Well, the gentleman and the schoolboy set to work, and the lad landed more touches on his formidable opponent than the latter liked; he lost his temper, the youngster scored again on the leg, and as he was leisurely retiring to guard, this precious gentleman, instead of acknowledging the hit, struck him a furious blow right across the chest. The only remark the boy made was, "My hit, I think," and went on playing. In the dressing-room afterwards it was found, as he removed his jersey, that his chest had been laid open from shoulder to waist, and the guilty gentleman expressed a fervent hope that it was not he who had done it. People took to wearing leather jackets after that episode.

The Biter Bit.

In the early sixties, Mr. Rolland, a gentleman of middle age, a great traveller, and of much experience, was one of the most constant frequenters of Angelo's

School. He was the most chivalrous player that could be imagined, and one of the finest all-round swordsmen in England as well; but one day he met with a disagreeable experience. There was about at that time a certain Sergeant T——y, a non-commissioned officer in the Royal Artillery, who had gotten himself a name as a player in much the same way as the gentleman whose exploit we have just recorded. But he was a far worse customer to deal with; on the fencing floor he behaved with absolutely brutal violence; fair play or foul, it was all the same to him so long as he could manage to do his opponent some ugly damage. He was not, of course, a member of the school, but on a time he thought fit to present himself there. Mr. Angelo received him in his usual courteous fashion, and invited him to fence. The sergeant replied that he did not "fence," but that he would play sticks with anyone. As soon as he had changed his clothes he was introduced to Mr. Rolland, who chanced to be disengaged at the moment, and he immediately said to that gentleman: "I hope you do not hit inside the leg; it is so very dangerous; I regard it as foul play." To which Mr. Rolland replied: "Oh! we never allow that here. We consider it the very foulest of foul play." This was comforting to the sergeant; he felt himself quite safe. They commenced their game, and when Mr. Rolland the least expected it he laid a heavy blow with all his force on to the forbidden part, dropped his man, and went away to brag in the barrack room about how he had had the better of one of the best players in England. But he had made a mistake. Mr. Rolland, a man of almost quixotic chivalry of mind, was infuriated at the foul treatment he had received, the effects of which lasted him over a fortnight, and vowed to Angelo that if ever he met the brute again he would give a "Roland for his Oliver." Before very long the opportunity offered itself, for the fellow, emboldened by his success, appeared again. Mr. Rolland was sitting down at the moment, but as he caught sight of the man entering the room the bystanders noticed an ominous, savage, lightning flash of his eyes, and said to each other: "We shall see something presently." Mr. Angelo, ignoring all this, welcomed the newcomer with: "My dear Mr. T——y, I am so glad to see you again! Of course, you will have a turn with some of us; and, by the way, there is an old friend of yours here, Mr. Rolland. I fancy you had the best of him the last time; you might like to give him his revenge."

As the pair appeared ready for their bout, the whole room became suddenly quiet; instructors, pupils, and players ceased their work, and formed a ring round the two combatants. The previous story of foul play was fresh in their memories. They knew Rolland; they knew his consummate skill and his infinite resource; they knew his imperturbable command of his temper; and they felt that something out of the common was about to be seen.

The pair engaged; the sergeant led off in his customary violent fashion, but Mr. Rolland played in a manner that had never been seen before. This time he was serious. Usually he would lead off with a frank attack; now he was strangely quiet. He parried the furious blows, and only now and then replied with a riposte. T——y, fancying that his man was afraid of him, redoubled his energy, and gradually tired himself, which was exactly what his opponent intended that he should do. At last the supreme moment arrived. Rolland all of a sudden couched like a tiger, like a tiger sprang forward, and with all the force of his spring and the weight of his mighty arm landed a fearful blow exactly on the point of the inside of his adversary's right knee. The biter was bit. Sergeant T——y uttered a shriek of agony, and fell fainting on the floor. He was carried to the dressing-room, where they fomented his leg with hot water and did the best they could for him at the moment. He was taken in a cab to the hospital, where he remained over a month, and it was three months before he was able to mount a horse again.

The Last of Sergeant T——y.

After the "Roland" that this indefatigable slasher had received from Mr. Rolland, one would have thought that ever afterwards he would have given No. 32, St. James's Street a wide berth. But he was by no means a "thin-skinned" man; his moral epidermis was of stouter make than even the fleshly ones of his various opponents ought to have been, and he paid a third and last visit to that historic scene of mimic battle. On this occasion he again met his match, and again received just and final punishment. He had for his opponent an assistant instructor of the school, Jackson by name, a big, strong, active fellow, who recently had retired from the Household Brigade, and had been for some years in the employment of Mr. Angelo as well. Old Jackson was not an eminent foil-player—his great big fist was of too coarse a kind to manipulate that delicate little instrument—but at singlestick he was, as our old friend George Merriman of Stoulton put it, "a deadly mon." They had a pretty hot fight, these two, for Jackson, when his blood was up, could hit quite as hard as T——y. At last Jackson's stick broke short off within some three inches of the hilt, and he had nothing left of a weapon but the buffalo-hide "basket"! Well, in such a case any decent-minded man would have stopped at once to allow his opponent to get a fresh stick; but not so Sergeant T——y. Here was his chance of really hurting somebody; he rushed at his man, and gave him not one hit only, but five or six, as hard as he could put them in. Jackson was furious. He drew back his arm, and with all his might drove the buffalo hilt full into T——y's helmet. The fellow was not hurt, for the wirework saved his face; but the force of the blow sent him tumbling across the room, and he fell all of a heap on the doormat. Mr. Angelo, who had been busy in a room below, came upstairs just in time to witness the entire scene. He walked up to T——y, gave him a kick, and ordered him to put on his clothes, to go away, and never to dare to show his face in the School of Arms again.

The Walking-stick.

We cannot conclude without making some mention of a method of stick play which has been quite recently introduced to British athletes by M. Pierre Vigny, a professor from Switzerland, who unites in himself the qualities of a champion player and of a careful, judicious teacher of his art, and he possesses in a marked degree the natural gift of facility in interesting his pupil in the work which that pupil has set himself to learn.

The instrument he employs is nothing more than the ordinary walking-stick of daily life, say, for example, a lightly-mounted malacca cane. The exercise, when played merely as a game, is a remarkably attractive one, so brilliant, indeed, that our time-honoured English singlestick is not to be compared with it. In the first place, the player is not hampered with a buffalo or wicker hand-guard, a fact which of itself lends variety to the play, for the man can, and does, frisk his cane about from one hand to the other, so that his opponent can never precisely tell which hand will deliver the attack, and careful practice of the various lessons will shortly make the student pretty nearly ambidextrous. One of the first things to understand in such play as this is to preserve the hand which holds the weapon, a thing which an occasional tap on the knuckles impresses on one's memory. M. Vigny does not confine himself to teaching a mere exhilarating game of play; he shows his pupils also the more serious side of the system, instructing them carefully in what they should do if attacked by a gang of ruffians. But we must not enter the arena of technical detail; it is better left in the hands of M. Vigny himself.

INDEX

THE END

BILLING AND SONS, LTD., PRINTERS, GUILDFORD

SELECT BIBLIOGRAPHY

Amberger, J. Christoph, *The Secret History of the Sword.* Baltimore, MD, HammerterzVerlag, 1996.

Anglin, Jay P., *The Schools of Defence in Elizabethan London.* Renaissance Quarterly XXXII, London, 1984.

Anglo, Sydney (ed), *Chivalry in the Renaissance.* Woodbridge, Boydell and Brewer, 1990.

Anglo, Sydney, *The Martial Arts of Renaissance Europe.* London and New Haven, Yale, 2000.

Aylward, J.D., *The English Master of Arms from the Twelfth to the Twentieth Century.* London, Routledge and Kegan Paul, 1956.

Baldick, Robert, *The Duel: A History of Duelling.* London, Chapman and Hall, 1965; New York, Clarkson N. Potter, 1965, and Barnes and Noble, 1966.

Barwick, Humfrey, *A Breefe Discourse concerning the force and effect of all manuall weapons of fire.* London, 1594.

Berriman, Captain M. W., *The Militiaman's Manual and Sword Play without a Master: Rapier and Broad Sword Exercises copiously explained and illustrated.* New York, 1859.

Bertrand, Léon, *The Fencer's Companion.* Aldershot, Gale and Polden, 1934.

Blackwell, Henry, *The English Fencing Master, or the Compleat Tutor of the Small-Sword.* London, 1702.

Brown, Terry, *English Martial Arts.* Hockwold-cum-Wilton, Anglo-Saxon Books, 1997.

Bryson, Frederick, *The Sixteenth-Century Italian Duel.* University of Chicago, 1938.

Burton, Richard, *The Book of the Sword.* London, Chatto and Windus, 1884.

Canby, Courtland, *A History of Weaponry.* New York, Hawthorne Books, 1963.

Castle, Egerton, *Schools and Masters of Fence.* London, George Bell and Sons, 1885, revised 1892, and (revised) Arms and Armour Press, 1969.

Clements, John, *Medieval Swordsmanship: Illustrated Methods and Techniques.* Boulder, CO, Paladin Press, 1998.

Cole, Michael D. (ed), *Swords & Hilt Weapons*. London, Multimedia Books, 1989.

Cruso, John, *Militarie Instructions for the Cavallerie*. Cambridge, 1632 and facsimile edition with Explanatory Notes and a Commentary by Brigadier Peter Young, Kineton, The Roundwood Press, 1972.

Dobringer, Hanko, *Fechtbuch* (1389). Nuremberg, German National Museum, Codex Ms. 3227a.

Du Boulay, F.R.H., *Germany in the Later Middle Ages*. New York, St. Martin's Press, 1983.

Dürer, Albrecht, *Fechtbuch* (1512), in Friedrich Dörnhoffer, *Jahrbuch der Kunsthistorischen Sammlungen des Allerhöchsten Kaiserhauses*, XXVII. Wien, F. Tempsky, 1910; Leipzig, G. Freytag, 1910.

Edge, David and John Miles, *Arms and Armor of the Medieval Knight*. New York, Crescent Books, 1988.

Hergsell, Gustav, *Die Fechtkunst im XV und XVI Jahrhunderte* (The Art of Fighting in the 15th and 16th Centuries). Leipzig, K.W. Hiersemann, 1896.

Hergsell, Gustav, See Rector

Hooper, Nicholas and Matthew Bennett (eds), *The Cambridge Illustrated Atlas: Warfare: The Middle Ages, 769–1487*. Cambridge and New York, Cambridge University Press, 1996.

Hope, Sir William, *The Scots Fencing Master or Compleat Small-Sword-Man*. Edinburgh, 1687.

Hutton, Alfred, *Cold Steel*. London, 1889.

Hutton, Alfred, *Old Sword-Play*. London, 1892.

Keen, Maurice (ed), *Medieval Warfare: A History*. Oxford University Press, 1999; New York, Getty Center for Education in the Arts, 1999.

Lonnergan, A., *The Fencer's Guide*. London, 1771.

McBane, Donald, *The Expert Sword-Man's Companion*. Glasgow, 1728.

Matthey, Cyril G.R., *Catalogue of Works on Fencing, Duelling, and Allied Subjects forming the Private Collection of Captain C. G. R. Matthey*. London, 1900.

Meyer, Joachim, *Grundtliche beschreibung der freyen ritterlichen und adelichen kunst des fechtens* (A Thorough Description of the Free, Knightly and Noble Art of Fencing). Strasbourg, 1570.

MSS I.33 (c1280). Leeds, Royal Armouries.

Norman, A.V.B., *The Rapier and Small-Sword 1460–1820.* London, Arms and Armour Press, 1980.

Novati, Francesco, See Rapisardi

Oakeshott, Ewart, *Records of the Medieval Sword.* Woodbridge, Boydell & Brewer, 1981.

Oakeshott, Ewart, *The Sword in the Age of Chivalry.* London, Lutterworth Press, 1964; Woodbridge, Boydell & Brewer, 1994.

Olivier, J., *Fencing Familiarized or a New treatise on the Art of Sword Play.* London, 1771.

Oman, C.W.C., *A History of the Art of War in the Middle Ages,* 2 vols. London, Methuen, 1924, and Greenhill, 1991.

Peeke, Richard, *Three to one: being, an English-Spanish combat, performed by a westerne gentleman, of Tavystoke in Devonshire, with an English quarterstaff, against three Spaniards at once with rapiers and poniards.* London, 1626.

Prost, Bernard (ed), *Traités du duel judicaire, relations de pas d'armes et tournois.* Paris, 1872.

Rapisardi, Giovani, *Fiore Dei Liberi's Flos Duellatorium.* Padua, Gladitoria Press, 1998.

Novati, Francesco, *Flos Duellatorum il Fior di Battaglia di Maestro Fiore Dei Liberi* (Flos Duellatorum, The Flower of Battle, by Master Fiore Dei Liberi). Bergamo, 1902.

Rector, Mark, *Medieval Combat.* First English edition of *Talhoffers Fechtbuch.* London, Greenhill Books, 2000.

Hergsell, Gustav, *Talhoffers Fechtbuch aus dem Jahre 1467.* Prague, 1887.

Talhoffer, Hans, *Fechtbuch aus dem Jahre 1443* (Gotha Codex). Gotha, Research Library at Schloss Friedenstein, Ms. Chart. A 558.

Ringeck, Sigmund, *Fechtbuch* (c1440). Dresden, State Library of Saxony, Ms. Dresd. C 487.

Rolan, Joseph, *The Amateur on Fencing, or a Treatise on the Art of Sword Defence.* London, 1809.

Steinmetz, Andrew, *The Romance of Duelling in all Times and Countries.* London, 1868, reprinted, Richmond Publishing, 1971.

Talhoffer, Hans, See Rector

Wise, Arthur, *Art and History of Personal Combat.* Greenwich, CT, Arma Press, 1972.

London, 2003